She Hath Wings

Jeanette
Van Zanten-Stump

She Hath Wings

© 2020 Jeanette Van Zanten-Stump

Print ISBN: 978-1-09830-984-8

Dedicated to my beloved husband, Cliff, for your enduring love—my story wouldn't be complete without you. You are the wind beneath my wings.

Table of Contents

Acknowledgments

I am deeply grateful to:

My husband Cliff, for your support, encouragement, patience, and the space you give me to write.

My children, Brandi, Justin, Cherey, and Caleb for the forgiveness of raising you in a religion that deprived you of hope for a better future, a belief in your inherent goodness, the unconditional love you deserved and experiences you needed while growing up.

Corinne Zinni-Case, for your enduring friendship and for teaching me about grace and encouraging me to write a book twenty years before the idea had entered my conscious mind.

Nancy Gerber, Rose Brody Schaut, Margo Pfingstler, Corinne Zinni-Case and my brother Jack Van Zanten, for your proofreading, attention to detail, and interest in my writing.

Melinda Marconi for your photography and the inspiration for the cover image of *She Hath Wings*.

Nancy and Richard Lazarus for the opportunity to spend a weekend writing at your cabin on Lake Cayuga.

The BookBaby publishing team who do amazing work formatting and publishing books.

And most of all to God, who I know without a shadow of a doubt, orchestrated the writing of this book. My deepest gratitude for giving me wings to fly.

You were born with wings.

You are not meant for crawling, so don't.

You have wings.

Learn to use them and fly. Rumi

Preface

———•———

O n a warm spring morning, as I was walking to the rough cut, hemlock pole barn to milk our small herd of goats, I brushed past the blueberry bushes full of white, delicate blossoms. A bird's nest tucked in the branches caught my eye. I gingerly lowered the boughs laden with green leaves, to get a peek at the nest made of twigs, strands of goat hair, tufts of lamb's wool, and a lining of soft down feathers from our chickens. Four tiny eggs, each the size of my thumbnail, and as blue as the sky above, rested inside. In a nearby pine tree, the mother robin scolded me with her unending chirping.

The sight was picture perfect, so I ran back to the house to get my digital camera. I focused the camera above the nest to capture the moment. Without touching the nest, I peeked in daily to monitor the progress of the eggs. The mother robin continued to squawk at me each time. After a couple of weeks, I was delighted to see hatched eggs replaced with tiny balls of feathers. When I returned the next day, to my dismay, the little fledglings were gone. The nest was empty. A deafening silence replaced the mother robin's scolding. I thought perhaps a squirrel or chipmunk had devoured the peeps.

In the spring of the year, it's common to find nests on our four acres of land, located six miles north of Ridgway, Pennsylvania. Tall Pennsylvania red pines, Eastern hemlocks, birch, and fruit trees are a haven for songbirds, robins, sparrows, cardinals, blue jays, finches, and woodpeckers. Little Mill Creek flows behind our homestead, providing the birds with a running water source and land lush with earthworms.

Sometimes we find interrupted nests resting on the ground underneath the boughs of the trees. The fragile nests, made from delicately interwoven twigs, are occasionally interrupted by the gusts of wind frequent in springtime.

In early November of 1960, when I was three years old, my father passed away, leaving my six siblings and me orphaned, bereft of parents. My mother suffered from mental illness and wasn't able to parent her brood, leaving us in the care of an orphanage. Mooseheart, located thirty-eight miles west of Chicago, is supported by local Moose Clubs throughout the United States and Canada. The one-thousand-acre institution founded in 1913 by James J. Davis, who was a member of the Sharon, Pennsylvania Moose Club, is still in operation today.

At the time, the Moose organization--who were predominately men--promised to take care of member's families if they passed away or were incapable of caring for their offspring. My father was a Moose member before he died. He knew my mother was unable to provide for seven children. In the event of his death, his wish was that his family would go to Mooseheart. When we went to Mooseheart, I was grateful to have a roof over my head, clothes to wear, and food to eat, but the separation from all I knew was unbearable. Like a fledgling from an interrupted nest, I grew up without parents to guide me and teach me how to fly. There were mishaps along the way. I experimented with drugs, married in my late teens, and became a mother at a young age. I relied on instincts to parent my children. I wrote about this time of my life in a memoir, *The Red Caboose-An Orphan's Journey*, published in 2018.

Readers of that book inquired as to how I met my husband Cliff and how I rose above the trauma of my childhood. *She Hath Wings*, chronicles how I found my wings and was able to finally attain freedom from the bondage of my past, a troubled marriage and the religion I had been involved in for twenty-five years. The arduous journey picks up when I moved from St. Marys, Pennsylvania, to Emporium, Pennsylvania, in the spring of 1983.

I have tried to recreate events, locales, and conversations from my memories of them. In order to maintain their anonymity in some instances, I have changed the names of individuals and places. I may also have changed some identifying characteristics and details such as physical properties, occupations and places of residence.

Trapped

●——————————————————————————●

As I navigated the 1979 red Zephyr station wagon through the tall mountains, referred to as 'God's Country' it felt as if my family and I were moving to the last track at the end of the railroad. Underneath the maroon and black striped maternity top, my protruding belly touched the steering wheel, and I felt the baby kick, tickling my insides. The hit song *Roseanna* by Toto was playing on the radio. I thought perhaps it might be a suitable name for the baby. The car was packed with cardboard boxes of clothes, toys and odds and ends that didn't fit in the U-Haul, including all the emotional baggage from the past twenty-five years of my life which I hadn't yet unpacked.

Brandi, my seven-year-old daughter, who was wearing a Rainbow Brite shirt, velour slacks, and Velcro sneakers rode in the front passenger seat of the vehicle, clinging to her tattered ki-ki, a worn piece of a salvaged baby blanket. The road we were traveling, once known as an Indian path, was Route 120 and commonly known as the Bucktail Trail. While driving, I wondered how early settlers managed when they moved to unknown places. As the car meandered the twists and turns in the road through the Pennsylvania State Forest from St. Marys to Emporium, I began gasping for air as the mountains closed in on me. I rolled down the window to breathe in the fragrance of the evergreen trees and wildflowers scattered along the roadside.

The borough of St. Marys, located in Elk County in north-central, Pennsylvania, was where I lived for the past twelve years of my life since leaving the orphanage at thirteen years old. St. Marys, founded in 1842 by German immigrants, was now populated by seven thousand people, consisting of two high schools, several Protestant and Catholic churches, twice as many taverns as places of worship, and the Straub Brewery. I was moving to a little town with about two thousand people, one Catholic church, a handful of Protestant churches, half as many taverns, and no brewery. In the 1860s, people settled in Cameron County and established the community of Emporium as a trade center. The town was also known for the Sylvania plant and large powdered metal plants.

As I crossed the railroad tracks, which marked the halfway point between the two towns, I glanced up at the sky to see a raptor soaring above the mountains and swooping into the valleys; I admired the bird's freedom. I wondered what it would be like to soar without being caged in by rules and regulations. If someone had told me I was going to face a dark night of the soul, I might have turned the car around on a dime. I was already isolated from society. I didn't have any friends who weren't Jehovah's Witnesses since I joined their religion in 1978. I quit watching TV because of the 'worldly influence,' and I didn't read newspapers because of the bad news. I didn't know or care who was the President of the United States, although I was familiar with Reaganomics. One of my witness friends had to go back to work teaching after being on public assistance because of the economic policy. All I knew for sure was that we were living in the 'last days of this system' and 'Armageddon' would come any day. Paradise was around the corner. If I had been aware of what was going on in the world, maybe I would have learned more about the People's Temple led by Jim Jones. Nine hundred people drank his Kool-aid and committed suicide. If I were paying attention, maybe I would have put two and two together and realized I was in a cult.

From the time I was three years old until I was thirteen years old, I lived in an orphanage at Mooseheart, Illinois, surrounded by chain-link fencing. For ten years, matrons told me what to wear, made me do chores, forced me to eat, and wouldn't let me talk. My daily activities were regulated by a loud whistle when it was time for me to get up, when it was time to go to school, when it was time to come in at night and when it was time to go to church. If I had an internal clock, it was stifled. I yearned to be free, to live in the outside world where matrons and whistles didn't regulate my life.

Although I was now free from the physical confinement of an institution, I was now in another type of isolation; mental confinement of rights and wrongs--where I would suffer punishment--not of beatings and physical constraint, but of fear, guilt and social ostracizing of a group. The payoff of staying in this spiritual prison was I didn't have to think or make decisions for myself. The Watchtower Bible & Tract Society instructed me whom to talk to and whom not to talk to, what to wear and what not to wear, what to watch on television and what not to watch, what to say and what not to say, what to think, and what not to think. The religion had its own set of words that only Jehovah's Witnesses used. The language made me feel a part of the group. I was safe and had a place to belong, or so I thought.

The little town of Emporium was nestled in between tall mountains with the Sinnemahoning River running through the valley. Although the hills were stunningly beautiful, they were also isolating. I wouldn't see a sunrise or sunset for the next seventeen years. As I drove down the main street, delicate buds were falling from maple trees, making room for bright green leaves to shade the sidewalks and nicely built houses. I tried my best to see the positive points of living in the picturesque community where my husband had found a new job at GKN Sintered Metals. When Gary was in high school, his family had moved to Emporium and lived in Sylvan Heights--nicknamed Snob's Nob--when his dad took a supervisor job at a powdered metal factory in Austin, Pennsylvania. Gary had fond memories of living in Emporium and his four years at Cameron County High School. He was looking forward to living in Emporium again, although he wasn't prepared for life to be different for him. Instead of living in a well to do area of Emporium, we would be crowded in a small apartment on a side street.

Gary and our four-year-old son, Justin, were ahead of me in the U-Haul and turned onto a side street and parked in front of a two-story stone apartment building we were renting from a landlord named George Coppersmith. It was the only affordable place we could find and would suit us until we were able to buy a mobile home with the proceeds from the sale of the house in St. Marys. Just as we started unloading boxes, a 'sister' from the Kingdom Hall stopped by with a ham dinner and the trimmings for supper. We were all hungry and I didn't have anything planned for our supper. At the time, I didn't realize that this gesture of love-bombing was one of the practices that kept me entrapped in the religion.

A five-year-old little girl with black curly hair and large brown eyes, dressed in a matching purple and pink polyester pantsuit came running over from the house next door to play with Brandi. She didn't have a shy bone in her body and told me her name was Rachel. Her mom, who looked to be in her thirties, had long black hair with bangs, plastic-framed glasses, and wore blue jeans and a checkered blouse. Her warm and friendly manner made me feel welcomed to the neighborhood.

With the same extroverted personality as her daughter, she introduced herself as Martha and said she was studying the Bible with Jehovah's Witnesses and wanted to know if I was a Jehovah.

I had never been called a Jehovah and it would have been sacrilegious for me to claim to be God. She looked away when I corrected her by saying, "I'm not Jehovah, I am a Jehovah's Witness. My name is Jeanette."

Martha then introduced me to her husband Dick and her other two children. Nicole was a shy teenager with long red hair, and Dennis was a preteen with a good sense of humor and a wide smile. I couldn't believe how easy it was to make friends quickly and thought I would like Emporium. I was happy to be making friends for myself and my children-friends who didn't drink or smoke and seemed to be honest people. We hurried to get everything inside as dark clouds formed in the sky, and thunder rumbled in the distance.

Another 'sister' whom I had met at Jehovah's Witness assemblies came by to help unpack. Pam had short red hair, sparkly blue eyes, and was kind and friendly, as were her three children. Her husband, Tim, a stocky man with a sheepish grin, was an 'unbeliever' and had started attending meetings at the Kingdom Hall, which gave me hope someday my husband would become a Jehovah's Witness. Together, Pam and I unloaded heavy boxes of canned carrots and tomatoes and lined them on top of the kitchen cabinets in the small kitchen.

On Sunday, we attended our first meeting at the Kingdom Hall. Jehovah's Witnesses called their meeting places Kingdom Halls instead of churches. They taught that a church was a congregation of people, not a building. The verbiage was another way to separate them from other Christian faiths. The Kingdom Hall in Emporium was located about five miles out of town on the Sizerville Road. The first time I walked into the one-story meeting hall, it felt as if I stepped back in time twenty-five years. The decor was drab and the building had a musty smell. The children and I found a place to sit in the back row of retired moss green theatre seats for the meeting.

Jehovah's Witnesses prided themselves on their worldwide brotherhood. They claimed people would identify the true religion by the love they had for each other, and they were the only organization with brothers and sisters all over the earth. I believed this was true as I was love-bombed from the first time I attended one of their meetings. People who were strangers talked to me and took an interest in my children.

Also, at the beginning of every year, the Watchtower Bible and Tract Society released an annual report in book form. The book had stories about people from all over the world who were learning about Jehovah. I enjoyed reading about people who lived in unfamiliar countries. The journal included the hours spent in the ministry, the number of books and magazines placed, a count of visits made to households, a report on new Kingdom Halls built all over the world, and the numbers of publishers, pioneers, circuit and district overseers. The statistic all of Jehovah's Witnesses waited for each year was how many of the 144,000, called the 'remnant', remained on earth.

The religion believed only 144,000, male and female of Christ's followers would go to heaven to rule over the millions of other people who would be living on the paradise earth.

These 'anointed' ones had an unsaid honorary status in the congregations. I only knew of one person who partook of the bread and wine. She was a sister from DuBois, and when I met her, I thought she was eccentric. The friends believed every word out of an anointed person's mouth was sacred.

Each year a memorial service of Christ's death was held on Nisan 14, the Hebrew term for the correct time of Passover. Some years the date coincided with Easter and sometimes it didn't. Using the word Nisan separated Jehovah's Witnesses from other Christian religions who might be celebrating the pagan holiday Easter at the same time. For Jehovah's Witnesses, there weren't any stories about the resurrection of Christ, there wasn't an Easter Bunny and the children didn't get candy. The memorial was a serious time for the remnant of the 144,000, that began after Christ's death, to renew their covenant by partaking of the bread and the wine. Meticulous records of the number of people who drank of the bread and the wine were recorded and released in the annual report.

Theoretically, the number should have decreased, but when it didn't, the Watchtower explained, 'unknowing new people and disgruntled disfellowshipped members partook out of ignorance' so they didn't count.

In our minds, as the number of the remnant decreased, we were closer to the end of the world. To back this, they used Matthew 24:30

that reads: "This generation shall not pass away before these things (the end of the world) take place." This generation was now into their eighties and nineties, and the time of the end was right around the corner. The Memorial service took place in every country all over the world. Weeks ahead of the event, we handed out leaflets with the time and place of the event to anyone and everyone associated with Jehovah's Witnesses. Even though it wasn't an Easter celebration, I bought a new dress for Brandi. I felt unique being part of this elite group who was going to live on the paradise earth. It didn't dawn on me I was being relegated to a second-class place in the organization.

Nevertheless, I was happy to be included in this select group of people who were God's chosen people. I didn't know how I would have made friends if I weren't a Jehovah's Witness. Even Gary was surprised by how many 'friends' I had in Emporium. Gary thought that moving would get me away from Jehovah's Witnesses. He didn't realize there were Kingdom Halls throughout the area. What I didn't know at the time was the love of the brotherhood was not only conditional, it was sexist. As long as I talked, dressed, and acted like everyone else, and as long as I stayed in subjection to my husband and the brothers at the Kingdom Hall, I would be in good standing with my new friends.

After all the moving boxes were emptied--the emotional baggage would take me years to unpack--I signed Brandi up for her last months of first grade at the Cameron County Elementary School. When I met her new teacher, Mrs. Rose Haas, I informed her, "We are Jehovah's Witnesses, and Brandi won't be celebrating any holidays or saluting the flag."

With a look of concern and a wrinkle in her brow, Mrs. Haas replied, "I understand. I've had other students who are Jehovah's Witnesses." Thankfully, she was extra kind to Brandi and went out of her way to make her feel welcome and included in her new class.

On the warm spring days, Justin played outside and met a little boy named Kain, who lived across the street. When Kain's mom Linda saw me outside sitting on the front porch, she asked if Justin could swim in their pool with her son. I hesitated because I wasn't supposed to let my children play with 'worldly' children. Although Linda wasn't a Jehovah's Witness, her friendly smile and hospitality won me over, and I let Justin play with Kain. I sat on the pool deck with Linda to make sure nothing terrible happened. As the children were splashing in the pool, Linda said she knew about Jehovah's Witnesses from Martha. On more than one occasion, she told me to be careful of Martha's husband, Dick, who she thought was a peeping Tom.

When Martha and I met weekly for a home Bible study, I noticed Dick seemed preoccupied with how Nicole dressed. He would send her to her room to change her clothes if he didn't like what she was wearing. I felt uncomfortable around him and asked someone else to take over the bible study.

I would live in Emporium for the next seventeen years of my life. At the time, trapped in an unhappy marriage and a religion that controlled every aspect of my life, I didn't know how to listen to the whispers of my heart, which later became screams.

New Life

I spent the summer getting ready for the birth of my third child. If the baby was a girl, I wanted to name her Jasmine. I loved the name from the song *Summer Breeze* by Seals and Croft and the thought of the scent of Jasmine blowing through the air. While I was at the Cameron County Library located on the corner of Broad and Fourth Streets, I found a book on baby names. As I perused the book, the name Cherey, meaning "dear one" caught my eye. And Jasmine would be her middle name. I didn't consider a boy's name. In my soul, I knew the baby would be a girl.

Along with the baby name book, I checked out books about natural childbirth. *The Leboyer Gentle Childbirth Method,* where bright hospital lights are dimmed, soft music played, and the baby is given a warm bath after being returned to the mother for warmth and nurturing, appealed to me. I also read about a practice called rooming-in. Some hospitals in the area were now allowing the baby to stay in the mother's room instead of the nursery. I was determined to have this experience with my baby. I also learned about the pros and cons of circumcision and announced to Gary that if the baby was a boy, he wouldn't be circumcised.

In the five years between the time I had given birth to Justin to now, when I was expecting my third child, ultrasounds became available. When

Dr. Punzalon, a new OB/GYN in Ridgway, told me he would be doing the procedure to make sure the baby was developing, I asked about the dangers of ultrasound to the fetus. He didn't have an answer. I told him the procedure wouldn't be an option for me, and I would have a natural childbirth. Also, I wouldn't be using the fetal heart monitor during delivery as it increased the chances of Caesarean sections. I also informed him I wanted the baby to room-in with me, and lastly, I wouldn't receive a blood transfusion under any circumstances, even if it came to life or death because I was a Jehovah's Witness.

The blood transfusion issue was a significant teaching which set Jehovah's Witnesses apart from other religions. They used Bible verses from Genesis 9:4, Leviticus 17:10, and Acts 15:28-15:29, which ordered people not to use blood products for any reason. They believed that blood represents life and is sacred to God. Jehovah's Witnesses took this teaching seriously. Anyone who received a blood transfusion, for themselves or their children, would be disfellowshipped from the religion. Although it sounds primitive to people outside of the faith, to Jehovah's Witnesses, it was a rational decision. At the time, I shut off how I would feel emotionally if my baby or myself died from lack of blood. Shutting things out was easy for me because that is how I survived my childhood.

During the summer, I made monthly doctor visits, which turned into weekly trips from Emporium to Ridgway. With Brandi and Justin in tow, we would spend the whole day at Jane's two-story house on Metoxet Avenue. I met Jane when I first became a Jehovah's Witness. Over the past five years, she had become a role model, teaching me what my mother wasn't able to, such as how to feed my children healthy nutritious food, how to live on a shoestring budget, how to discipline children, and how to be a kind person. She had seven children. Two of her younger boys, and my son Justin, spent the day playing with toy trucks and cars in the backyard in a sawdust pile under a large pine tree. Her girls, who were older than Brandi, played Barbie dolls, using Celestial Seasoning tea boxes and whatever else they could find for furniture. For lunch, the girls made stacks of peanut butter, mayonnaise, and dill pickle sandwiches for everyone. In the afternoon, the girls would take all the kids to the Ridgway Community pool to swim.

Jane always had a hearty meal of hamburger gravy over mashed potatoes, or sausage biscuits and gravy and sometimes "Snake Stew," which was beef stew roasted in the oven for supper to feed everyone. Jane handled crises with ease and calm. When Justin stepped on a rake lying in the backyard, the sharp end caught him in the lip. As blood was gushing from his mouth, Jane applied a warm cloth and told me to take him to the emergency room, where Dr. Thompson stitched him up.

Jane knew I didn't have room for a crib in the crowded apartment and let me borrow a small handcrafted white crib where each of her children slept. She also offered to watch Brandi and Justin when the baby was born. Jane was like a mother I never had, like a sister I always wanted, and a friend I thought I would have for life. The 'sisters' from Emporium had a baby shower for me at Sizerville State Park and gifted me with beautiful clothes and all that I needed for the baby.

When I went into labor on September 8th, 1983, Gary and I drove over to Ridgway with Brandi and Justin. I dropped the children off at Jane's house and went to the hospital to find out the progress of my labor. The nurse told me I was two centimeters dilated. I told her I wanted to go to my friend's house in Ridgway and would return to the hospital as the labor progressed. I spent the rest of the day and evening visiting with Jane, while Gary and her husband Dennis sat in the kitchen drinking beer. When my water broke in the evening, Jane encouraged me to go to the hospital. I knew her husband Dennis had delivered her children and was hoping I could have the baby at her house. When I brought up the idea to Gary, he insisted we get to the hospital.

As the nurse examined me, she told me I was fully effaced and ready to deliver anytime. She paged Dr. Punzalon, who arrived within minutes. After examining me, with a look of horror on his face, he said, "The baby is in a face presentation. You need a Caesarean section. Nurse, notify the surgery team."

While my arms were being strapped to insert an IV, the doctor lectured me about waiting to come to the hospital. I felt my face turning red with anger and started to shake. It felt as if I was going into shock. I tried my best to ignore him and concentrated on breathing during the contractions. I stared at the cement block walls and ceiling, praying to Jehovah for strength and safety. And I used my coping skill of dissociation.

I felt myself rise above the table where my body was lying, and I watched everything from above. The lyrics to the song *Roseanna* by Toto ran through my mind. While waiting for the surgery team to arrive, the baby proceeded down the birth canal to the point at which a Caesarean section wasn't possible. Dr. Punzalon ordered the nurse to cancel the surgery. I ordered the nurses to remove the IV and the straps holding my arms down, which they did. The labor progressed, and within minutes I gave birth to a healthy baby girl. As the doctor handed her to the nurse to be weighed, I requested to hold the baby to breastfeed. The nurse begrudgingly put the eight-pound bundle of joy in my arms.

As I held her and gazed into her beautiful eyes, I again thought about calling her Roseanna but stayed with the name Cherey Jasmine. Cherey wasn't only a beautiful name, but it was a cheerful name. It reminded me of Mary Poppin's song Chim Chim Cher-ee. I loved the part in the movie where Bert rose out of the ashes singing such a cheerful tune.

As the doctor stitched up a small vaginal tear, he started lecturing me again, about not wanting a blood transfusion and waiting to go to the hospital. I told him I didn't ever want to talk to him again. When the nurse took me to the small room where there was barely room for a bassinet, I told her the baby would be rooming-in with me. As she handed me admission forms to sign, she informed me rooming-in wasn't in hospital policy. I read through the papers, and before I signed my name, I wrote in 'The baby has my permission to room-in with me.' I handed the papers back to her and said, "Now it's in the policy the baby can room-in."

She abruptly walked out of the room and returned minutes later with the baby. She squeezed the bassinet in between my bed and the wall and told me the baby would be returning to the nursery at night. I said, "No, the baby will be staying with me for the night, and tomorrow I will be going home." I was informed the required stay was three days to educate me about caring for a baby. I told her I had two other children at home and didn't need any educating.

In the morning, when the doctor made his rounds, he said in his broken English, "I wasn't taught about natural childbirth in school and didn't believe it possible. The baby is healthy and beautiful." I was still angry with him and said I would be going home that day. He nodded his head yes as if he understood and signed the release papers.

A few weeks after Cherey was born, my mother was hospitalized for a large tumor in her abdomen. My brother, Jack, and his wife, Connie, drove from Wisconsin with their three children. My oldest brother, Paul, and his wife, Dottie, traveled from Michigan with their young daughter. Both of my sisters-in-laws brought beautiful gifts for Cherey. My brother Bob and his wife Gloria, who lived locally, had a little boy and were expecting another baby due to arrive six weeks after Cherey was born. Warren and Bill were living in St. Marys.

Everyone except for my sister Ginny, from Connecticut, were present for the surgery. While we were visiting together, I tried to 'witness' to Dottie. She had a sharp mind and told me in no uncertain terms not to take the Bible literally as there were a lot of discrepancies if I took it at face value. Despite our differences in religion, we got along well.

My mom required a hysterectomy to remove a benign tumor. While she had been distant before the surgery, she seemed more disconnected afterward. After Paul and Dottie moved to Michigan, my mom had moved in with my brother Bill on Rightmeyer Street in St. Marys. Bill took her to see a psychiatrist in Ridgway. As her condition worsened, she was admitted to the psychiatric unit located on the fourth floor of the Ridgway Hospital, where she received Electric Shock Treatments. After being released, she began attending the Dickinson Mental Health Partial Hospitalization Program for outpatient therapy.

The only thing I knew about mental illness was learned when I visited the North Warren State Hospital in Warren, Pennsylvania, with a Jehovah's Witness friend who was visiting her cousin. The eerie place, with concrete walls, locked gates, and drugged patients walking around in hospital gowns reminded me of the movie *One Flew Over the Cuckoo's Nest* that I had watched in 1975. The thought of my mother being in a psych unit felt shameful and embarrassing.

Against my better judgment, I visited my mom, when she was hospitalized again for the second time. The psychiatric floor at Ridgway Hospital was much nicer than the State Hospital, but my mom wasn't much better than the other patients. She seemed like a zombie, staring into space and uncommunicative. I felt helpless and ashamed. I called Dr. Ordiway, her psychiatrist, to see what I could do to make the situation better. While talking with him, I broke down crying. He suggested not to get involved with her care and to take care of myself. I took his advice.

Our little apartment in Emporium was crowded with the new baby, and by spring, we were ready to move into a larger home. Gary and I picked out a three-bedroom mobile home from Owl Homes in Olean, New York. Land was hard to find in Emporium, so we rented a lot at a trailer court on the Four Mile Road, about four miles out of town. Brandi made quick friends with a neighbor girl named Barb Skinner. I got along with her mom Peg and enjoyed chatting with her even though she wasn't a Jehovah's Witness. Barb's dad, Leroy, was retired from the military and served in Viet Nam. He was suffering from the effects of Agent Orange; a chemical used to defoliate the Asian jungle. I asked him if he knew the chemical was dangerous, and he said, "No, ma'am, I believed everything my government told me, and they assured us it was safe."

Jehovah's Witnesses took a strong stance against war and refused to be any part of the military, including making weapons or supporting a war in any way. It was offensive to Leroy that we didn't pledge allegiance to the flag or believe in serving in the military. For me, his experience verified Jehovah's Witnesses had a valid stance. This belief precluded boys from joining Boy Scouts because it was considered pre-training for the military. If drafted, Jehovah's Witnesses would be conscientious objectors, so they would never have to go to war.

After my brother Jack served in Viet Nam, he re-enlisted in the Army to eventually spend over thirty years in the military. When Cherey was a little over a year old, we drove out to visit Jack and Connie, who then lived in Southern Illinois. I did my best to keep my religious beliefs to myself, and they made it easy by having activities planned. While there, we went to the zoo and visited the Gateway Arch in St. Louis, Missouri. I felt conflicted, wanting to have a relationship with my brother and his family, but my thinking that the military was an evil entity caused unease between us.

Even though we were living over fifty miles away from my friend Jane, I kept in touch by driving over to Ridgway once a month. In July of 1985, the two of us piled the kids into the back of her station wagon and drove up to Northeast, Pennsylvania, to pick cherries and take the kids swimming in Lake Erie. On the way up, I felt myself getting nauseous. When I returned home, I bought a home pregnancy kit. It read positive. I was now expecting my fourth child.

I found a country doctor located in Port Allegheny, who was willing to deliver the baby without any interventions. The hospital in Coudersport was much more progressive than the hospitals in Elk County. Caleb Marc arrived on March 15th, 1986, at the Coudersport Hospital with the lights dimmed and calm music playing. The doctor stepped in as soon as the baby was ready to be born and stepped out as soon as Caleb was in my arms. The only room available for rooming-in was one the doctors used. I stayed overnight and was delighted to go home the next day.

Although Caleb was a good baby, I felt overwhelmed and stressed with caring for four children nearly on my own. Gary worked two jobs to provide for the family and thought he needed time to himself. He took an annual vacation to the Jamboree in the Hills in West Virginia. I cut back on how much time I spent in the door to door ministry to take care of the children.

One sign of a cult is that it separates people from their family members. Jehovah's Witnesses accomplished this by not permitting its members to celebrate holidays or attend weddings and funerals in churches. We were kept so busy in the preaching work and going to meetings that we didn't have time to spend with the family who weren't Jehovah's Witnesses. Also, we called each other brother and sister, making us feel that people in the religion were our family. In the end, blood is thicker than water, and despite being a Jehovah's Witness, I tried my best to stay in touch with family. I also felt as if I were trying to keep together the family that I lost as a child when we went to Mooseheart and we were all separated.

My brother Warren moved to a camp outside of St. Marys, where we had family reunions in the summer. My sister Ginny started visiting Pennsylvania with her family. Brandi and her daughter Tammy got along well and had fun riding the four-wheeler at my brother's camp. We did our best to be a family, but my brothers drank a lot and it scared me when they took the kids for rides while they were drinking.

During the summer, the children and I rode with my mom and my brother Warren out to Connecticut to see my sister Ginny and her family. Brandi was breaking out in the chickenpox, and it was a long hot ride for her. When we got to Ginny's, she told us we would be camping for the duration of the visit and put us up in a beat-up camper with uncovered foam mattresses and a leaky roof. She fed us peanut butter and jelly sandwiches for breakfast, lunch, and supper.

Although we planned a three-day visit, my mother had enough and decided we would leave the next day after driving over ten hours to get there. My brother Warren and I decided to stay another day so the children could swim and play with their cousins. In the evening, Ginny's husband Dick took Brandi and Justin to an auction and didn't return until after midnight. I stayed up waiting for them to return. The next day I was exhausted and tired. I cried tears of disappointment, shame, and embarrassment the whole way home and vowed I would never travel to see my sister again.

After Gary's mom had passed away, his dad sold the house on Mark Street, where he lived. He built a house on a piece of property he purchased from Gary's Aunt Bert on Brusselles Street. With money from the sale of the house on Mark Street, he gave each of his three children $5000, which he insisted we spend on a satellite since there wasn't any television service where we lived at North Creek. On holidays we gathered at the new house with Gary's sisters and their families for holiday dinners until it became too crowded with all the grandchildren. I felt guilty for celebrating the holidays so I started making excuses as to why we couldn't attend. I didn't realize that holidays weren't only about celebrating an event, they were important times for families to gather and connect with each other. My belief that I was doing something 'right' and they were doing something 'wrong' fed my false ego and created distance me and my family members.

In 1990, one of Gary's cousins, Tom Rung, who lived next door to Gary's dad on Brusselles Street, shot and killed his partner, Vera. Vera and I attended high school together. The couple had a little girl. I remembered Vera to be a backward, quiet girl. Before the murder, Barry, Tom's brother, who was a Viet Nam vet, shot himself in the face trying to commit suicide. No one knew about Post Traumatic Stress and chalked it up to Barry's drinking. After Vera's murder, the family didn't know how to talk about or handle death. We all buried the shame no one ever talked about on top of layers of other buried emotions. Everything was swept under the carpet.

Gary's dad met a woman from St. Marys and remarried. The marriage was short-lived. Not long after the break-up with his second wife, he developed prostate cancer and passed away within a few years. I tried to hang on to the idea of whatever semblance of family there was on my side. It was like hanging on to a frayed rope ready to snap anytime.

My brother Paul and I stayed in touch by calling each other once in a while. He and Dottie now had two children. Whenever they came back to Pennsylvania from Michigan, we met at a playground or a hotel to visit. In our conversations, the subject of the extended family would come up. Paul was never able to let go of the bitterness he felt about going to Mooseheart after our father passed away.

Once a year, Gary and I would set aside one hundred dollars from our income tax and take the children out to see Paul and Dottie in Michigan. We had fun going to waterparks, an old-time village, and a restaurant called Frankenmuth for the best chicken dinners around. Paul and Dottie enjoyed seeing everyone have fun and always paid for all our meals and any expenses.

Jack and Connie moved to Wisconsin, so we drove out to see them. On our way to their house, we stopped for a tour of the Kellogg cereal factory in Battlecreek, Michigan. During our visit, Jack tried to give me the book, *Thirty Years as a Watchtower Slave*, but I wouldn't take it because it was prohibited reading, according to the Watchtower Organization. I knew that being a Jehovah's Witness was a strain on our relationship.

On the way home, I 'm not sure what possessed me, but I got the idea to drive down to Illinois to see Mooseheart before we headed back to Pennsylvania. Perhaps I had listened to John Denver's song, *Take Me Home* too many times and was looking for a place I belonged. My children heard my family talk about living at the orphanage, and I thought perhaps they would like to see the institution. I didn't know the toll it would take on my family and on me.

I planned the trip to miss the Chicago traffic hour. Gary drove the car as I read the map to navigate our way to Illinois. It was just about dusk when I could make out the large red letters which spelled MOOSEHEART above the football stadium. Justin was sitting in the back seat looking out the window. When he saw the chain link fence, he asked, "Mommy is this a prison?"

"No, this is where mommy lived when I was a little girl," I answered.

As we entered the grounds of Mooseheart, Gary stopped at the stop sign posted outside the guardhouse. When he rolled down the window to talk to the guard, I told the man standing watch, "I used to live here and am taking my children to see where I grew up."

I had no intention of asking anyone for permission. I instructed Gary to keep on driving, which he did. The grounds of the campus were vacant. I expected there to be children playing outside like I had to until dark, but there wasn't one child in sight. I told the children about Baby Village, thinking they could get out and play at the playground for a few minutes. We drove past the massive three-story, cement block building called Loyalty Hall, where my mom lived. I explained to them that this is where I went to visit her for one hour a day. Brandi asked, "Why didn't you live with your mom?

When I didn't have an answer, tears welled up in my eyes. 'Why?" is a question I never ask, much less try to answer. I only knew how shitty it felt. Thinking I could hide my sadness from the children, I told them to stay in the car with Gary while I walked to Baby Village alone. I forgot about letting them play at the playground.

The first place I went to was to Schuylkill Hall, where my mother had dropped me off over thirty years before. I no longer felt like a grown-up as I walked up the red brick steps and opened the same wooden white painted gate. Instead, I felt like a helpless little girl. Rather than knocking on the door, I walked into the building where a matron who wasn't Mommy Cox met me. In the background, I saw five little girls peeking around the corner to see who was at the door. I heard voices of little girls who sounded like Vita York, Tammy Ruple, and Kathy Brasch. They were in the background jumping up and down on the beds.

I introduced myself to the matron. "My name is Jeanette, and I came here to tell you to love these little girls. Hug them and take good care of them." I turned around and walked out of the hall.

My children and Gary were walking around the heart-shaped baby pool, centered in the middle of Baby Village. We all got back in the car, and I told Gary to drive to Virginia Hall. The kids and Gary stayed in the car while I got out and went up to the hall. I felt a little older now and was feeling more angry than helpless. The front door of the building was locked, so I had to knock. When a matron came to the door, I told her I used to live in the hall and wanted to see it again. I pushed the door open to take a walk through the hall and, as clear as day, saw myself dressed in a nightgown on my hands and knees, scrubbing the floor with a toothbrush.

When I noticed the matron dialing numbers on the telephone, I quickly left the hall and returned to the car. Gary was getting nervous and suggested we leave. I agreed. Rather than exiting through the front gate, I directed him to the dairy farm where we could escape the campus through the back gate. As we drove past the large dairy barn, I longed to get out and show the kids where I had pleasant memories but knew by now the guards would be on our trail.

It felt as if I had two more children in the car- a three-year-old little girl from Schuylkill Hall and a ten-year-old girl from Virginia Hall-who were fragmented parts of myself that I lost from trauma-induced dissociation. I was helping them escape from Mooseheart like I wished someone would have done for me. I kept my eye out for headlights in the rearview mirror. I was relieved we made it out without getting stopped, and no one coming after us. A full moon was shining in the sky, and I prayed that God would watch over us and get us home safely. By the time we arrived at the Indiana state border, my heartbeat had slowed down, and I didn't feel so disoriented. The children, including the two extra I now had in tow, all fell asleep. I stayed awake to help Gary navigate our way home.

Caged Bird

———————————————

G ary enjoyed working at GKN and made friends with his co-workers, who invited us to suppers and parties. Even though they weren't
Jehovah's Witnesses, I enjoyed their company. He also connected with a
family who had a farm and processed the meat from their own cattle. Justin
and his dad enjoyed butchering and spending time at the farm together.
On one occasion, Justin came home with his front tooth broken due to a
side of beef hitting him in the face. Instead of being grateful that he wasn't
seriously hurt, I screamed at Gary for allowing the accident to happen.
Thankfully, there was a pediatric dentist in Coudersport who was able to
fix the broken tooth.

Living in the trailer court became challenging when Cherey made
friends with a family who moved into a trailer across from ours. They had
a two-year-old girl the same age as Cherey, who swore like a sailor a few
times while the children were outside playing. When I told Cherey it was
time to come inside, the child called me a bitch. When Cherey repeated the
word a couple of times, I washed her mouth out with soap. I wish I had better parenting skills and could have explained to her the difference between
right and wrong words.

An older woman named Miss Hackett, who was a retired librarian, lived in the trailer court and invited the girls into her mobile home for story hour once a week. She prepared a snack for them and made them wash their hands before eating. When I saw how much Cherey enjoyed going to Miss Hackett's for story hour, I signed her up for story-time at the Cameron County Public Library on Wednesday mornings. Each week, the librarian, greeted us with a warm smile and made sure Cherey felt included.

It didn't take long to feel crowded with four children in the mobile home. I found myself hollering at the children for playing too loudly. Sizerville State Park was only a few miles up the road, so we started spending time there swimming in the pool and taking walks in the woods. We waded in the cold creek water, stepping gingerly on the slippery rocks. It felt good to be free. There was no one watching our every move and telling us what to do. The aroma of the hemlock and white pine trees filled my lungs. It was refreshing to be able to breathe freely. Just as I found comfort in nature while living at Mooseheart, I found solace in the natural surroundings of the Elk State Forest.

When it was too hot to cook in the trailer, I packed up a picnic basket, and we headed to the park to grill hamburgers and hot dogs over a wood fire. I imagined the park was my own personal country club that I had access to at no cost all year round. The soothing sound of the wind swaying the tall pines gave me the strength to face life's challenges. I became familiar with the melodious songbirds and thought I might like to have a bird as a pet. I found a woman who sold songbirds and purchased a couple of apricot-colored canaries. I didn't like that they had to stay in a cage and tried to let them fly free in the mobile home, which ended in their demise.

The birds were a metaphor for my life. I felt like a caged bird, contained to a cage for fear of something catastrophic happening to me if I ever flew free. At the meetings, we were warned that leaving Jehovah's Witnesses would end in our demise, people who left the religion ended up becoming alcoholics, drug abusers, and living immoral lifestyles. The talks always ended with a scripture reading from John 6:68, where Jesus asked his twelve apostles if they wanted to leave. "Simon Peter replied, Lord, to whom would we go? You have words of eternal life." They claimed Jehovah's Witness was the true religion and led us to believe there was no other source for truth.

Sizerville wasn't only a spiritual place; I would later learn it was also a magical place full of miracles. The park became a sanctuary for me. While walking through the forest trails, carpeted with golden pine needles, with the beautiful blue sky above, I found myself conversing with God, asking him to help me raise my children. I didn't have conversations with God at the Kingdom Hall. The peaceful Elk Forest was a respite from the austere meeting place of Jehovah's Witnesses.

The drab Kingdom Hall had orange carpeting, puke green theater seats, and tapestry curtains. There weren't any pictures, flowers, or statues; only chairs and a podium on a small stage. A banner quoting a scripture hung on the wall above the stage. We sang Kingdom songs to the accompaniment of music played on a turntable. Most of the music had a dark tone and was part of the brainwashing, which drilled the teachings of Jehovah's Witnesses into our minds.

Several times a week, the children had to sit still and listen to monotonous talks for hours at a time. If the children misbehaved, they were taken to the bathroom and spanked. I regret to say that I participated in this disdainful practice modeled by the elders. If children didn't behave at the meetings, parents were instructed to punish them at home. One mother made her children pick a branch from a lilac bush for their switching. I was a little more lenient with my children as I allowed them to draw during the meetings and read secular books until a brother chastised me for bringing a book with fairy tales. He cautioned me and said the stories were demonic. I questioned his sanity.

The highly controlled meetings were monotonous and mind-numbing. On Sundays, a brother conducted the Watchtower study. Sisters were allowed to answer the questions after a brother read each paragraph from an article we studied the night before by underlining all the answers. The meetings were guilt-inducing and addressed the gamut of human behavior from gossip to masturbation. I started to feel guilty about every move I made. Unlike mainstream churches, there wasn't any avenue for forgiveness, such as confession. We were only encouraged to tell the brothers of our sin; then, we would be punished by having 'privileges,' such as answering at meetings or going out in service, taken away. To relieve the burden of guilt from ourselves, we all watched for other people to fall short of the rules, and would go to the elders and tattle, feeling like we were helping those who were falling short.

When I was at Sizerville, I never felt guilt; all judgment was suspended in this sacred place where I was about to meet people who would become close and dear friends. At the time, I felt like I was in a dark tunnel, but I found people who were beacons of light at the other end. We attended nature programs offered at the park. The park naturalist Lisa Bainey, a young woman in her twenties, with light brunette hair and a welcoming smile, took us on hikes in the park and taught the children and me about the fauna and the flora of the area. We followed Lisa through the forest like she was the Pied Piper of Hamlin, catching crayfish in the creeks and picking daylily buds, which we steamed over a campfire. Lisa taught us about songbirds, and I volunteered to help repair bluebird boxes. From the time Caleb was a baby, I took him to every nature class at Sizerville, pushing him in an umbrella stroller through the woods. He grew up learning the names of birds, plants, and mammals. We dissected owl pellets, learned about spittlebugs, made cough drops from coltsfoot, and learned Velcro was inspired by the burdock plant.

At one of the nature classes, Lisa read a beautiful poem, *Be the Best of Whatever You Are* by Douglas Malloch to the children. As she read in her soft voice, I thought about how I wanted to instill the meaning of the poem in my children and myself. I copied the poem and carried it with me for many years.

If you can't be a pine on top of the hill
Be a scrub in the valley—but be
The best little scrub by the side of the rill;
Be a bush if you can't be a tree.
If you can't be a bush be a bit of grass,
And some highway some happier make;
If you can't be a muskie, then just be a bass—
But the liveliest bass in the lake!
We can't all be captains, we've got to be crew,
There's something for all of us here.
There's big work to do and there's lesser to do,
And the task we must do is real.
If you can't be a highway then just be a trail,
If you can't be the sun be a star;
It isn't by size that you win or you fail—
Be the best of whatever you are!

On weekends, Gary and I would pitch a tent and camp at the camp-ground. At dusk, we watched movies about bats and went hunting for the nocturnal mammals after dark.

Learning about the dark side of life alleviated fears I had acquired in my childhood; fear of mice, fear of the dark, fear of getting lost, fear of the unknown. Lisa taught me to embrace the darker side of myself, the me who felt lost, even though other parts of me thought they had all the answers to life.

When Justin was in kindergarten, he came home and said, "Mom, there's a little boy at school who has bread that breaks apart, like mine." He had asked me on several occasions if he could have soft white bread like the other kids. I always answered, "Absolutely not. White bread is full of chemicals and preservatives."

I longed to know the little boy's mom who made him sandwiches on homemade bread as I did. I met her at the school's first open house.

While I was talking with the teacher, Justin started playing with a boy his age named Micah. He was as quiet and shy as Justin. His mom, Pat, introduced herself and told me she had recently moved here from eastern Pennsylvania and lived at Sizerville. She invited us to her cabin located at the far end of the park.

While visiting, I learned she also ordered healthy food from Genesee Natural Foods, and we began combining our orders. It didn't take long for us to become friends. The only glitch was she was a devout Catholic. To justify being friends with her, I had to witness to her. Thankfully, she was kind and didn't seem to mind talking about the Bible. We met at the park while the children played, to discuss the Bible. Pat told me how much the rosary and Catholic faith meant to her, and I never pushed her to give up what brought her comfort. Although I had 'friends' from the Kingdom Hall, I didn't have as much in common with them as I did Pat. I called them friends because we were of the same religion, but few appreciated the outdoors and nature as I did. Pat's friendship was a shining light in a dark sky.

It was refreshing to have a true friend who valued caring for children holistically and took pleasure in the outdoors. Justin and Micah spent a lot of time together, riding around the park on their bicycles. Pat and I sewed forestry badges on khaki shirts, and they pretended to be forest rangers. Brandi and Cherey played with Pat's two daughters. In the winter, I took Justin and Brandi up to the park to ice skate on a little pond. They learned to skate by pushing the younger children in the umbrella strollers. It was a happy time for all of us, although Pat seemed to get sick often and was always cleaning the house with bleach to kill whatever germs were affecting her.

Pat was the epitome of kindness who loved her children from the depths of her heart. She gave me a book titled, *Love You Forever* by Robert Munsch to read to my children. The first night I read the book to Cherey, who was in kindergarten at the time, I couldn't stop crying as I read the singsong verses, "I'll love you forever, I'll like you for always, As long as I'm living, my baby you'll be." I cried for the mother who wasn't able to cherish me, and for the first time in my life, I understood a mother's unconditional love. I now had an idea of how to love my children through the various stages of growth they would be going through.

When Pat became pregnant with their fourth child, I was invited to her baby shower at June Hornung's house, where I met her friends Mary Solveson and Mary Gelnett. All of the women attended St. Mark's Catholic Church together, and I got along with them, as we all lived earthy lifestyles. However, I never fit into the group because I was a Jehovah's Witness. There was always cognitive dissonance going through my head. I enjoyed their company but felt like I was doing something wrong. I wouldn't let myself belong.

Justin and Micah stayed friends until Micah was old enough to join Boy Scouts and play sports, then they parted ways. Jehovah's Witnesses didn't allow children to join Boy Scouts due to it being patriotic and preparatory for the military. Any sport was out because of the worldly association. Justin wanted desperately to play football but wasn't allowed. Micah's dad, Ken, got a job at a state park in another part of the state, and the family moved. We were all sad to see Pat and the kids leave. Not soon after, I learned Pat had cancer and passed away. Because she died before Armageddon, I found comfort in the Jehovah's Witness belief that she would be resurrected to paradise.

When Brandi started second grade and Justin started kindergarten, I worried about 'bad' associations on the school bus and their friends at school. At the Kingdom Hall assemblies, we were constantly warned about bad associations. I did my best to keep them away from 'worldly' kids, but when I went to the school for a play or open house, all the teachers and other parents were kind. Justin made friends with an eager little boy named Archie, who lived with his Aunt June because his mom had recently passed away. I met June at Pat's baby shower, and to my surprise, she showed an interest in the Bible and accepted a Bible Study when I stopped at her house in my door to door work. When I would visit June at her home, Brandi would go with me and play with her little girl Candace, who was Cherey's age. June was a friendly person, and I felt justified associating with her since she was studying the Bible. We became good friends and started spending a lot of time together.

When I needed time for myself while living at the trailer court, I would take long walks up the Four Mile Road where an elderly 'sister' named Ann lived in an old farmhouse. She was as odd as she was kind and always appreciated having company. She cooked with a wood cookstove and didn't drive so other brothers and sisters would take her to the meetings and out in service.

Although everyone was kind, I felt crowded living close to people at the trailer court. Sister Ann offered to sell us an acre of her land. After it didn't pass the septic perk test, we began looking for another place of our own. Gary and I found a piece of property for sale in North Creek, which we were able to buy for a reasonable price. We had the land excavated by Dale Fox, who had graduated with me from high school. His mother-in-law owned the property we bought. I was a little nervous about seeing him again as he was one of the 'red neck' kids, but after getting reacquainted, we got along well. He had a good sense of humor and liked to joke around.

After we had the mobile home moved to North Creek, Gary started working with Dale part-time, driving the dump truck. On weekends, Justin went with Gary and enjoyed riding in the heavy equipment. To make extra room for the kids, we built an addition with a loft onto the mobile home. Brandi and Cherey now had a bigger bedroom, and we had a dining space heated with a kerosene heater and wood burner. Gary wasn't adept at finishing projects, so I made do and painted a hopscotch pattern on the plywood floor and hung a trapeze swing from the rafters where Cherey had hours of fun playing.

Gary's dad gave Justin a band saw which we set up in the addition. We started making cut-out birdhouses from scrap wood and giving them as gifts to friends. In the winter, the children enjoyed playing in the woods and sledding down a pipeline behind the trailer. In the summer, they used the hill for a waterslide. I had room for a little garden and planted a few vegetables, although the deer ate most of what grew.

We also made friends with other people who lived in North Creek. The families with children Justin and Brandi's age invited them to neighborhood ball games and other events. We got to know Rick and Lucy, who lived at the other end of North Creek. Lucy invited me to their trailer for tea, and we asked them to our place for a cookout. Rick liked to drink and was loud after having a few beers. He started swearing around the kids, and when I asked him not to curse, he asked me what I would do if he didn't. I was holding a banana cream pie Lucy made and told him, "If you say one more swear word, I'll throw this pie at you."

He replied, "You don't have a mean enough bone in your body to do that."

I turned to Lucy and asked if I could throw the pie.

Lucy was always up for a good time and laughingly shook her head up and down. When the next swear word came out of his mouth, I picked up the pie and threw it at him. As he wiped the yellow pudding and cool whip off his face, he repeatedly said he couldn't believe I did it. Thankfully he also quit swearing for the rest of the evening.

The Witnesses also had picnics and gatherings throughout the year, but I enjoyed the company of Gary's 'worldly' friends. They were more fun and weren't as stiff as the people from the Kingdom Hall. At the meetings, there were continuous warnings about associating with worldly people, and my conscience began to bother me. I was again experiencing cognitive dissonance, a state in which someone holds two or more contrary beliefs. As much as I enjoyed being with people who weren't Jehovah's Witnesses, I did value a few close friends I made over the years. Although I moved to Emporium, I still considered Vickie--a high school friend--my best friend. Vickie's little girl, who was a year younger than Brandi, became close friends, spending time at each other's houses. I also became good friends with her sister, Cookie, who had become a Jehovah's Witness. We no longer got high together but instead spent time together while the children played. Cookie now had four children. When they were little, we cared for each other's children and became closer than I ever felt to my biological siblings. I couldn't bear the thought of not having them in my life.

I also became close to Sandy and Pat Maietta, who had moved to Emporium from Long Island, New York with their three children, Ami, Erin, and Jeff. They learned about the remote area from a circuit overseer who encouraged them to move where the 'need was great.' Intending to live in the country, the family bought a ranch-style house in Rich Valley. The children thought they were moving to an area where rich people lived but instead found themselves in the middle of nowhere, on a property next to a creek, for their entertainment.

Sandy was a mechanic of short stature with sandy brown hair and a good sense of humor. Although he was baptized, he never attained a position as a ministerial servant or elder in the congregation due to his fun-loving nature. Pat was a tall, lovely woman who spoke quietly. I felt an instant connection with her and found out later it was because we were both abused as children.

Sandy and my husband Gary got along well, drinking beer and talking about cars while Pat and I enjoyed preparing meals and gardening. We spent many days together, working in her gardens, while our children played outside together. We also spent many hours going door to door together. I felt as if Pat and I were more than 'spiritual sisters.' Pat seemed like a real sister that I hoped to have for eternity.

Another Witness friend who still lived in St. Mary's was Mary. Her husband wasn't a Jehovah's Witness, and she had five children. We enjoyed each other's company and spent many hours out in field service. While traveling back and forth to assemblies together, she once shared a poem by Victor Hugo which resonated deep in my soul: "*Be like the bird who, pausing in her flight awhile on boughs too slight, feels them give way beneath her, and yet sings, knowing she hath wings."* I typed the poem out in a large font and framed it. It hangs above my writing desk to this day. I knew if I ever wrote a book about my life, the title would be *She Hath Wings*.

Mary and I enjoyed the same music and listened to The Indigo Girls and other folk music. She invited me to go to a Mary Chapin Carpenter concert at the Chautauqua Institute in New York. I fell in love with the lake and the ambiance of the closed community. When her daughter Debbie got married, I attended the wedding and helped with the food preparation. When her mother passed away, I drove three hours to attend the out of town funeral.

After I moved to Emporium, Mary and her husband divorced. I introduced her to a man who was attending meetings in Emporium. He lived outside of Austin, Pennsylvania, in a log cabin he built himself. It wasn't long before the two of them married, and Mary moved to Coudersport with her two teenage sons. Mary's daughter, Debbie, moved to the Philippines with her husband, who was in the Air Force.

When Debbie was diagnosed with cancer, I tried to be a good friend to Mary by listening and showing her compassion, even though her daughter wasn't a Jehovah's Witness. I thought my relationship with Mary was what it would be like to have a real sister. I thought we would be friends for eternity.

I always had to consider that if I continued to associate with worldly people, I would be 'marked' as a danger to those inside the group, and my friends would quit associating with my children and me, except for at the meetings and out in field service. I sided with Jehovah's Witnesses and began giving Gary excuses as to why we couldn't visit our 'worldly' friends.

Dark Night of the Soul

Jehovah's Witnesses encouraged adult children to care for their elderly parents. Out of obligation, I tried to help my mother. My mom was living on Rightmeyer Street with my brother Bill, but the two of them didn't get along. She called and said she wanted to move to Emporium. I called around and found available apartments, but when she came down to look at them, she said they were trash. Instead, she moved into the Elk County Towers, a government housing unit. I felt a sigh of relief; she wouldn't be living near me.

When I went to St. Marys for groceries and saw her walking through town, she looked like a bag lady with her uncombed hair and misbuttoned coat as she shuffled her feet on the heels of her shoes. I felt embarrassed and hoped no one knew she was my mother. She developed lung problems and I drove her to Pittsburgh for tests. It was one of the longest drives of my life, not being able to talk to my mother because she had no idea what was happening in the world or my life.

Trying to care for my mother was challenging as she complained about everyone and everything. I decided the least I could do was bring her a hot meal and eat with her once a month. I made her a meal of meatloaf, mashed potatoes, and carrots. I knew taking all the kids would stress her out, so I decided to only take my five-year-old daughter, Cherey, with me. After driving up from Emporium and carrying the food up to her apartment, I knocked on the door. As I waited for her to answer, standing in the long narrow hallway, I felt myself going back in time to when I visited her at Loyalty Hall at Mooseheart in a similar apartment building. Other resident's doors had flowers and people's names on the front. My mom's door only had a number. When she opened the door, it seemed as if she didn't recognize me. I told her my name and said I had supper for her. She opened the door wider, letting us into the apartment. She was wearing a polyester pantsuit with stains down the front. The apartment reeked of urine.

Cherey held the door open for me as I carried the box of hot food into the apartment and set the warm cardboard box on the table. In the living room, my mom sat on the couch, staring into space. Cherey had to use the toilet, so I took her into the bathroom located next to the bedroom. The floor was scattered with dirty clothes, the sink was littered with gray hair, and the toilet splattered with feces. I used a piece of toilet paper to wipe the seat off for Cherey. Afterward, we used the dried cake of Ivory soap, which looked like it wasn't used in months, to wash our hands.

In the kitchen, the sink was full of dirty dishes and grime-covered the stove and door of the refrigerator. I tried to stay cheerful as I washed three plates and forks and serving spoons. As I filled the sink with hot soapy water, I wondered why my mom didn't take care of herself. I wondered what happened to her in her life. I decided to ask what her life was like when she was younger. Buying time to formulate my words, I nervously dried every tine of the forks before I put them in the silverware drawer. As Cherey set the table, I lifted the warm casserole dishes out of the box and told my mom it was time to eat. She shuffled over to the kitchen from where she was sitting on the sofa.

When we were all seated at the table, I said a prayer, thanking Jehovah for our food. As I cut the meatloaf in slices, with my voice shaking, I asked, "Mom, what was your life like when you were younger?"

In a split second, her catatonic state turned to hysteria. "Get the hell out of here. Who do you think you are coming in here and acting as if you care about me."

"Mom, I love you and brought you a warm meal so we can eat together." I lied. I didn't love my mom. I never even liked my mom.

With saliva coming out of her mouth, she screamed, "You don't love me. Nobody loves me." I wondered if she could read my mind. Feeling the same rejection that I experienced when I was three years old when she dropped me off at Schuylkill Hall at Mooseheart, I felt as if I wanted to collapse to the floor. I looked over to see tears welling up in Cherey's eyes and had enough sense to put the casserole dishes back into the box and leave. It didn't dawn on me that my little girl didn't have any supper and needed to eat before we drove back to Emporium.

Tears rolled down my cheeks, and I thought I would cry an ocean if I didn't distract myself. When we were in the car, driving back to Emporium, Cherey asked me what was wrong. I told her nothing as I fumbled around for a cassette and pushed it into the tape player. Within minutes we were singing, *Down by the Bay* and other songs by Raffi.

This experience sent me into a downward spiral. It would take me years to climb out of a deep abyss of depression. I began to experience excruciating headaches, making me unable to get out of bed on some days. Physical symptoms of stabbing pain in my chest and overwhelming exhaustion worried me, so I made an appointment with my family physician.

Dr. Richard Freeman, who had a practice at the Cameron County Health Center on Third Street, was nearing his forties, with graying hair and a kind smile, and wore wire-rimmed glasses that accented his intelligence. He was soft-spoken and listened more than he talked. I first began seeing him when a doctor in St. Marys tried to diagnose Cherey with Failure to Thrive Syndrome because of her low weight on the growth chart. The doctor wanted to hospitalize her to prove I wasn't feeding her. I opted for a second opinion, and when I took her to Dr. Freeman, he reassured me she appeared healthy and her weight was proportionate to her height. He was a thorough doctor and sent us to Geisinger Hospital to rule out anything serious. She received a clean bill of health. Dr. Freeman received my confidence and trust, which would be invaluable to me in the months ahead.

When I related my physical symptoms, Dr. Freeman immediately ordered blood work for the Epstein Barr Virus, which came back positive. He prescribed bed rest. After a physical exam, he asked, "Are you experiencing any stress?"

I replied, "No, everything in my life is perfect. I am one of Jehovah's Witnesses."

He raised his eyebrows and said, "Really? Where there aren't problems, there isn't growth. No one's life is perfect. I would like to see you again in a month."

At my next appointment, despite trying to get more rest, the headaches and chest pains continued. Dr. Freeman started asking me questions about how I was sleeping and was concerned I was losing weight. He gave me the book *Happiness is a Choice* by Minirth and Meier and instructed me to do the self-test for depression in the back of the book and to bring it back in two weeks at my next visit.

When I returned with the test in hand, it verified what Dr. Freeman suspected. I was clinically depressed. When he suggested taking an antidepressant, I broke down crying. The thing I feared most was happening; I was crazy like my mother. Dr. Freeman suggested I see a psychologist. I adamantly refused, telling him I wasn't crazy like my mom. He explained that depression is a physical illness and medication could help. I agreed to take the prescription. When I went to the pharmacy, I felt ashamed and waited until there weren't any customers in view before I had the prescription filled. When I went home, I hid the pills in my top drawer underneath my socks and underwear so Gary wouldn't find them.

I continued to see Dr. Freeman every week. He sat down and listened intently to me. When I shared with him that people made me feel one way or another, he helped me understand no one could make me feel anything; how I felt was my choice. He understood the strict religious dogma of Jehovah's Witnesses, as he was a Seventh Day Adventist. He helped me set goals and objectives other than my religion.

When I said I enjoyed growing plants and gardening, he shared that he enjoyed horticulture, in particular, growing herbs, and invited me to his house to see his greenhouse. When I stopped by his home, his wife was welcoming. When he saw my interest in herbs, he invited me to a class he was conducting in Bradford. I traveled to the classes once a week and learned how to germinate and propagate a variety of herbs, including parsley, basil, and lavender. The scents of the plants had a relaxing effect on my frazzled nerves. Caring for the seedlings lifted my spirits and gave me a sense of purpose.

At the same time, I was seeing Dr. Freeman, my daughter Brandi's best friend, was diagnosed with cancer. Chastity was fifteen and had moved nearby to Howard Siding, a little settlement halfway between St. Marys and Emporium, with her step-mom, Ginger. The family came to the Kingdom Hall and Brandi and Chasity became instant friends. They both liked New Kids on the Block music. Chastity began to have severe stomach pains, which was chalked up to psychosomatic illness. When her symptoms didn't subside, she was diagnosed with a fast-growing abdominal cancer.

When I went to visit Dr. Freeman, I talked to him about Chastity, and he recommended I read the book *Death and Dying* by Elisabeth Kübler Ross. I checked the book out of the local library and read it cover to cover within a few days. The book helped me understand the stages of grief. Chastity was dying physically, and I felt as if I were dying emotionally.

Chastity often stayed at our house between treatment visits at Roswell. Her brunette hair fell out from chemo treatments, and her weight went from a well-rounded teenager to a thin skeleton. The two of us stayed up late into the night talking while she was at my house. I did my best to listen and tried to understand what she was going through. She thanked me and said, "No one else knows how to listen. Everyone else thinks I'm going to live to be sixteen and get my driver's license, but I know I'm not going to live long."

At the Kingdom Hall, the elders pressured Chastity not to take a blood transfusion if needed during any surgeries. One brother, Frank Scarpelli, who spoke with a strong Midwest accent, was extremely forceful with Chastity, accompanying her to doctor appointments and talking with surgeons. He was part of a 'liaison' committee organized by the Watchtower Bible and Tract Society. The group included a legal team who used a lot of legalese in case a doctor tried to use a court order for a blood transfusion, especially when it came to a minor.

Frank was a middle-aged man with black balding hair and wire-rimmed glasses who wore well-tailored Armani suits. He reminded me of one of the thugs in the Godfather. His wife Sharon and two teenage boys moved to Emporium from Michigan. Their reason for moving there was to help where the 'need was great,' which was a term to define small rural congregations who didn't have many 'publishers,' or people as everyone else would say.

My son Justin, who was then twelve years old, and their son John became instant friends. John was a mischievous boy who liked to joke around and make people laugh. His extroverted personality complimented my son Justin's quiet nature. John's older brother Dan was tall and thin, with dark black hair, and was introverted. Frank adopted both of the boys after their father committed suicide when they were younger.

Their mom, Sharon, a petite woman, dressed neatly and wore straight skirts and high-heeled shoes. Her short haircut was styled perfectly, her perfect make-up never smeared, and a perpetual smile was always painted across her face. I could never figure her out. If someone was sick or died, she still had a smile on her face.

Frank began ruling the small congregation of people with an iron fist. He gave talks at the Kingdom Hall on proper dress and how many times people should be getting up during the meetings to use the bathroom. He condemned us for having hobbies and said we should spend our time studying and spending time out in field service. The teenagers developed a strong dislike for Frank's rules and started saying the Book of Frank was a new book to the Bible.

Quick Build Kingdom Halls, where Witnesses from other congregations remodeled or rebuilt a Kingdom Hall in a weekend, were happening all over the United States. Brothers who had skills in building, roofing, wiring, and plumbing took time off their secular jobs to join the Quick Build team. Frank jumped on the bandwagon and spearheaded a remodeling project of the Emporium Kingdom Hall even though the congregation was small and not well off financially.

The Emporium Hall was stripped down to the foundation and rebuilt. Although the project was called a Quick Build, it took days and days of prep work, tearing down the old building. On weekends, months ahead of the actual building project, brothers in the congregation, along with sisters and young teenagers from neighboring congregations, worked laboriously tearing out moldy carpeting and wood paneling. Even Chastity, who was dying of cancer, pitched in and worked on occasion. We hauled heavy block and mixed cement to build a foundation for an addition to the building. The sisters who weren't able to work prepared meals for the working crew.

After the project was completed, we had a brand-new meeting place with light-colored wallpaper, mauve carpeting, new matching chairs, bright lighting, modern bathrooms, and a new podium from where Frank could deliver his shaming talks. Next to the podium was a little room, no bigger than a closet, where the elders would have clandestine meetings between themselves and publishers who needed counseling. When a person was caught doing something wrong, 'judicial meetings' would be held in the room. The only thing missing from the building was windows; the previous windows that provided natural light were torn out and covered over.

The rationale was that potential break-ins would be minimal; therefore, insurance rates would be lower. Because there wasn't any ventilation, the fumes from the new building products caused me to feel sick each time I entered the building.

Before the project began, publishers pledged how much money they could donate each month to the building. Many of us were cash strapped and couldn't afford much. The Watchtower Bible and Tract Society provided a loan to cover the cost of the project. On the Thursday night meetings, a financial report was given, reminding everyone how much was still owed on the building. Many of us believed Armageddon was right around the corner and we wouldn't be responsible for paying off the loan.

After multiple surgeries, Chastity would be praised at meetings and conventions for not accepting blood transfusions. Annually, the elders distributed wallet-size cards, which were legally binding documents to all baptized members of the congregation. The cards were filled out and signed by at least two other Jehovah's Witnesses as witnesses. At the time Chastity was dying, she, along with my daughter Brandi and my son Justin, and other teenagers were baptized as Jehovah's Witnesses. They were now required to follow all the rules of the organization, including refusing blood transfusions or be disfellowshipped, which would require their family members to disown them.

At the end of Chastity's illness, with the help of the Make-A-Wish foundation, she attended a New Kids On the Block concert. Chastity and her family also went to Disney World in Florida. And then there were simple experiences Chastity dreamt of doing. She had never been on a boat before, so we took her to the East Branch Dam for a boat ride. Friends and family showered her with gifts, including dozens of porcelain dolls and teddy bears.

Chastity passed away shortly after her baptism, leaving her stepmom, Ginger, her sister, Tiona, and all of her teenage friends heartbroken. At the funeral service, Frank Scarpelli extolled her for not receiving a blood transfusion. He assured everyone she would be resurrected to the paradise earth where we would see her again if we stayed faithful to Jehovah and his organization. According to him, there was no reason to grieve.

The only grief support my daughter Brandi received for the loss of her friend was from her classmates, who all wore black the day she returned to school after Chastity's death. One of her friends wrote her a poem. While Brandi was out in service, she told a 'sister' what her friends at school did for her. The woman scolded Brandi, saying the kids at school weren't her friends, they were her acquaintances. Brandi was deeply hurt by this rude comment and lack of love. It was at this point she started to question the validity of the religion.

I continued to see Dr. Freeman, who walked me through the stages of grief from losing Chastity. At the same time, I was watching Oprah on television, and she was talking about how childhood sexual abuse affects women throughout their lives. Memories of abuse flooded into my mind. When I shared this with Dr. Freeman, he again suggested I see a psychologist, but I flatly refused. I insisted I wasn't crazy. I told him other people were doing worse than I was. He told me it didn't matter if there is one drop or fifty drops of poison in a glass of water; any amount would make you sick. I opted to be sick for a little longer.

A Good Shepherd

———•———

The beige rotary phone hanging on the wall next to the back door of the mobile home started ringing while the older children were in school and my youngest son, Caleb was watching Reading Rainbow on PBS. I was in the midst of hand washing the breakfast dishes. The only caller ID available at the time was my intuition. Before I picked up the receiver, a list of callers went through my head. A bill collector? My mother? My brother Paul? One of the sisters from the Kingdom Hall? Not knowing who was on the other end of the phone, I lingered from the kitchen sink to the phone until I thought perhaps it was the school calling to inform me one of the kids was sick. I hurriedly picked up the handset with my sudsy left hand and rested my right forefinger on the silver cradle so I could hang up quickly in case it was an unwanted caller.

"Hello?"

A familiar, but unidentifiable voice asked, "Jeanette?"

"Yes."

"This is Uncle Henry. I'm calling from your brother Bill's house. I am in St. Marys and would like to see you."

Feeling as if I could faint, I wiped my hands on a dishtowel and sat down at the kitchen table. I hadn't heard my Uncle Henry's voice since my Oma, his mom, passed away over ten years ago. He proceeded to tell me that he separated from Aunt Evelyn.

Uncle Henry was sixteen years younger than my father. He was the only one in his immediate family born in the United States. His brothers, Jacob and my father, Paul, and his twin sisters, Lena and Jeanette, were all born in Holland. After my father passed away in 1960 and I went to Mooseheart, I didn't have any memories of Uncle Henry except for the story my brother Bob told, about how mean his wife Aunt Evelyn was and how a black sheep named Sammy broke her leg. In 1971, when we left Mooseheart, my mother took me to Mercer County, Pennsylvania, to visit relatives I hadn't seen in over ten years. Some of the relatives felt strange and were boring. But when I met Uncle Henry at his farm, it was as if I found my father. My uncle was outside tending the sheep; the smell of their wool reminded me of my early childhood. His tan leathery skin, black-rimmed glasses, and warm smile were comforting. I felt like a little lamb who wanted to follow him wherever he went. True to my brother's stories, his wife, Aunt Evelyn, wasn't friendly. Because she didn't invite us into the farmhouse, we sat outside at the picnic table on a hot summer day to visit with Uncle Henry. He offered us a bowl of ice cream, but we declined. We knew better than to bother Aunt Evelyn.

I hadn't seen Uncle Henry since then and was ecstatic and surprised to hear from him again. My brother Bill invited him up to my brother's camp for the weekend and arranged a family reunion. Although I didn't feel comfortable in my brother's territory, I couldn't get enough of being with my long-lost uncle. We both smiled ear to ear the whole weekend.

Within a few weeks, Uncle Henry returned to Elk County with his girlfriend to visit me in Emporium. Georgie was the opposite of Evelyn. She was personable and had a welcoming presence. When she walked in the back door of the mobile home, I welcomed her with a warm hug. I felt as if I were in Mrs. Gulley's arms again. She paid attention to the children and gave each of them a hug.

The aroma of homemade rye bread I had just removed from the oven swirled in the air. A kettle of rendered lard was cooling on the stove, and a venison pot pie with homemade crust was in the oven baking for supper. Uncle Henry gave me the biggest hug ever and asked me where I learned to bake and cook. I told him I read cookbooks and taught myself. He couldn't get over how I knew how to do what my dad and Oma did, even though I wasn't raised around them. He brought photo albums of my ancestors and showed me old sepia-toned photographs, telling me who everyone was. I didn't have the heart to tell him I wouldn't remember any of their names but listened to the stories of how his mom and dad immigrated to America from Holland and started a celery farm in Newton Falls, Ohio.

It was nearing Christmas, and Uncle Henry and Georgie unloaded a bag of gifts for the children. I felt uncomfortable. I didn't know how to handle the situation, as we didn't celebrate Christmas because, according to Jehovah's Witnesses, Jesus' birth was unknown, and Christmas was a pagan holiday. Uncle Henry was the last person I wanted to alienate, so I told the children it was OK for them to open the beautifully wrapped gifts.

I thanked both Uncle Henry and Georgie and gently said, "Thank you, but you don't have to buy the children anything. We are happy to see you."

With tears in his eyes, Uncle Henry replied, "After your dad passed away, I always wanted to send you presents at Mooseheart, but Aunt Evelyn wouldn't allow it. Now I want to do something for your children to make up for what I didn't do for you."

Georgie invited our family to her house in Sharon for the Memorial Day weekend, where she made homemade perogies and other treats. While staying at her home, I never felt we were a burden. She made sure we had comfortable beds to sleep in and enough food to eat. Uncle Henry asked if I wanted to visit my dad's grave with him. After getting out of Mooseheart,

I had been there with my mom and remembered feeling cold and sad. I didn't care to go, but I didn't want to disappoint my uncle. Georgie said she would watch the kids, so the two of us could have time together.

On a bright sunny day, with the trees beginning to bud and robins pulling worms out of the ground, I climbed into Uncle Henry's old pick-up truck and pulled the door shut. He turned the key, and the engine fired up. The drive to the cemetery was silent, as I imagined it was on the day of my dad's funeral, over twenty years before.

When we arrived at the Hermitage Park Cemetery, lines of American Flags waved at us like kites flying in the slight breeze. My eyes began to water, and I rubbed them, thinking the wind was causing me to tear up. Uncle Henry drove slowly through the cemetery, meandering through the grounds as he looked for a large tree that marked the place where my father was buried. He shifted the truck into park and turned off the engine. We both got out and walked to the marked grave together. Uncle Henry had a polaroid camera in hand and snapped a photo of the copper headstone engraved with my dad's name, the date he was born, and the date he died.

When Uncle Henry handed me the photo, I held it by the edges, hoping it and my tears would dry quickly. The film on the photo dried, but my eyes wouldn't quit watering. It was as if a dam broke; tears flooded my face and poured onto the ground. I collapsed into Uncle Henry's arms and laid my head on his shoulder and sobbed harder than I had ever cried in my life. I felt as small as a three-year-old child. As I dried my tears on the arm of his worn flannel shirt, I felt cleansed, but a little embarrassed and ashamed. As we silently drove back to Georgie's house, I thought about how good it felt to have Uncle Henry in my life. Like a link in a broken chain, he was my connection to a father I never knew. I looked forward to spending time with him, learning more about my ancestors from Holland, and what life was like for him as a child.

When we returned to Georgie's house, nothing looked the same, and I wondered how my children and Gary got there. It was as if I were in the show Time Tunnel, I had watched as a child. It took some time for me to slowly reorient myself to the present time. I didn't realize that not everyone had lapses in memory like this.

Since being reunited with Uncle Henry, my family seemed to be getting along better than ever. Georgie brought warmth, love, and healing to the family. She felt sorry that Brandi was being raised a Jehovah's Witness, and although she never said anything, her actions spoke louder than words.

She invited Brandi to spend weekends with her and Uncle Henry, which I allowed. She bought Brandi new clothes and took her to get her hair styled. Brandi deserved every bit of attention Georgie gave to her, and I never balked at her spending time with a 'worldly' person who was having an immoral relationship with my uncle. I remembered how Mrs. Gulley treated me as a young girl at Mooseheart and couldn't deny Brandi the same unconditional love from an older woman.

To make up for time lost after my father passed away, my brother Bill and Uncle Henry took a trip out West together. Years later, I learned that Uncle Henry drove out to Michigan to make amends with my brother Paul, who was hurting himself by holding on to anger like a burning ember of coal. He was resentful that after our father died, Uncle Henry didn't step in to take him and Bill, so they didn't have to go to Mooseheart. After making peace with my brother Paul, on the way home to Pennsylvania, my beloved Uncle Henry died instantly of a heart attack. I was happy to hear the two of them made amends.

My fragile life of cards came crumbling down when Gary delivered the news to me. I sobbed and cried for days. The salty tears were my only food for the next few weeks. My heart felt as if it had been ripped out of my chest. It was as if I lost my father all over again. I found comfort in the Jehovah's Witness teaching that Uncle Henry would be resurrected to the paradise earth because he died before Armageddon.

I traveled to the funeral in Sharon with my husband Gary and four young children. This would be the first time my mom, five brothers, and one sister and I were together in over twenty-five years since my sister had left Mooseheart in 1963. It would also be the last time. My sister Ginny had traveled from Connecticut, my brother Jack from Wisconsin, and my brother Paul from Michigan. My mother, Bob, Warren, Bill, and I all lived in Pennsylvania.

At the funeral home, I felt awkward seeing Aunt Evelyn--she and Uncle Henry weren't officially divorced-- dressed in black and praying for my Uncle's soul, who she deemed was in purgatory. I thought my uncle was the kindest man I ever met in my life and was sure he was in heaven with the Good Shepherd, Jesus Christ. In my eyes, Uncle Henry's only fault was that he was a heavy smoker. Aunt Evelyn tried to talk to me, but I was feeling angry at how she treated my Uncle Henry. I turned and walked away from her. I did speak to his two sons, one who was now a medical doctor and told them how much I would miss their dad and related the kind acts he did for me.

They told me they didn't know that side of their dad. All I knew of Uncle Henry was his kind, gentle spirit. I felt confused and wondered if Uncle Henry was riddled with guilt his whole life for not caring for his deceased brother's family. Uncle Henry was denied a mass in the church, but a short service was held at the funeral home, where the priest also prayed to deliver him from purgatory. My mother attended, but just stared into space and seemed a million miles away. I wondered if she was thinking about my dad's funeral.

After the funeral, we went back to Georgie's house. She didn't attend the funeral out of respect for the family. She served a banquet of ham, perogies, cottage potatoes, and desserts. Since we were all wearing dress clothes, I requested we get a nice family photo together. You would have thought I was asking for blood. My brothers retorted they weren't staying in monkey suits for any picture. Paul's wife, Dottie, and Jack's wife, Connie, set them straight right away and tried to help organize everyone for a family photo, but the other three boys continued to balk. Everyone finally got together for a picture, with all of us awkwardly standing about a foot apart from each other. I was upset at my family and didn't feel like getting in front of the camera. Gary used a little 110 camera to take a picture for me. After the film was developed and I received the photo in the mail, I ripped the picture up and threw it in the garbage. It might have helped if I would have known about Post Traumatic Stress and remembered how much we all hated the propaganda photo sessions at Mooseheart.

Life felt harder than ever without Uncle Henry's presence in my life. I wish he would have been there for support when my brother Paul passed away two years later. I wish he could have been here for support when my mother passed away. I wish he could have been here when I went through a divorce. I wish I could have celebrated Christmas with him after I left Jehovah's Witnesses. I would have made him Speculaas cookies at Christmas and Ole Bollen on New Year's Eve.

I heard from Uncle Henry ten years later. When I got the bright idea to barter two kid goats for two lambs, my husband, Cliff, obliged and brought home two little lambs. They weren't tame and fled as soon as we let them out in the pasture. Cliff rounded them up with a rope and corralled them into the goat kid pen where they couldn't escape. I made a point to pet and talk to them every day. When I ran my hands through their fleece, their wool felt like a beautiful, warm sweater with the lingering scent of lanolin. Soon they were eating out of my hand.

About a month after we had the lambs, an older model, brown pick-up truck pulled in the driveway. After turning off the engine to the truck, three men stepped out of the vehicle. I greeted them and asked, "Where are you guys from?"

They replied, "Pymatuning. We're on our way home from a camp in Tionesta and stopped to buy fudge." They had seen the sign in our yard advertising the Goat Milk Fudge.

I commented, "I lived in Sharpsville, Pennsylvania, near Pymatuning, in the late 1950s before the Shenango Lake was built."

The oldest man gazed at the two lambs grazing in the little pasture while we continued to chat about what flavors of goat milk fudge they wanted. They opted for chocolate with walnuts and butter pecan. I noticed the older man walk over to the pen to pet the goats. He wore the same plastic-framed glasses and had the same slim build and dark leather skin as my Uncle Henry. After easing my way over to where he was standing, I asked, "What do you do for work?"

"I'm retired from Sharon Steel."

"My Uncle Henry worked at Sharon Steel."

He winked his eye, smiled knowingly, and said, "Jeanette, you have two nice little lambs and a beautiful little farm." In the meantime, the two other men got back into the truck and waited while he stayed by the sheep. I didn't remember exchanging names and wondered how he knew my name.

I walked him back to the truck and thanked the men for stopping. I wanted to give "Uncle Henry" a big hug goodbye but didn't want to alarm him. My heart was brimming with the approval and fatherly love I longed for my whole life. I found comfort knowing the Good Shepherd was watching over me.

Two years after my Uncle Henry passed away, my brother Paul died suddenly of an aneurysm. He had just built a beautiful home for his wife Dottie and their two children, in Owosso, Michigan. After Uncle Henry's death, Paul called me frequently to talk. I remember the last conversation we had about what color stain he was using to paint the outside of the house. He was only forty-two years old. Paul became my father figure after my dad's death. He helped my brother Warren and me get out of Mooseheart before we graduated. He was a genius with computers before they were household items and he was part owner of a powder metal business.

While I was in Michigan for the funeral, Dottie, her sisters, Jane and Pat, who also lived at Mooseheart and I were sitting at the kitchen table talking about the abuse which happened at Mooseheart. They were discussing a new PBS series they found helpful to heal the abandonment and abuse they experienced at Mooseheart. The program was "Homecoming" by John Bradshaw. Jane and Pat looked at me and asked if I was ever sexually abused at Mooseheart. At that time, I vaguely remembered the orphanage and shook my head no.

When I returned to Emporium, I started watching the Homecoming series on PBS. It was one of the only channels we had on our TV. Everything John Bradshaw talked about sounded familiar, especially the parts about the inner child. I always felt like a little girl who never grew up. I started doing the exercises Bradshaw suggested. One was guided imagery of seeing one of your first memories. The first memory that came to mind was a scene I couldn't get out of my head. It was indelibly etched in my memory, just as if someone carved their initials into a tree. The only problem was every time I thought of it, tears welled up in my eyes, and I felt a sadness larger than the planet earth.

The memory was clear as day as if it happened yesterday instead of twenty years ago. I was walking on a sidewalk to a gray stone building that looked like thunderclouds, with a red tile roof that matched the porch. On the front of the building was a sign that read Schuylkill Hall. I was three years old and wearing a cotton plaid dress tied in the back, white ankle socks, stiff patent leather shoes, and a spring coat and hat as I counted the concrete steps one, two, three, leading up to the porch. My mom opened the white wooden gate and knocked on the door. An older woman with graying hair opened the paned glass door with a brass doorknob and said, "Hello. You must be Mrs. Van Zanten." Afterward, to suppress any emotion, my mind was blank, as if someone erased a blackboard slate, leaving behind the smudged dusty white lines reminiscent of rain clouds.

Guided by John Bradshaw's deep, slow voice, I allowed myself to name the feelings of abandonment and loss. His instructions were to go back and reclaim my inner child, but instead, I fell right into a black hole with her. There was no separation between my adult self and my child self.

After this experience, life at home felt overwhelming. I found myself in places without realizing how I got there, and I was beginning to experience periods of rage when I felt as if I could kill myself or someone else, such as the time when I invited my daughter's teenage friends over for a pizza party. As we were stretching the dough onto the baking sheets, the conversation turned to nicknames.

One of the girls asked: "Jeanette, did you have a nickname when you were little?"

Before I could change the subject, my daughter Brandi innocently said: "Yeah, her nickname was Brat."

The girl kiddingly called me the name. The second I heard "Brat," leave her mouth, rage swelled up from my gut. My blood began to boil, and all the anger I held in for thirty years exploded. I grabbed the snotty fifteen-year-old by the locks of her curly brown hair and took her out on the back porch and began to choke her.

"Don't you ever call me that again," I screamed.

Out of the corner of my eye, I saw the other teens scatter like scared little kittens to the bedrooms at the far end of the mobile home. After the rage had subsided, I felt like a piece of shit. I realized I ruined my teenage daughter's sleepover. If I had that moment to do over again, I would have said, "Brandi, open the jar of pizza sauce."

And when Heather called me Brat, I would have said, "Heather, the bag of mozzarella cheese is in the fridge."

But that's not how the story ended. I returned to the kitchen and finished the pizza myself without the girl's help. After everyone finished eating, I told the girls to clean up the kitchen. I slipped on my shoes and took the keys to the car, not telling anyone where I was going or when I would be back.

In the pouring down rain, I ran from the mobile home to where the car was parked a hundred yards away. I inserted the key into the ignition, started the engine, turned on the windshield wipers, and backed the maroon hatchback down the long country driveway that turned onto the main highway.

I planned on driving a few miles up the road to cool off and have time to myself. The windshield wipers were swishing back and forth, and the lights of a tractor-trailer were coming toward me. I was surprised by the voice in my head. "Turn into the front of the semi! Turn now, and it will all be over." The car veered to the left when I thought of my four children and what it would be like for them not to have their mom.

"Beeepppp!" The sound of the tractor-trailer horn startled me, and I swerved the car back across the double yellow lines and pulled over to the side of the road. I leaned my head on the steering wheel and sobbed for half an hour. I realized this was an over-reaction to a teenage girl calling me a name, but didn't understand why or what to do about it. I knew it was time to take Dr. Freeman's advice to see a psychologist.

My friend Jane had moved to an old farmhouse in Rockton, a little settlement outside of DuBois, Pennsylvania. Jane was a hard-working, petite woman with wide hazel eyes and a kind nature. Her husband, Dennis wasn't employed, so Jane found cleaning jobs in the area. Dennis remembered Gary from when Caleb was born and permitted his wife to have us over for supper while he was there. The house had gaping holes in the floors and didn't have running water or heat. It was so old that the kids found newspapers clipping in the walls about President Lincoln's assassination.

Jane now had seven children; her daughters were teenagers and enjoyed playing with Brandi when we visited, although neither of them seemed happy. They were always busy helping with chores, making bread, canning food, doing laundry in an old wringer washer by carrying water in from a well, weeding the large garden, and taking care of the younger children.

Justin enjoyed playing with Jane's two young boys, who were close to his age. The boys were now old enough to go hunting, so during hunting season, we spent weekends staying overnight while the 'men' went out hunting. Afterward, we cut up venison and canned it, so the family had food for the winter. In the late summer of the next year, while Jane and I were picking elderberries, she told me that she had decided to leave Dennis. I was shocked. Jehovah's Witnesses frowned on divorce and separation, except on the grounds of adultery.

Jane told me about seeing a psychologist, Dr. Ray Francis, who she had met when she lived in Ridgway. He now had a practice in DuBois and she was cleaning his office in exchange for counseling. When she shared this news, I raised my eyebrows. The Watchtower Organization looked down on getting counseling from 'worldly' sources. We were instructed to rely on 'elders' who had no background in psychology or counseling for direction.

Without going into detail, Jane told me that her grounds for leaving Dennis were abuse and neglect. I had noticed the abuse when Gary and I were visiting. He and Gary were sitting at the kitchen table of the kitchen, drinking a beer.

David winked at Gary and said, "Watch this."

Jane and I were at the sink washing dishes when Dennis barked, "Jane, get out there and weed those beets in the garden."

She jumped like she saw a mouse, dried her hands on the dish towel, and ran out to the garden. I followed to help her. She was nervous and scared of how Dennis would react when she left, so at Dr. Francis' instruction, she arranged for the constable to be present on moving day. Dennis didn't become violent as she expected, but to her surprise, he sat down and cried. Jane moved into a house in DuBois that was owned by a 'sister' who was also a victim of her 'unbelieving' husband's abuse and understood what Jane was going through.

At the new house, we had more time to talk openly.

Jane told me about her childhood growing up in the Midwest, and I told her a little about my childhood in the nearby state of Illinois, although

I put most of it out of my mind. Dennis showered her with gifts trying to woo her back. He even began studying with Jehovah's Witnesses. Jane stood her ground and never looked back. When I visited, it was refreshing to see the children laughing and playing without worrying about disturbing Dennis. I was a fledgling, watching and taking note of what Jane was doing.

After Jane left Dennis, and he started to study the Bible, the elders firmly persuaded her to get back together with him, but she held her ground. She lost privileges such as answering at meetings and going out in field service for a time. Jane wasn't alone in her situation, as there were several women who were Jehovah's Witnesses in abusive relationships, including women whose husbands were elders and ministerial servants. Being in subjection to men was strongly enforced. I watched many women suffer in silence. They didn't come to meetings with black and blue marks, but they came with bruised souls, their eyes cast toward the floor.

Women were not allowed to lead a prayer without a scarf on their heads, and they weren't allowed to have teaching parts at meetings. If a teenage boy in a home were baptized, his mother was to be in subjection to him. If a woman spoke her mind, she was labeled a Jezebel, an evil woman from the Bible who ruled over men. Due to my outspoken nature, I acquired this label. Many talks were given at the Kingdom Hall, scolding women for speaking out of turn and not being in subjection to their husbands.

Will There Be a Morning?

———●————————————●———

While the children were in school, I made an appointment with Dr. Raymond Francis, the psychologist that Jane had told me about. Caleb was still home during the day so I made the appointment in the morning so Gary could watch him before he went to work in the afternoon.

Dr. Francis' office was located downtown in DuBois in a two-story office building on West Long Avenue. When I entered the office with comfortable chairs facing each other I instantly felt as though I were in a safe space. Dr. Francis' welcomed me with a soft-spoken voice and blue eyes that didn't look away when he talked. When I told him I had four children, he told me he had seven children.

He then said, "Tell me about you."

I responded, "I'm a Jehovah's Witness and live in Emporium."

He gently asked, "Are you married?"

"Yes."

"And how is your marriage?"

"Good."

He raised his eyebrows as if he could see right through me. "Really? So, what brings you here."

At the time, I was working on an eight by ten-inch family tree cross stitch. At the trunk of the tree, I stitched May 3, 1975, the date Gary and I were married. The pattern had branches and leaves for scripture quotes and my children's names and birthdates.

Wanting the whole family to someday be in the paradise earth together, at the top of the tree, I stitched in the quote, "As for me and my household, we will serve the Lord." Joshua 25:15. I told Dr. Francis about the project I was working on but explained that I was having a hard time finishing it. He asked what part of the project was challenging. I told him the roots of the tree. I was trying to stitch together my broken family, whose roots felt tangled and confusing.

I proceeded to tell him about the depression and medications Dr. Freeman prescribed. When I told him how lost I was feeling, he took note and suggested I return to see him within the next week. I thought I must be really bad if he wanted to see me so soon.

After my first session with Dr. Francis for the first time in my life, I felt there was light at the end of the tunnel, and I found someone to show me the way out. A poem by Emily Dickinson summed up how I was feeling:

> Will there really be a 'Morning'?
> Is there such a thing as "Day?"
> Could I see it from the mountains
> If I were as tall as they?
> Has it feet like Water lilies?
> Has it feathers like a Bird?
> Is it brought from famous countries
> Of which I have never heard?
> Oh, some Scholar!
> Oh, some Sailor!
> Oh, some Wise man from the skies!
> Please to tell a little pilgrim
> Where the place called "Morning" lies?

The next week, Dr. Francis inquired about my childhood and I told him about Mooseheart. He again raised his eyebrows and said how hard it must have been to be raised in an institution without love and nurturing. I broke down crying. I had never been able to put into words what it was like to live at Mooseheart, but he nailed it in a few words. He handed me a box of tissue and waited until I was done sobbing before I asked, "How do you know what it was like for me." I thought perhaps he was a psychic.

He said, "I did photography and journalistic work at St. Joseph's Orphanage in Erie." I didn't know about St. Joseph's orphanage, but I did know he understood. His words were like snowflakes gently landing on the ground.

"Do you ever get angry?" he asked.

"No, because the Bible doesn't approve of being angry."

He explained when emotions are held inside it's akin to holding a hose to the ground; sooner or later the water is going to come out spurting all over. He recommended that I stop at the bookstore and pick up a copy of *A Gift to Myself* by Charles Whitfield MD.

The book was a spin-off from John Bradshaw's work of healing the inner child. After reading the book, which included assignments, I told Dr. Francis that after watching *Homecoming* I felt as if I had a nervous break-down and I wasn't sure if I liked Whitfield's book. Dr. Francis told me I needed to take it more slowly and shore up my resources before I explored any more childhood memories.

We spent the next few months talking about the problems I was having at home with the children and my husband. He gave me some great parenting advice and suggestions to improve communication with Gary. He called and invited Gary to come in to talk with him, but Gary refused. Due to our incompatibility, Dr. Francis recommended that I separate from Gary. I told him that I didn't have spiritual grounds for a separation.

Memories from my past, like labor pains giving birth, were becoming unstoppable. When I drove past a playground, I had flashbacks of the little boy who jumped off the red caboose at the Mooseheart playground. Excruciating headaches would plague me for days. It felt as if my head was going to crack open. When I found myself screaming at my children, I had visions of matrons screaming at me. Dark basements scared me; I was deathly afraid of mice and rats--being in a dark room without lights sent me into a panic. I hated men and didn't trust anyone.

Dr. Francis had a good sense of humor and would chide me a little to get me to lighten up, but I felt small and helpless and started to cry. He was sensitive and cut back on the jokes. He told me about Post Traumatic Stress Disorder which was attributed to soldiers returning from the war but said it was also applicable to child abuse victims.

When I couldn't stop the memories of my early childhood and Mooseheart from surfacing, I started to write about my experiences and mailed them to Dr. Francis. He recognized that I had several different handwritings and at one of my visits suggested I had a Multiple Personality Disorder. I read the book, *Sybil*, when I was in high school. When he delivered the diagnosis, I felt like a freak from the circus and broke down crying.

Dr. Francis explained that mental illness is no different than having a broken arm or leg; it's a part of the body that is broken but could be fixed. On a tan rotary phone, he telephoned a woman named Beverly who lived in Florida and taught him about MPD (Multiple Personality Disorder). She was a kind woman who assured me I wasn't crazy and was in good hands with Dr. Francis. He told me at first, he didn't buy into the diagnosis but was later convinced after seeing Beverly for a few years. He went on to tell me people who have MPD are generally creative-minded children who came up with a unique way of dealing with severe abuse that had to have happened over many years. He recommended an in-patient facility in Maryland that could help but I didn't have anyone to care for my children and wouldn't leave them.

In one of our conversations, Dr. Francis said the only thing someone couldn't take from me was my mind. At the time, I disagreed because I felt as if my mind were hijacked by the matrons at Mooseheart and by Jehovah's Witnesses. He recommended I read *In Search of Meaning* by Victor Frankl. When I returned home, I checked the book out of the library and read it cover to cover within a few days.

The book was a game-changer for me. The author was an Austrian psychiatrist and Holocaust survivor who observed that the people who had hope were the ones who survived the concentration camps. The teachings of logotherapy helped strengthen my mind and attitude toward life. I no longer felt like a victim, after reading the quotation, *"Everything can be taken from a man but one thing: the last of the human freedoms--to choose one's attitude in any given set of circumstances, to choose one's way."*

Dr. Francis told me we needed to work on the integration of the different selves. He used the illustration of baking a cake; when all the separate parts were combined, they made the cake. If one was missing, then the cake wouldn't be good. First, we had to find all the missing parts buried deep within my psyche. He taught me that I created different personalities to protect myself from painful experiences. Some of them were working overtime, protecting me from perceived threats. Everything he said made sense, but integration wasn't something I could grasp. It would take many years for memories to surface. I also had to learn not to dissociate and create new selves when life got stressful.

I tried to make sense of these new insights by writing poetry. When I heard thoughts in my head, I began writing them down and dropped them in the mail to Dr. Francis. He patiently read everything I wrote and helped me process what was happening. Some of my writings were perfectly printed in a child's handwriting on lined tablet paper. Other writings were typed, and others were written longhand. When I balked at the idea of having different personalities, Dr. Francis brought the different handwritings to my attention. When I saw them, I didn't recognize some of the writings and realized there were parts of myself I didn't know.

Trying to integrate was something of which we couldn't agree, but we did agree on everyone getting along and listening to each other. I started reading other books about MPD, such as *When Rabbit Howls* and *Fractured Mind*. Self-help books such as *The Road Less Traveled* by Scott Peck and *The Courage to Heal* by Ellen Bass began to line my bookshelves. As I read the books, I didn't feel alone; there were other people who shared my experiences.

The writing was the key to opening Pandora's Box I shut many years ago. Now that the box was opened, painful memories buried deep in my psyche and body began to surface. I didn't have words for many of the memories because they happened before I began talking. There were also parts of me, that although they were old enough to speak, couldn't voice because they were terrified of the consequences of punishment or of not being believed. These memories called abreactions started to surface through physical pain. When my right thigh felt as if it were on fire, I was able to talk to a little girl that showed me pictures of the toilet cleaner which burned a hole in her leg. Each time a memory would surface, Dr. Francis patiently told me that he believed me, that it wasn't my fault and that I was safe. He repeated this to me many times until I finally believed it. I came across the quotation, *"Life can only be understood backwards; but it must be lived forwards,"* by the philosopher Soren Kierkegaard, that I cross-stitched and framed. The saying was like a map for me when I felt disoriented and confused.

The experience was so traumatic that on more than one occasion I was unable to drive home because I felt disoriented after our sessions. Dr. Francis made arrangements for me to stay overnight at a women's shelter in Clearfield so I could see him the next morning. After I was rested, he was able to help bring me back to the present.

As a coping skill, I created another personality after Dr. Francis and named him Walter, which was the doctor's middle name. I didn't realize it at the time, but I got the name from his license which hung on the office wall. Initially, the thought of having a male personality was bizarre, until I read all humans are androgynous and have male and female characteristics. I now understood it was OK that I wasn't a girly girl and didn't like make-up and feminine clothes with lace and such. Walter proved to be an ISH (inner self helper) whom I would summon when I needed strength and wisdom, which was quite often.

As I became acquainted with different parts of myself, I began to give them names I identified with and liked at the time they came into being. Along with nice names, like Elizabeth, Liz, Caroline, and Anna, there was a personality named Brat. I acquired the name from my brothers and hated it. When I told Dr. Francis about how much I detested the name, he suggested we call her Miriam. Through the simple act of giving that part of me an acceptable name, she was able to integrate and communicate her hurts, desires, and wishes.

Through therapy, I was able to understand why it scared me to be in a dark room with the door shut, why I gagged at the thought of cream of wheat cereal, why I didn't trust people and that my deepest fear was abandonment. Instead of seeing myself as an adult with all the confusing anxieties and perplexing fears, it helped to know the child part of me was feeling this way and that the feeling stemmed from a traumatic event in my childhood. Some of my parenting skills, such as listening to emotions and not shaming the children when they made mistakes, were weak. Dr. Francis taught me how to use words and body language to get the children to listen. He gave me names for the wide range of emotions I was experiencing and showed me how to accept them and helped me let them go. I applied this not only to myself but also to the children.

I worked hard to educate myself on parenting by reading books. One day Justin came home and told me he was angry and was going to kill someone who made him mad. I was scared and didn't know what to do. When I told Dr. Francis, he suggested the next time Justin threatened someone, to tell him he wouldn't look good in stripes. His words worked like a charm. Justin quit making threats and we were able to talk about what was making him angry.

When the elders at the Kingdom Hall learned I was seeing a psychologist, they started giving talks on Thursday nights about the dangers of seeing worldly counselors. Since the congregation was small, everyone knew that I was the person they were talking about. People who I thought were my friends started to distance themselves from me. After I didn't comply by ending my visits with Dr. Francis, the elders arranged a meeting with me. When I arrived at the Kingdom Hall, I was surprised to see five elders there, including the presiding overseer from the Port Allegheny congregation. They said that they were a special team appointed by the society to help publishers with psychological problems. They decided that I was demonized, and they were going to perform an exorcism.

I sat for hours while they prayed and prayed, expecting me to go off the deep end when the demon left me. After a few hours, I got up to leave the meeting and found I was locked in the Kingdom Hall. I started to scream my brains out until they finally unlocked the door. I drove home exhausted and unable to care for my family

When I told Dr. Francis about the experience, he told me that they had no business doing what they did. He instructed me to tell them I am under a doctor's care and need to refrain from any further meetings with them. His advice made so much sense to me. Afterward, they left me alone but I was now unable to enter the Kingdom Hall without having anxiety attacks. Being locked inside the building had triggered memories of being trapped in closets and rooms for punishment at Mooseheart. I attributed the claustrophobia to the fact that there weren't any windows in the building. During the meetings, I would sit out in the foyer, next to the front door I propped open with books so I could get out in an emergency.

Along with the brothers pretending they were exorcists, they also started to counsel sexual abuse victims. The teenage girl, Nicole, who lived next door to me when I first moved to Emporium, was finally able to tell the elders her stepdad, Dick, was sexually abusing her. Rather than contacting the authorities, the elders told her to keep it to herself because if people knew about the abuse, it would ruin the congregation's reputation. A rule from the Watchtower Bible and Tract Society said there needed to be two witnesses to accuse someone of wrongdoing before they could take action. The stepdad wasn't baptized so the elders couldn't disfellowship him. The brothers assured Nicole they would talk to her stepdad to tell him to stop. When that didn't happen, she went back to the elders, multiple times, for 'counseling' until she had enough and contacted the authorities.

The fallout in the congregation and community was tremendous. Nicole's stepdad was arrested and her mom, Martha was so disgusted with the elders that she quit going to the meetings. Nicole's younger sister, Rachel, who was a young teenager was severed from her only friends because she no longer attended meetings and was now considered worldly. At school, she thought no one from the Kingdom Hall was allowed to talk to her until her friend Ami found her crying in the bathroom. Ami assured Rachel that she would never quit talking to her.

At the same time, another teenager who went to school with Brandi confided in my daughter that her stepdad was sexually abusing her. Her mom was recently baptized as a Jehovah's Witness and was also told not to go to the authorities. Her daughter confided in the school nurse and the situation was then made public with her stepdad going to jail. While imprisoned, he started studying the Bible with Jehovah's Witnesses and the mother blamed her husband's deviant behavior on her daughter. Both of these situations were reminders of my own sexual abuse as a child and of not having anyone to tell or help me.

Any time I had contact with my siblings and mother, I relapsed psychologically. When my mother was hospitalized for a kidney infection, I went to visit her. When I walked into her room, she looked at me with a blank stare and told me she wanted to die. I was hoping she would be happy to see me, perhaps thank me for visiting, but she didn't seem appreciative at all. I walked out of the room and started crying. When I couldn't quit sobbing, a nurse came and put her arm around me and asked me if I was alright. I shook my head no and escaped into the elevator. This was the last time I saw my mother.

When I visited with my brothers, I didn't know how to deal with their lack of social skills when they talked loudly, interrupted, or didn't listen when I talked. After my brother Bob and his wife divorced, I started witnessing to Bob and started giving him Jehovah's Witness literature on getting through a divorce. He took an interest in what he read and started a Bible study with a couple from the Kersey congregation and was baptized as a Jehovah's Witness. He began giving talks at the meetings and I started getting concerned someday he could be an elder in the congregation. Even though he was now a witness he had a knack for pushing my buttons and I didn't enjoy being around him. When I was around my family, I felt as if I were being dragged back into a swamp and couldn't get out.

Then one day, I hit bottom when the phone rang.

"Hello. This is the senior center in St. Marys. Is Dorothy Van Zanten your mother?"

Feeling as if I were going to faint, I sat down in the chair next to the phone. "Yes. Why?" I thought perhaps they were calling to tell me she died.

"We need you to help your mother. She comes to the senior center and her clothes are unclean and she smells so bad that no one wants to be around her." I remembered her shuffling, downtown St. Marys, on the heels of her shoes, with her coat misbuttoned and her stringy, uncombed gray hair hanging in her eyes. I couldn't get the image out of my mind. The shame and embarrassment were more than I could bear. I felt like I wanted disappear from the face of the earth.

"I'm sorry, ma'am, but I am barely taking care of myself and my four children much less my mother." I didn't wait for a response. After I hung up the phone, I began crying. I felt as if I were drowning in my own tears.

When I shared the experience with Dr. Francis, he reminded me that embarrassment and shame were only appropriate if I intentionally did something to make someone feel bad. He helped me to acknowledge the feeling of sadness for my mother's condition. He recommended ending contact with my family since it was causing me distress. I told him I didn't know how to stop them from contacting me. I felt so guilty about cutting contact with my mother. He told me this was doctor's orders and the only reason for feeling guilt was if I had done something intentionally wrong such as rob a bank.

I asked if he would call her and tell her I didn't hold anything against her. I knew she never did anything intentionally to hurt me. She wasn't capable of giving me what I needed. He offered to call her for me. He also called the senior center and told them not to contact me, but to call one of my brothers if my mom needed anything.

When I returned to his office the next week, I asked if he called my mother. He replied, "I did and she's as far away as Oregon." It comforted me to know it wasn't only me that felt she was distant. I took solace in his words and believed on some level she had heard what he said. As painful as this experience was, it helped me process the shame I felt was at the core of my being from the time I was a child. After I wrote a poem about shame the feeling dissipated:

Shame

Shame for breakfast
Shame for lunch
Shame has been my
Daily portion.
I don't know what I did
To deserve so much.

Shame from mother
Shame from brothers

Shame from teachers
Shame from friends
Shame was their way of having fun
Their finger pointed outward
Chanting, "Shame, shame on you."

Shamed for the way I walked.
Shamed for the way I talked.
Shamed for having human needs.
Shame pours out through my tears.
Shame wells up in my heart, as it bleeds.

Shame is yours.
Shame is not mine.
Shame is being given back.
Shame won't stop me from holding up my chin.
Now I have a friend who likes me
and looks me straight in the eye and
says, "You're fine just the way you are."

My mother passed away a few months later. When I received the news, I felt as if the biggest weight in the world were lifted off my shoulders. I no longer had the responsibility to make my mother happy. Her sadness had finally come to an end. When I talked to Dr. Francis, he told me not to attend the funeral. The night of her viewing, Gary took the kids to the funeral home. I attended a National Alliance for the Mentally Ill meeting in a church basement. I was warmly welcomed by Reverend Bruce Burkness and other people who had family members who were mentally ill. I took note of Bruce's warmth and kindness compared to the judgmental elders at the Kingdom Hall. In a broken voice, I teared up when I told the group my story about my mother's mental illness. I broke down crying when a woman named Crystal shared her story of having a mentally ill mother. For the first time in my life, I felt as if I wasn't alone.

The next day there was a knock at the door. It was my brother Jack. He was my one brother I didn't feel uncomfortable around and I welcomed him into the house. I wasn't sure how he felt about me not attending the funeral and we didn't talk about how either of us felt. He wanted to know how I was doing. His visit reminded me of the story in the Bible about the shepherd who went looking for the lost sheep.

At the same time, I was trying to put myself back together, my home life was falling apart. Gary lost his job at GKN and I worried about how the bills would get paid. I called Dr. Francis crying. He said there was a lot of talent between Gary and me. When I then told Dr. Francis that I wouldn't have insurance to pay for my visits, he told me he could afford to go without a few meals and we would get through this. With Dr. Francis' encouragement of my writing skills, I prepared a resume for a reporting job with *The Bradford Era*, a regional newspaper that covered Elk, Cameron, and McKean Counties.

To my surprise, I was called for an interview. I prepared for the event by reading books and watching videos from the Cameron County Library. Dr. Francis provided a glowing reference and I was hired for the job, writing human interest stories and reporting local school board, borough council meetings, and the police report. Some of the meetings conflicted with the meetings at the Kingdom Hall. The elders counseled me about missing meetings, but I wasn't about to give up my first real job. The pay was only twenty-five cents a word. I lived by the mantra "A penny saved is a penny earned."

One of my first human interest stories was about a man from Emporium who made a part for the Hubble telescope. I also did a feature article on the park naturalist, Lisa Bainey. I enjoyed taking photographs and seeing articles I wrote printed in *The Bradford Era*. My self-esteem soared, as I began meeting people in the community. During Child Sexual Abuse month, the paper was doing articles about child abuse and I offered my story, which I submitted anonymously. I subscribed to *The Bradford*

Era and scoured the job ads as I needed a job that paid more than a few dollars a week. I also knew that I needed more references and experience. Dr. Francis encouraged me to keep writing and suggested I buy a word processor to write my story. There wasn't an extra penny in our budget for a typewriter, much less a word processor, so I continued to journal by hand.

Gary and I decided to sell the mobile home and buy a little house in town. I noticed the house while going door to door with Jehovah's Witnesses. The two-story white house at 8 West Fifth Street had been empty for a few months. Whenever I drove past the house, lyrics from Crosby, Stills, and Nash song Our House lingered in my head. "Our house is a very, very, fine house, with two cats in the yard, life used to be so hard. Now everything is easy because of you." I felt as if Jehovah was telling me to buy the house and deep down thought the house might fix our marital woes.

When I called the realtor, he told me an older woman who was in a nursing home owned the home, and he thought we would be eligible for a government loan. As devastating as it was for Gary to lose his job, it put us into an income bracket that qualified us for the needed money to buy the house. After filling out a ton of paperwork and selling the trailer on North Creek, the home was ours.

With the help of friends from the Kingdom Hall, we moved in on a cold January day. The house reeked of cigarette smoke, so we decided to paint the ugly green walls white. Justin, Brandi, and her friend Stacy pitched in and helped with the painting. When we applied the paint, nicotine seeped through the wet paint and dripped down the walls like muddy streams of water. The only solution was to wash the walls first and coat them with Kilz primer. At the time, the paint wasn't odor-free, so we opened the windows and painted in the frigid January temperatures.

Justin excelled at art and had won a cash award from the Catholic Daughters of America for an art contest he entered at school. We had to keep it under our hats because we weren't supposed to have anything to do with other religions. I believed in fostering my children's talents and allowed Justin to sketch and paint life-size Looney Tune figures of the Tazmanian Devil and Tweety bird on the white bedroom walls.

When people from the Kingdom Hall saw the paintings, they scoffed at me for allowing my children's self-expression. One brother scolded me by telling me the Tasmanian Devil, along with the Smurfs, were demonized. I was also chastised for allowing my children to read fairy tale books at the meetings because they had demonic origins. I began to question the validity of such claims but kept my thoughts to myself for a while. The paintings remained on the walls.

As much as I missed living in the country, I liked being in town and started to feel connected to the community. The Cameron County library was only a block away. In the evening, while Gary was working, I would take Caleb and Cherey to the library. We met our neighbors, John and Marge Simons. Mr. Simons was a football coach, and Mrs. Simons was the librarian at the elementary school and always spoke to Brandi and Justin. In the fall, they invited us up to their camp on Moore Hill to make apple cider. I was still a little wary of spending time with 'worldly' people, so Gary took the children.

While carrying a load of laundry down the steps of the house, I slipped on the bottom step and broke my ankle. When I came home from the hospital with a cast, Mr. Simons carried me up the flight of outdoor steps. I hated feeling like a burden to someone but was grateful to have Mr. Simons help. I felt safe in his arms. Our backyard neighbors, John and Linda Reid, owned the local Sears store, and when we needed new appliances, they gave us a good price and delivered them to the house free of charge. I was learning Jehovah's Witnesses didn't have a monopoly on being kind and trustworthy.

At home there was just enough money to pay the bills. Gary and I were receiving unemployment, and I signed up for food stamps. With my foot in a cast, I hobbled down the steps to the car and drove to the Northern Tier Community Action building on Fourth Street for a free box of food from the food pantry. As I was waiting in line, propped up by crutches, I felt as if this were the lowest point in my life. I felt alone, humiliated, and ashamed and wondered if this was how Jesus felt having to come to earth after living in Heaven.

I was unable to carry the box, so I waited for a volunteer to put it in the car for me. While standing at the curbside, tears streamed down my cheeks. I prayed God would help my family through this difficult time. I thanked him for the box of non-fat dry milk, generic peanut butter, pasta, canned vegetables, and boxes of government cheese, which would help feed my children. At the time, I didn't realize living on a shoestring would be my ticket out of poverty and out of the spiritual prison I was in.

While my ankle healed, I decided I would like to learn to play the piano. Dr. Francis was helping me get in touch with my inner children, one of whom regretted getting kicked out of the music program at Mooseheart for ruining the violin bow. She didn't enjoy playing the violin but did like the piano lessons and wanted another chance to learn the piano. My ten-year-old self found a free piano and asked Gary to move it. She didn't realize how heavy pianos were. Gary got some guys from the fire department to help him drag it up the steep bank to our house. Trying to please my inner child, I found a piano teacher, Mrs. Sebring, who only lived a block from our house. She was a strict older woman who was an accomplished pianist. After two months of lessons, she had a stroke and passed away. Although I never learned how to play a complicated piece of music, I could plunk out some folk songs, and my child-self was satisfied.

Over the years, we racked up quite a bit of credit card debt and daily phone calls from collectors were more than I could handle. I felt as if I were drowning, and there wasn't anyone to ask for help until I saw a television ad for an agency in Altoona which assisted people to get out of debt. I called for an appointment for Gary and me. The agency had us cut up our credit cards and made arrangements for lower interest rates with the debtors. Each month I sent them a set amount of money, and when one bill was paid, they applied the payment amount to the next debt until finally all of our debts were paid. I learned not to rely on credit to get by and vowed I would never let credit get out of hand again.

While Gary was out of work, he joined the volunteer fire department across the street. Justin was able to join the fire department also. The volunteer work gave the two of them something to do together and a way to contribute to the community. Brandi started babysitting full time after school and on weekends, so she had the money for school clothes.

While perusing classified ads in the Bradford Era, I came across a job located in Eldred for a Family Service Worker for the Head Start Program. I didn't like the idea of traveling forty miles to work but living on a shoe-string budget wasn't paying the bills. The qualifications didn't require a college degree, so I sent in a resume and cover letter.

To my surprise, I received a call for an interview. I was asked to bring in a letter of recommendation for the interview. I had no idea who to ask for such a letter. When Cherey was five years old, I signed her up for kindergarten at the Woodland Elementary School. Cherey started to cry before getting on the bus in the morning. I began volunteering in the classroom, helping the children with a visual perception program and figured out quickly why Cherey didn't want to go to school; the teacher was loud and screamed at the children. I made arrangements with the principle to have her teacher changed.

Mrs. Marty Lewis was her new teacher. She was small in stature and soft-spoken, which calmed Cherey's anxiety. I continued to volunteer in the classroom. Cherey made friends with a little boy named Nick, who was also quiet and shy.

When I asked Mrs. Lewis if I could bring Caleb while I volunteered, she readily agreed. Nick's mom, Biz, also volunteered in the classroom. She was friendly and kind, as was her son, who played with Caleb while we helped the children with their projects. Mrs. Lewis and Biz were like two twinkling stars on a very dark night.

Each week, I looked forward to volunteering at the school. I called Mrs. Lewis and asked her for a letter of reference. Within a day, she sent me a letter describing how helpful and good I was with the children in her class. Other than Dr. Francis complimenting me on the writing and photography work I was doing for *The Bradford Era*, no one had ever spoken so highly of me.

At the time, all I knew about Head Start was its location at the building on Fourth Street in front of the food pantry, where I received boxes of free food each month. I brushed up on my interviewing skills by checking out VCR tapes on job skills from the library. I learned the Northern Tier Community Action Corp agency managed Head Start, a government-subsidized preschool for low-income children, which included parent involvement.

On the day of the interview, as I sat in the foyer of the Northern Tier building with other interviewees, I felt underqualified. My palms were sweaty, and I could barely breathe. When it came time for the interview, I was summoned to a meeting room in the basement of the building where five people would be interviewing me. I recognized Mike Kuleck, who went to school with Gary, and I knew his wife, Robin, from the yarn shop she managed from their home on Sizerville Road. Since Head Start includes parents in the decision-making process, Nancy, a woman I had met in the door to door work, was on the interviewing board. She had custody of her grandchildren; the other three people were strangers. I decided to be myself. I told myself that it wasn't a life or death matter if I got the job.

When the group of people started asking questions, I answered them as honestly as possible.

"Have you ever visited people in their homes?"

"Yes, in the door to door work as a Jehovah's Witness."

"What would you do if a child needed medical care? Would you take them to the hospital for a blood transfusion?"

"I would make sure they had all the proper permission forms filled out. I would call the ambulance to take them to the hospital. It would be up to their parents to decide if they should have a blood transfusion."

"What are your strengths, and what are your weaknesses."

"My strength is my sensitivity, and my weakness is my sensitivity."

After Nancy commented on the letter from Mrs. Lewis, she stated that if I was good enough for her, I was good enough for Head Start. Everyone in the room nodded their heads in agreement and informed me there were other people to interview, but they would get back to me. I sighed a breath of relief. Within a week, I received a phone call and was told the job in Eldred had been filled, but there was a job opening in St. Marys for a Family Service Worker. Was I interested?

Without hesitation, I told the team, yes. What I liked best was that I would have vacation time off when my children were off school for the holidays and during the summer.

I received a stipend from the assistance office for clothing and bought some dress slacks and tops. My job included health benefits, so I was able to tell the assistance office I didn't need their help any longer. I was ecstatic--I would no longer have to get food from the food pantry. On my first day of work, Caleb, who was five years old and had just started kindergarten, came down with the chickenpox. Thankfully, Gary was home to take care of him during the day.

The Head Start classroom in St. Marys was located at the Spruce Street School, where Brandi had attended kindergarten when we lived in St. Marys. Mrs. Debbie was the teacher for the seventeen pre-school children. The classroom was decorated with colorful leaves and fall decorations. My first assignment of going on home visits to do intake forms was a stark contrast from going door to door as a Jehovah's Witness. Most of the homes were clean enough, but some of them were disgusting. My heart went out to the children who had to live in these substandard conditions.

More than once, I was reminded of my early childhood. Still, I acclimated to the job and got along well with the teachers, parents, and children.

My job description also required that I recruit children for the Head Start program. I did this by putting up posters around town and handing out flyers at the food pantry to limited-resource families. On one occasion, just as I was ready to go home for the day, I met a mother and her little girl, standing in line waiting for their food.

I introduced myself, "Hi, I'm Jeanette from Head Start. What is your name?"

"Connie."

"Would you be interested in enrolling your little girl in the Head Start Program?" I asked.

She told me, "I don't think so. Angelina is much too shy." When I looked down to say hello to the little girl she hid behind her mom's back.

I persisted and told her, "Head Start is a family program and you are more than welcome to come to the center with your little girl as a volunteer."

The mom took an application and said, "I'll look it over."

When we received the roster of students for the upcoming year, I was surprised to see Angelina's name on the list. Connie came with her daughter to the center and was a fantastic help with the children. When a position for an assistant teacher opened up, Connie applied and was hired for the job. She went on to become a lead teacher and received a national award for her exemplary rise from being on public assistance to a Head Start employee.

When I received my first paycheck, I felt as if I had conquered Mount Everest. We weren't out of the woods financially. It was a start, not only in getting out of debt but of getting out of Jehovah's Witnesses. I was glad to be putting money aside for retirement as I was having doubts about the world coming to an end any time soon. While Gary was laid off, the 'friends' at the Kingdom Hall took advantage of him being home. The brothers started stopping by the house while he was home. I was startled when Gary agreed to have a Bible study with a brother and began attending meetings with the family. He didn't have any dress clothes, so we took a trip to the Blair Outlet Store in Warren to buy him a polyester tan suit and casual slacks he could wear with dress shirts and a tie. To my surprise, he began attending all the meetings, quit smoking, started going door to door, and was baptized as one of Jehovah's Witnesses at a circuit assembly. I lost my victim status as a sister with an unbelieving mate. I was relegated to a sister who had to be in subjection to her husband in all matters. This was a hard pill for me to swallow as I felt as if I were now out to sea with no one at the helm.

Within a couple of months, Gary was hired as a second shift supervisor at Emporium Specialties in Austin, Pennsylvania. The elders counseled against him taking the job, as he would miss meetings. They told him Jehovah would provide. We both knew it was up to us to provide for our family. Gary worked hard to make up for the lost wages and also took a part-time job at Intech, a powdered metal factory in Ridgway, leaving him little time to be with the family or attend the meetings. We bought a second-hand Renault for him to drive back and forth to work, so I had transportation to go to the meetings. When Justin turned sixteen, he learned how to operate the standard car. After getting his driver's license, he got a job at Luigi's restaurant, making hoagies for Joe DiBello. It wasn't long before Joe had him delivering hoagies to local businesses in the area.

True to the elder's advice, Gary did not stick with the Jehovah's Witnesses. He tried to hide his smoking by chewing Big Red gum, but it didn't work. The kids saw him smoking at the fire hall, and when they told me, I told the elders. They gave him the benefit of the doubt the first time, but after some of the friends from the Kingdom Hall caught him lighting up, he was disfellowshipped. This put our family on the outskirts of the religion. No one would come to our house because Gary was disfellowshipped. It also put a strain on our marriage as Gary was back to secretly spending money. When I talked to Dr. Francis about our marital woes, he suggested a separation. I told him the only grounds for separation were abuse or adultery. He patiently listened and helped me with coping skills the best he could.

Dr. Francis taught me not to judge myself or other people as well as not to compare myself to others. During the summer, rather than drive out to Sizerville, I took Caleb and Cherey to the community pool located behind the high school. While walking into the pool, when I started to feel as if I didn't belong. I told myself, "You aren't better than anyone else here, and no one here is better than you." That simple statement was a turning point in my life. I began to socialize and make friends with people I knew from the community without trying to witness or convert them to the Jehovah's Witness religion.

When I took the kids swimming to Sizerville State Park, I started to socialize more with people. After attending a nature program on identifying wildflowers, Lisa, the park naturalist, asked me if I knew anyone who made hard tack candy. She was planning an Autumn Festival in which artisans would be crafting wood toys, homemade soap, spinning wool, carving spoons, and pressing cider. Dulcimer and fiddle musicians were scheduled to perform. Little did I know that my future beloved husband, who I hadn't yet met, would be one of the artisans. The event sounded right up my alley with all the canning, quilting, and sewing I did at home. When I agreed to participate, Lisa said, "Let me know what you'll need, and I'll buy all the ingredients."

Making hard tack candy was a wintertime activity I learned from my witness friend, Jane. The candy was made by measuring sugar, corn syrup, and water into a heavy saucepan. Over medium heat on a stovetop, the mixture was brought to three hundred thirty degrees. After removing the mixture from the heat, the children stirred in flavoring, then I poured the candy onto a baking sheet greased with shortening and set it outside to harden. After the candy hardened and looked like a pane of glass, Justin was always the first to get the hammer from his dad's tool pile to crack the candy into small pieces. After dusting it with confectioner's sugar, they would bag it up and take it to school to share with their friends. I told Lisa I had never made the candy over a wood fire but was willing to give it a try.

When the day of the festival arrived, I knew from camping experience that I would need a heavy-duty saucepan to prevent scorching. I unearthed an old pressure cooker I had found at a yard sale, some old spoons, and a candy thermometer. Gary drove up to the park with us to help get the fire started and afterward went up to the Sizerville Inn to drink for the afternoon. Caleb was six years old at the time and helped me measure out the sugar and corn syrup. It took a little finesse trying to manage the fire and keep an eye on the temperature of the candy at the same time. The thermometer, which was clipped to the side of the saucepan, dropped into the fire, so I learned to judge the right temperature by dropping a spoonful of the hot liquid into ice-cold water.

Cherey and her eight-year-old friends picked out the flavors and food coloring to match. After the candy was poured onto baking sheets coated with lard, it hardened quickly on the crisp October day. Children came by and cracked the brittle candy, which looked like pieces of glass and tasted each one to decide the flavor they liked best. Hundreds of children filled up on hardtack as they rounded the scenic park to experience how old-time crafts were made.

After the festival, the demonstrators gathered in the nature center to have a potluck supper. Lisa provided a pot of chili, and others brought side dishes and desserts. I liked being part of the group and contributing positively to the community. Because I was a Jehovah's Witness, holidays and family rituals were sorely missing in our lives. The Autumn Festival filled this void. I didn't see anything wrong with participating in an event labeled 'worldly' by Jehovah's Witnesses.

During the school year, when Caleb was in elementary school, I volunteered as a chaperone when his class went on environmental field trips to Sizerville State Park. After the children got off the bus and were organizing into groups, Lisa approached me and said someone called in sick, and she needed someone to conduct one of the workshops. Without asking what was involved, I agreed. Lisa and I jogged through the woods to the pavilion where I would be stationed. She hurriedly showed me what I would be presenting by pulling a frozen rodent out of a cooler. I didn't have the heart to disappoint her and tell her I was petrified of mice and rats. She proceeded to show me a star-nose mole and gave me a book to read to the children. She then demonstrated an activity using cardboard egg cartons and yarn to make a nose for the children to tie behind their ears.

When the first group of children arrived for the lesson, I nervously held the star-nosed mole by the tail and dangled it in front of the group. The story about the rodent was endearing, and by the time the second group of children arrived, I found myself holding the mole more securely while wearing gloves. After teaching five groups of kids about the star-nosed mole, I no longer felt petrified of rodents. After the program, Lisa thanked me profusely for filling in and told me what a great job I had done with the kids. My self-esteem gained ten points.

When I knocked on Lisa's door while out in service with the witnesses, she invited me into her house. I appreciated her kindness. We talked more about our children than we did the Bible. She had just given birth to her second child, Ryan, who was born premature. It was a tender time for both of us. I encouraged her as a new mom, and she helped me through her acceptance despite my being a Jehovah's Witness.

New Beginnings

While working at Head Star in St. Marys, a position at the Emporium Head Start for an assistant teacher opened up. I applied and was hired. I was happy to be closer to home and not be driving back and forth to St. Marys every day. I was now known as "Miss Jeanette" and began working in the classroom caring for seventeen preschool children, planning menus, and preparing food for their breakfast. My co-workers, Freda and Ellie, were extraordinarily kind and never judged me for being a Jehovah's Witness, although challenges did arise.

At Christmas, a little boy named Adam asked me, "Teacher, is there really a Santa Claus?"

I cleverly told him, "That's something you will have to ask your mommy."

A week later, he approached me and asked, "Teacher, do reindeer fly."

Without realizing the question was connected to Christmas, a matter of factly, I answered, "No, reindeer don't fly, Adam."

That night I received a phone call from his mom who was upset I ruined Christmas for the whole family, including Adam's younger sister who was only three years old. I apologized and told the mom I didn't intentionally ruin their Christmas, but Andrew asked a bright question, and I gave what I felt was a bright answer.

Other situations arose that I was in no way prepared to handle. This was during the time of the sexual abuse scandal with the Boy Scouts in Emporium. A little girl named Laura had an older stepbrother who was a victim of the abuser. He, in turn, abused his little sister. After doing a "Good Touch, Bad Touch" program to educate the children on how to handle sexual abuse, Laura started acting out the abuse while playing with dolls during free playtime. I tried to get help from my supervisors, but no one seemed to know what to do about the situation. I called Dr. Francis, and he told me that was one of the downsides to talking to children about sexual abuse in group settings. He gave me the phone number to John Yates, the director of Dickinson Mental Health Services, who he said would place me with a counselor to help Laura. When I called Mr. Yates, he was kind and helpful. After I told him Dr. Francis told me to call him, he took a particular interest in the situation and set up an appointment for the family to talk to a counselor. I learned later that Dr. Francis had worked for Dickinson Mental Health and had hired John for the director position.

While I worked at Head Start, First Lady, Barbara Bush started a literacy initiative for children and families. Mrs. Bush believed 'the home was a child's first classroom, the parent was a child's first teacher, and reading was a child's first subject.' Unfortunately, for many children who attended Head Start, the first two beliefs weren't true, but we were determined to make the last one happen. Head Start classrooms received thousands of dollars to buy books for children. The teachers and assistant teachers attended literacy workshops, where we learned about the importance of reading to children. We were instructed to set up a library corner in the classrooms.

Being a lover of reading, my children had a bookcase full of books at home which I read to them every night. We enjoyed books such as *Alexander and the Terrible, Horrible, No Good, Very Bad Day* by Judith Viorist, *The Very Hungry Caterpillar* by Eric Carle, *Where the Wild Things*

Are by Maurice Sendak and *The Mitten* by Jan Brett. I ordered these books for Head Start and each month studied a featured author, hoping to instill a love of reading and literature in the children's lives. Each day at circle time, I would read the children a book aloud.

Reading children's books helped me to grow as a person and to nurture the emotionally stunted child in myself. While reading *The Runaway Bunny* by Margaret Wise Brown, I broke down crying. The story was about a little bunny who kept running away from his mommy, who in turn, chased after the rabbit, no matter where he went or what he became. When a little girl named Vicky, with blonde hair and blue eyes, asked me why my eyes were wet, I told her, "Because when I was little, I never had a mommy who would find me when I was lost or ran away." Vicky got up from where she was seated in the circle and gave me a big hug. The two of us become quite close. One morning she came to the classroom crying, and I asked her why her eyes were wet. She told me her dog chewed up her favorite teddy bear. I told her to bring it to school the next day and I would fix it. When she brought in the worn teddy bear, I took it home, stitched the ear up and bandaged it with white gauze.

Caring for children who sometimes lived in abusive homes, pushed buttons for me, but I learned first-hand how to care for the abused little girl inside of me. When a little girl named Jessica started hitting other children, rather than punish her and put her in time out, I got out crayons and paper, and we colored together. While she was coloring, with a black crayon, I asked her about her mommy and mommy's boyfriend, who I knew to be violent and abusive. As I talked with Jessica, she began tearing up the picture she was coloring. I named the feeling as anger and said it was okay to feel that way. Afterward, she threw the paper in the garbage and never hit another child. I learned to process my feelings about the abuse I experienced.

I read a book titled *Strong at the Broken Places* by Linda Sanford based on the quotation, "*The world breaks everyone and afterward some are strong at the broken places."* by Ernest Hemmingway. I found this to be true while working with children from abusive homes. I understood them in ways that other caregivers could not understand.

Head Start is a government-funded program, and after working there, I started to see that the government wasn't an evil entity. I began to wonder how Jehovah's Witnesses could go to doctors and send their children to school, but not believe in educating them beyond high school. Although I hadn't gone to college, I saw the wisdom in education.

Educational training was mandatory for Head Start employees, so I started attending Better Kid Care Seminars sponsored by Penn State Cooperative Extension and organized by Barb Miller, the Family Living Agent. Childcare providers were introduced to a puppet named Chef Combo, who taught the children about eating healthy meals that included vegetables and fruits. I started incorporating weekly lessons in nutrition using the puppet. Chef Combo was a forgetful older man with a white mustache and wore a white chef's hat. The children became quite fond of him and started telling him secrets they didn't ordinarily tell me. When they were talking to him, it was as if I were not present. I made sure Chef Combo repeated what they said, so they knew he was listening. Then I would give them a few words of advice and encouragement.

Ellie Pellam was the family service worker for Cameron County and had worked as an extension agent for many years before getting married and having children. Ellie invited me to be on the Penn State Cooperative Extension Advisory Board for Cameron County, which met four times a year on Thursday evenings. I had no idea what that meant, but it sounded important, so I agreed, even though it meant missing a few meetings at the Kingdom Hall. The board meetings involved listening to fiscal reports, hearing about programs the Extension office was conducting, including 4-H, nutrition and horticulture programs. At my first meeting, I was welcomed by the president of the board, Jim Shoup, who knew Gary from his high school years of going to school with his son, Dennis. I was a little nervous that Mr. Shoup was going to judge me for being a Jehovah's Witness, but he was kind and accepting. I also met Corinne Zinni-Case, who had moved to Emporium from Massachusetts. I was immediately drawn to Corinne's warmth and ability to listen intently to anyone speaking.

After working at Head Start a few years, a job opening as a nutrition education advisor advertised in the *Cameron County Echo* caught my eye. A 'sister' from the Kingdom Hall was looking for employment, so I told her about the job, but she wasn't interested. When I told Ellie Pellam, the family service worker at Head Start, about the position, she asked me why I didn't apply. For some reason, applying for the job never entered my mind. I sent in a resume, and to my surprise was called for an interview. The job I applied for was with the Expanded Foods and Nutrition Education Program (EFNEP)for low-income families funded by the government. Barb Miller, who knew me from the Better Kid Care seminars, would be my supervisor. She was happy to have someone she knew on board. I would work under Cathy Harrington from Penn State, who was present for the interview.

During the interview, I was asked, "What would you do if a client wants to bake Christmas cookies."

I replied, "I would help them bake the cookies."

I was then asked, "What would you do if there were cockroaches in a house you were visiting."

I replied, "I would silently think that's a good source of protein."

When I was offered the job, I felt as if my status in life escalated about ten steps. The pay was decent, with vacation and sick days off, a retirement program, education, and health benefits doing a job I loved and felt qualified to do. I loved to cook and knew the importance of proper nutrition. What more could I ask for? I didn't realize this job would be my ticket out of Jehovah's Witnesses in just a few months. I was required to attend a four-day training at Penn State University in State College. While I was packing for the event, my daughter Cherey, who was about twelve at the time, became extremely worried.

"Mom, who are you going to stay with while you are away?"

"I'll be rooming with someone who is starting the same job I am."

"But you don't know her."

"I'm sure we will get along."

I had never been to Penn State before, and the minute I drove onto the campus grounds, a whole new world was opened up to me. My first roommate was a woman named Leslie, who lived in the State College area. We roomed at The Atherton Hotel and stayed up all night talking about health, growing herbs, and eating naturally. God couldn't have put me with a better person. A group of about ten other women, who were hired as Nutrition Education Advisors for the central region of Pennsylvania, were also in attendance. We felt like royalty dining on delicious food prepared by chefs. We were given a tour of the campus and treated to ice cream from the Penn State Creamery, where I had my first taste of coffee ice cream. I began to realize how small my world had been.

For four days, we learned about Penn State and how to do our job. I received my first email address and learned desktop publishing. I would work from home and had access to a computer at the Extension office located less than a block from my house. This was the first time in my life that I turned on a computer and was introduced to the dial-up internet.

At the conference, I had time to leisurely read in the evening and picked up a booklet about Jesus. Out of curiosity, I opened the book and started reading it. The book suggested saying a prayer to ask Jesus to come into your heart. Even though I felt like a heathen, I closed the book and said a silent prayer, inviting Jesus into my life. Afterward, instead of feeling guilty, I felt an immense amount of peace, and for the first time in my life, I felt truly loved.

Each month, I traveled to Penn State and other campuses in the region for training and got to know the State College area quite well. I took Cherey and Caleb swimming at the pool on campus and shopping at the mall. My favorite store was the Barnes and Noble bookstore. While browsing the clearance section of the bookstore, I picked up a paperback titled *When A Church Goes Bad--Dealing with the Pain of Spiritual Abuse* by Casey M. Sabella. When I returned home, I hid the book in my bedroom. At night I began reading the book and stayed up all night until I finished it. Although the book wasn't specifically about Jehovah's Witnesses, it made references to the religion. I no longer felt alone about my perception of elders at the Kingdom Hall and how spiritually abusive they were.

The next day, I found the author's telephone number by calling directory assistance from my upstairs bedroom. My fingers were trembling as I turned the dial on the rotary phone. When Mr. Sabella answered the phone, compassion poured from his voice.

"Hello, this is Casey Sabella." The minute I began talking, tears poured out of my heart.

"Mr. Sabella, my name is Jeanette. I just read your book, *When A Church Goes Bad,* and want to tell you I don't feel crazy anymore. I'm one of Jehovah's Witnesses. When I read your book, it was as if you were writing about the Kingdom Hall I attend."

"Thank you, Jeanette. Are you okay?" No one, other than Dr. Francis, had ever asked me if I were okay.

"I'm not sure. I don't know what to do. I've been a Jehovah's Witness for twenty-five years, and if I leave the religion, I will be destroyed at Armageddon."

"Jeanette, I want to tell you, that isn't true. It's only what you were taught. I know you are feeling alone right now, but let me tell you there are thousands of people waiting to welcome and support you."

"Really? How do you know?"

"Because I know what it feels like to leave a religion you thought was the truth. I'm going to give you a man's name, and I want you to call him. His name is Randall Watters, and he was a Jehovah's Witness."

I jotted down the phone number on a scratch piece of paper. After thanking Mr. Sabella, I called the phone number and talked to Randy. He was just as kind and offered to send me some tapes and material to read. I gave him my address and told him not to use a return address. I didn't want anyone to find out I was reading 'apostate' information. When I received the packet in the mail, I couldn't put it down. Everything I read rang true. A suggested book *Crisis of Conscience* by Raymond Franz interested me because my conscience was now in crisis. How could I continue to belong to a religion which was hurting more than helping me? I told myself, maybe it was just the Emporium congregation under the toxic rule of Frank Scarpelli. When the thick 440-page book, published in 1983, that I mail ordered, arrived I knew I wasn't going to be able to read it in one night. Franz was a former member of the governing body at the Watchtower in Brooklyn, New York. Because the book was written by 'an apostate,' I hid it in my clothes closet on the top shelf. I didn't want any of my kids finding it and telling someone at the Kingdom Hall what I was reading. My thinking was so distorted that I thought if I was in a car accident and died, I wouldn't be resurrected to the paradise and would never see my children again. Each night after the children went to bed, I read the book. I couldn't quit turning the pages and thought it would take me forever to read the book. I stayed up reading into the wee hours of the morning until I finished the book in less than a week.

Tears of sadness rolled down my cheeks as I read about brothers and sisters in Malawi who were murdered by government authorities because they wouldn't buy a card saying they belonged to the government while allowances were made for Jehovah's Witnesses in Mexico. I didn't understand how United States citizens could have social security cards, and people from other countries were forbidden to have ties to their government. I shook with anger when the author went into detail, describing the hypocrisy of the blood transfusions. Many people, including children, died, believing it was wrong to receive a blood transfusion, while the governing body was making allowances for other people by approving the use of blood platelets for medical emergencies. Raymond Franz tried to alter the rules internally, but there was no changing the dictates, which resulted in people being disfellowshipped. He was eventually disfellowshipped for socializing with 'an apostate.'

After reading the book, I realized the religion was rotten from the top down, not the bottom up. How was I going to extricate myself from the faith that had been my identity for the past twenty-five years? How could I tell my children that what I believed in and taught them their whole lives was a farce? I felt like I was standing at the edge of a large cliff, ready to jump off the edge into an abyss of darkness. The bough I was pausing on was a little limb at the end of a tree ready to snap. If I believed I had wings, I could have jumped, knowing I would fly instead of fall. I tucked the books away and didn't talk to anyone about what I knew. I remembered reading in *A Search for Meaning* by Victor Frankl that some people in concentration camps didn't survive once they were released because the light from the outside world was just too bright for them. I now understood how that happened.

Rather than pouring myself into Jehovah's Witnesses, I slowly started to transfer my identity to Penn State, another institution that told me what to do and when to do it. I had to set aside my beliefs about such things as to whether it was healthier to eat butter versus margarine. I did have the freedom to inform people that there were two schools of thought. Despite having to educate people about the harmful effects of butter, I was able to hold on to my belief that butter was the better choice. It was natural and not made from chemicals, which I believe are more harmful.

Barb Miller and I started a program called Super Cupboards for women with limited resources in Elk and Cameron Counties. Barb was a single woman and was one of the most resourceful people I had ever met.

If I were stranded on an island, the one person I would want to be with, was Barb. She was extremely resourceful and saved everything from bread ties to every paper which crossed her desk. The classes were generally held in church basements and included lessons on budgeting, nutrition, parenting, and health. Together the women prepared a full course meal, while they learned cooking skills and food safety. Barb also conducted Better Kid Care Seminars, in which nutrition was a component and invited me to teach a lesson using Chef Combo. Barb helped me spread my wings by believing in me and supporting me in my new job.

It was more than ironic that one of my first mentors at Mooseheart was my home economics teacher, whose name was Miss Miller. The only difference between the two women was that Barb was tall and slender, and Miss Mae Miller was shorter and plump; both of them were kind and resourceful. I carried fond memories of Miss Miller in my heart. She taught me how to follow recipes, how to cut out patterns, and how to sew.

When everyone else thought I was a troublemaker, Miss Miller saw the best in me. She noted my neat handwriting and nominated me to copy recipes onto a large poster board to use in group cooking classes.

Visiting people with limited resources in their homes was challenging. Many of the clients didn't seem interested in cooking or eating healthy. When I received referrals from Children and Youth Services, some of the kitchens were so filthy that it wasn't possible to do any cooking. I was required to teach clients about nutrition and food safety, which seemed tedious and useless. I was feeling depressed about the job until I turned my thinking around. I remembered being a mother with four young children at home, feeling like a slave, cooking and washing dishes all day until I changed my viewpoint.

When I began looking at cooking as a culinary art form, I became more creative and enjoyed being in the kitchen. I used the same technique and told myself that nutrition and cooking were essential skills. After my attitude change, I started to meet people interested in learning how to cook and prepare healthy meals.

I began visiting a woman named Liz, who recently moved to Ridgway from Oregon with her three young children. She had just gone through a family crisis and was trying to recover. I had recently attended a seminar at Penn State University in State College by Mary Pipher, Ph.D., author of *Reviving Ophelia-Saving the Selves of Adolescent Girls*. In the book, she discussed how resilient families are and that growing plants can inspire hope. When I visited Liz, she said she wanted to grow a vegetable garden but didn't have the outdoor space. I brought her a container, potting soil, and pumpkin seeds to start on her kitchen windowsill, knowing the plants would probably never produce a pumpkin. I believed that caring for the plant and watching it grow would inspire Liz, and it did.

I helped Liz polish her employment resume for a position broadcasting with a local radio station-which she obtained with ease-by providing a personal reference. I did my best to help her through the grief of losing her teenage daughter in an automobile accident. Liz wasn't only a client; the two of us became friends.

While working for Penn State, I learned about the 4-H Program. I liked the curriculum and the idea of children learning life skills hands-on. Lori McDowell was the youth extension agent for Elk and Cameron Counties and worked out of my base office. Lori was accepting and seemed to have a good rapport with youth. Her fiery red hair and bright blue eyes reflected her zest for life and interest in having fun.

Lori organized 4-H camps and other activities. I decided to become a 4-H leader, thinking it would benefit my children. After attending extensive leader trainings, I started arts and crafts and cooking clubs with a couple of 'worldly' kids Cherey and Caleb knew from school. None of the Jehovah's Witness kids were allowed to participate. I signed the kids up to attend a four-day summer camp where they stayed overnight. We entered projects in the Cameron County fair and won blue ribbons for the entries.

Caleb won first place in speaking contests and was invited to go to Harrisburg for Capital Days, where he won the first-place trophy for his speech on how to make chicken wings. He also met Dan Surra, the state representative. Lori asked if I would be interested in attending a 4-H conference in Vermont. The extension office would pay for the plane ticket and hotel. It was exciting to travel to Lake Champlain. I made a teddy bear where the first teddy bear, named after Teddy Roosevelt, was made, visited the von Trapp family home and learned more about the 4-H Program.

Through a tobacco-free grant, to help kids to avoid smoking, Lori hired a woman named Mary Ann to develop and deliver programming to youth. Ironically, Mary Ann was raised in St. Joseph's Orphanage in Erie. It was comforting to meet someone familiar with life in an orphanage. We had a connection between us that no one else seemed to understand. After meeting Mary Ann, I felt less alone in the world. I also met Jan Hampton, who worked with the Conservation Department. Her office was in the bank annex building with the Extension office. Even though I was a Jehovah's Witness, Jan never shied away from being friends with me, as other people sometimes did. She was Gary's second cousin on his mother's side and treated me like one of the family.

During the holiday season, Jan brought in a white sweatshirt with blue morning glories with Jeanette inscribed in the vines of the shirt. I wondered how she knew the morning glories were one of my favorite flowers. At Christmas, instead of giving me a Santa Claus ornament like she gave the other co-workers, she made me a snowman. Her exuberance and happiness for life and people were contagious. Jan's smile made me feel accepted. In turn, I started to smile at people while walking down the street and noticed people smiled in return. For the first time ever, I began to feel joy in my life.

Jan invited Caleb to attend the Black Forest Conservation Camp in Potter County, where he enjoyed meeting new people and learning about the environment. I signed Caleb up for art programs at the recreation center. I was trying my best to make up for the lost time by helping the kids fit in socially.

When Cherey was entering tenth grade, she asked to be home-schooled, and I obliged. Other Jehovah's Witness families were home-schooling their children to protect them from the worldly association. Even though I was having doubts about the religion, the indoctrination was so deep that I still believed worldly friends were bad for my children. Cherey had a shy nature, and social situations were hard for her. I thought home-schooling would be suitable for her.

Cherey participated in school plays and music programs. At one of the programs, she was required to sing the main part in a patriotic song. I was in the audience, frowning because it wasn't allowed by Jehovah's Witnesses. Afterward, the music teacher approached me and told me what a beautiful voice Cherey had. I refrained from shaming Cherey for singing the song, but I'm sure she picked up on my disdain from the stage. I wish I could turn back time and stand up and clap for her at the performance.

After researching home computers from a book, I checked out of the library, I ordered a NuTrend computer recommended by the author. With the skills I learned at Penn State, I figured out how to connect the computer to the phone line and was able to access the world wide web for the first time in my life. I started searching for information on Mooseheart to find classmates that I went to school with from the time I was in nursery school to eighth grade. When I discovered the Mooseheart Alumni website, I was ecstatic find contact information for my brother Jack's graduating class of 1970. Jack was listed in the directory and had an email address.

I typed a letter to him:

> Dear Jack,
>   I hope you are well. I know it's been awhile since we've been in touch and I apologize for the distance. I wanted to thank you for

taking the time to visit me when our mom passed away and I didn't attend the funeral.

I don't know if I told you or not, but I have been seeing a psychologist for depression and childhood trauma and he recommended that I not attend as being around some of my family is too exhausting for me.

I'm now working for Penn State Cooperative extension and have access to the world wide web. I'm glad to have found a way to correspond with you.

Much love,

Jeanette

I sent it off, not knowing if he would get it or even if he would respond. Within a few days, I heard back from him, saying that he would also like to keep in touch. He was living in Oklahoma at the time and was still in the military full time. I was glad to be in touch with him again.

The computer was not only useful to me for work and keeping in touch with Jack but was helpful to Cherey in her schoolwork. For a science and health requirement, I signed Cherey up for one of Barb Miller's nutrition classes on diabetes. The only thing I knew about diabetes were stories Gary's mom told me about her mom having diabetes and needing to eat chocolate bars. At Barb's diabetes class, Cherey and I learned there were two types of diabetes. Because the subject wasn't applicable to us, when we finished the course, the difference between type 1 and type 2 diabetes, still wasn't clear to either of us. The class seemed to be an omen. In a few years, both of us would get a crash course in type 1 diabetes.

By the end of tenth grade, Cherey was bored with staying home, and I was overwhelmed with trying to get her to do chores such as dishes and helping with meals, much less getting her to do schoolwork. She returned to Cameron County High School for her junior year. It seemed like the homeschooling backfired as she worked to fit in socially by making friends with kids who weren't doing well. It seemed that homeschooling contributed even more to her social unease. Now she had to try to make friends after missing a year of school.

As the older children entered their teen years, the challenge of parenting tested my mettle. I wasn't alone in this situation as many of the teenagers who attended the Kingdom Hall were acting out by smoking, drinking, and God forbid, dating. The consequence of their behavior was being disfellowshipped. If your kid was caught doing something wrong, the other kids weren't allowed to associate with them. It seemed that the children whose parents were elders were treated with more leniency. The unfairness caused a lot of resentment between the adults. When I was out in-service waiting in the car with Sharon Scarpelli, while her husband, Frank, and another brother were conducting a home Bible study, she pulled a piece of paper out of her purse and handed it to me.

"What is this?"

"It's a picture that my son, John, drew."

I unfolded the piece of paper to see a pencil drawing of a mouse under a trap and replied, "Interesting picture."

Even though we were alone in the car together, she leaned over and whispered, "What do you think it means?"

Without hesitation, I replied, "It looks as if he's feeling trapped."

The perpetual smile she always wore turned to a frown, and she asked, "I wonder why he feels this way."

I wanted to say because your husband controls every little thing he does. He puts Tabasco sauce on a cotton ball and makes him hold it in his mouth. He also beats him with a belt buckle whenever he does something wrong. But I couldn't say anything because I was sworn to secrecy by my children, who confided in me. They were close friends with John and knew first-hand how John, and his brother Dan, were treated. If Frank Scarpelli ever found out John told, he would be in more trouble. I felt like a caged bird and knew not to sing.

Another parent was frustrated with her teenage daughter for wanting to date a boy. Despite her daughter being a straight-A student, she had her sent to a children's home outside of the county for her rebellion.

I heard rumors about some of the adolescent boys being sexually abused by an elder in the Kersey congregation. The boy's parents were told not to go to the police and the elder was sent off to a congregation in Kentucky. One of the boys, who I had known since he was a baby, started using drugs and within a few years died of a drug overdose.

During the teen years, I tried to take Brandi and Justin to see Dr. Francis, but they wouldn't talk to him because going to counseling was discouraged at the Kingdom Hall. After Brandi graduated, she wanted to go to school for business in Olean, New York but I wouldn't allow her to go because Jehovah's Witnesses didn't believe in going to college. Instead, she started working at a powdered metal plant where her dad worked and moved to St. Marys. While working at the factory, she was severely injured when her arm got caught in one of the machines, requiring surgery and multiple trips back and forth to Pittsburgh to repair nerve damage. She moved back to Emporium and tried to attend meetings but decided that she didn't want to be a Jehovah's Witness anymore. Brandi wrote a letter to the elders saying she no longer wanted to belong to the religion. Now she was disassociated, and I wasn't supposed to talk to her. As I'm writing this, I feel heartsick.

For a short time, I tried not talking to Brandi, but it broke my heart, so I established contact with her. I started letting Caleb and Cherey visit her in Kersey, where she had moved after she married a man she had met in Emporium. I did my best to support her by making sure she had groceries and sending her cards. In June 1998, I was present when Brandi gave birth to my first grandchild, William Alfred Peluso III.

Justin wanted to play football but wasn't allowed. Not only because the Witnesses didn't allow it but because I felt it was a dangerous sport. He became angry and resentful. The only thing that interested him in high school was a shop class with Mr. Murray, who became a mentor to him. Not long after Brandi left the religion, Justin, along with his friend John Scarpelli, were disfellowshipped for smoking. Again, I was expected to disown my son. After thinking long and hard, I decided this wasn't something I could do. I didn't have a family as a child, and I wasn't going to give up the only family I had as an adult.

I confided in Dr. Francis about the doubts I was having about the religion's teachings-in particular the edict not to talk to my children. If I had shared my thoughts with a Jehovah's Witness, it would have led to instant disfellowshipping. I felt safe with Dr. Francis. Instead of telling me what to do, he asked, "What merit is there in what Jehovah's Witnesses teach, and what merit is there in what you believe and what makes you feel most comfortable?"

I felt most comfortable talking to my children. I also would use this litmus test to guide me through the turbulent waters ahead. I remembered Dr. Francis had told me earlier no one could take my mind from me. Even though I felt my mind was hijacked, I realized that instead of giving me answers, Dr. Francis was teaching me to think for myself. I started to view the religion from a new perspective. Dr. Francis opened the door to the cage I was in, but I wasn't yet ready to fly free.

Grace

Being employed with Penn State meant attending monthly staffing meetings and quarterly board meetings in Elk and Cameron Counties. The boards consisted of people in the community from a wide variety of backgrounds, including farmers, clergy, homemakers, and retired teachers, including my former biology teacher, Mr. Yaccabucci, who was now retired. When I walked into the meeting room, I wanted to hide my head in shame for how I behaved in high school.

Thankfully, he didn't remember me. I don't know if it was him or me who changed, but he didn't seem as strict. We got along well, and after a few meetings, I was able to tell him I graduated with his daughter, Amy.

Corinne, from the Extension Board, invited me to her house for tea. She had two young children, Caleb and Olivia. Corine had moved to Emporium from Massachusetts and had a strong New England accent. She didn't treat me differently because of my religion. From some of our conversations, I knew she didn't agree with the teachings of Jehovah's Witnesses, but she was respectful and cautious not to criticize me. Corinne had a background counseling battered women and was well aware of mind control.

On a snowy winter evening, she invited me cross-country skiing with her while her husband Tim took care of the children. I remembered dreaming about cross country skiing while working with Head Start. A guest speaker came in with her cross-country skis and talked to the class about the winter sport. While listening to her talk about how beautiful and quiet it is in the woods in the wintertime, I thought that's something I would like to do someday. I couldn't believe something I dreamed of doing was coming true. In the starry night, we skied the unplowed, snow-covered streets. The glide of the skis on the snow was mesmerizing. For the first time in my life, I felt exhilarated and free.

When spring arrived, Corinne was now expecting her third child. Together we took evening walks, pushing Olivia in a stroller. On one of our walks, Corinne mentioned the word grace in reference to God's love for us. The only grace I knew was saying a prayer before eating.

Without trying to sound stupid, I asked, "What does grace mean to you?"

She answered, "It's God's unconditional love for us. There is nothing we can do to earn God's love. He loves us just the way we are."

That was the most beautiful thing I had ever heard.

When I went home, I cried at the thought of God loving me for who I am. It dawned on me I didn't have to go to meetings, I didn't have to go out in the door to door ministry, and I didn't have to be perfect for God to love me. I felt free of the shackles of Jehovah's Witnesses. At the same time, the bough I was perched on was giving way, and I felt I had wings to fly.

This new perception of God didn't feel masculine, so I imagined God to be a feminine Goddess. I named her Rose. When I prayed in this manner, I didn't feel like I was going to be punished for some wrongdoing. Talking to Rose was like talking to other parts of myself, except it felt as if Rose were outside of myself. I felt loved by her unconditionally, and whenever I needed help beyond my human abilities, Rose came through. As I look back, she was my Divine intelligence.

At the board meetings, I also met John and Lois Shoemaker, who had retired from teaching and were now managing The Faircroft Bed and

Breakfast in Ridgway. Lois was starting an herb garden and introduced me to a woman named Stephanie Distler, who was the proprietor of Sweet Posie's Herbary in Johnsonburg. Little did I know at the time that the entrepreneurs I was meeting were lining me up for one of the greatest blessings of my life.

To distance myself from all the trauma and injustice that was going on with the religion, I poured myself into my work with Penn State and working with children. For the past twenty-five years, my identity was a Jehovah's Witness, going to meetings five times a week, studying for all the meetings, going out in field service, reading all the Watchtower and Awake magazines, attending conventions three times a year and spending time with the other Witnesses. The religion had consumed me. Shedding this identity felt as though I were removing a mask. I felt like a snake shedding its skin except it didn't feel as if I had an identity underneath the mask. I started to construct one with activities I enjoyed doing. I was always good at cooking, so I began holding Kids Cooking Classes afterschool in church kitchens and the kitchen at the Northern Tier Community Action Building on Fourth Street. I taught children how to make quesadillas, pizza, and other simple dishes they could prepare for themselves. I felt good about myself when children and parents sent me thank you notes for the classes.

To reserve the kitchens for the classes, I had to meet with the pastor of the church. The first time I met with one of them, I felt an overwhelming sense of guilt. It felt as if I was robbing a bank. Each of the clergymen put me at ease with their kindness and willingness to help with the classes. Being in their presence was so unlike the elders at the Kingdom Hall who always seemed to be looking for issues to counsel me on. Pastor Davis from the Presbyterian Church on Fourth Street, and I got to know each other quite well. When I arrived to set up for the class, he would come to the church to talk and see if I needed anything. He showed me a sign he was making for the outside of the church.

At times it was a lot of work supervising the children, and plans didn't always turn out for the best. While I was teaching the kids how to make hardtack candy, instead of adding a teaspoon of cinnamon flavoring to the mixture, one of the students accidentally poured in a whole bottle. We had to evacuate the building because our eyes and noses were burning from the fumes. I was able to salvage the candy, and we all enjoyed eating red hot hardtack! The cooking classes were well attended, and I became familiar with children in the community.

At one of the classes, a young girl named Joyce came with her head down, not talking to anyone. When I asked what was making her so sad, with tears in her eyes, she said, "I think my mom is going to die."

"What makes you think that?"

"My mom has heart problems and told me she isn't going to live long."

I tried to comfort her. "That must be so frightening for you. But if she does die, everything will be OK."

With tears in her eyes, she asked, "How do you know?"

I replied, "Because when I was a little girl, my dad died, and my mom was unable to care for me. It was hard, but I survived." With the back of her hand, she wiped away the tears. Because her mom didn't drive, I gave Joyce a ride home from the weekly cooking classes. When I dropped her off, I noticed a large rock with Sleeping Beauty painted on the front. When I asked Joyce, who the artist was, she said her mom. Joyce invited me into her house to meet her mom, Diane.

Diane was a large woman with black hair that matched her daughter's. Beneath her rough exterior was a kind, creative woman who had inner strength. She was a single mom who raised Joyce and her older brothers. When I commented on Diane's painting outside, she broke into a wide grin and proceeded to show me through her house, where she had more paintings. We never talked about her dying.

On a Saturday afternoon, when I took Caleb to Memorial Hall to shoot a few games of pool, I took note of the bare walls of the building. When I went downstairs to use the restroom, I ran into the newly hired director, Carol Feibig.

Carol was a tall, thin young woman with shoulder-length brunette hair. I congratulated her on the new job. Out of the blue, I asked if she ever thought of brightening the recreation hall up by painting the walls with murals. Her eyes lit up and she said, "That's a great idea."

I told her about Diane's artwork and said I would ask Diane if she would be interested in doing some artwork for Memorial Hall. Carol said in the meantime, she would get permission from the recreation board. The next time I took Joyce home from the Cooking Class, I asked Diane if she would like to paint some murals at Memorial Hall.

Her response was, "Really? That would give me something to do, except I don't have money for paint."

I relayed the message to Carol, and she said the board was excited about the idea and had the supplies. I explained Diane's situation to Carol and warned Diane had a rough exterior but was a kind soul. The two of them connected, and Diane spruced up the interior and exterior walls of the recreation center. Over the time Diane was painting, she and Carol got to know each other quite well. When an opening came up for an evening position, Diane applied for the job at Memorial Hall and was hired.

After Diane received her first paycheck, she marched into the Public Assistance office and told the caseworker she no longer needed assistance because she had a job. When the caseworker told her she still qualified for food stamps, Diane told her she no longer needed them. For the first time in her life, she didn't need welfare. It was the proudest moment in her life.

A few months later, Diane passed away from heart failure. When I went to the viewing at the funeral home, Carol was there with tears streaming down her cheeks. She thanked me for introducing the two of them and told me Diane had just gotten her driver's permit and was planning on getting a car before she died. Just as I predicted, Joyce survived after her mom's death. Years later, she sent me a beautiful message with a picture of a cake she baked. She thanked me for teaching her how to bake and said she would never forget the kindness that I showed her during one of the most challenging times in her life.

In the summer, I attended a training event sponsored by Rodale Press on starting community gardens and learned that they were offering a grant for start-up projects. The project needed to include youth from juvenile probation to qualify for the seed money. I contacted the Cameron County Probation Office and spoke to Loretta, who put me in touch with Jan Burkness, the head probation officer. Jan was supportive of the project and wrote a letter of support for the program. On top of that, she suggested we use the space behind St. John's Lutheran Church. The pastor was her husband, Bruce, who I remembered from the mental health meeting I attended when my mother passed away.

Helping to relieve poverty in the community and world is a mission in the Lutheran faith. When Pastor Burkness presented the idea to the church board members, they permitted us to use the plot of land behind the church for a garden.

Adolescent boys on probation installed railroad ties for the raised bed gardens under the supervision of Doug Callen. Doug took a personal interest in the boys and believed that they should be doing purposeful work in the community. At the time, Doug's wife was suffering from health complications, and we spent hours talking and sharing our stories. He was a kind soul whom I would keep in touch with for many years.

A local business donated topsoil, and we bought garden tools with the grant money. Our only obstacle was the neighbors who didn't want troublemakers in their neighborhood. I was surprised when Pastor Burkness trusted me with a key to the church to hold the 4-H meetings. I expected the elders from the Kingdom Hall to say something about me spending so much time at churches, but no one seemed to be aware of what

I was doing. A children's community garden was started using the 4-H gardening curriculum.

Each child had their own piece of ground to grow vegetables with the help of women who were master gardeners. Each week we met to weed, water the garden plots. Using what I learned from Dr. Freeman, I started an herb garden using an old wagon wheel.

There weren't many greenhouses in the area at the time, but I was fortunate to have found a place in Johnsonburg where I could buy plants. The proprietor, Stephanie Distler, was a member of the Cooperative Extension Board and talked about her business at one of the meetings. I wasn't familiar with Johnsonburg and couldn't find the business located on Mill Street. At the time, we didn't have a GPS or cell phones, and I ended up in Wilcox before I turned around and headed back to Johnsonburg. After stopping at a gas station and asking for directions, I finally found the Sweet Posie Herbary located in the backyard of Stephanie's two-story white house on the corner of Mill and Church Street, across from St. John's Lutheran Church. Stephanie loved the language of flowers. Sweet Posie was another name for a Tussie Mussie or nosegay which was popular between the 1400s through the Victorian era.

Stephanie welcomed me with a tour of her backyard gardens, including a French en masse vegetable garden and a four-square garden bordered by roses and other perennials. I was impressed with her knowledge of plants. I wasn't familiar with many of the names, so I purchased the essential herbs of oregano, parsley, basil, and thyme for the pizza garden.

Stephanie invited me into her lovely kitchen that had plants drying from the ceiling and mixtures of herb blends in large glass jars. The relaxing fragrance of lavender and other aromatic herbs permeated the air. The windows were decorated with sheer half aprons from the 1950s, that let in streams of sunlight to nourish the plants on the windowsills. As Stephanie steeped a pot of herbal tea, she instructed me how to care for and use the plants I bought. Stephanie served me loose leaf tea in delicate porcelain cups that belonged to her grandmother. I had never tried loose leaf tea before and thought I would never make tea using a teabag again. After leaving her house that exuded her grandmother's love and warmth, I had a sense of nostalgia that I had never felt before. Visiting with Stephanie in her kitchen was like stepping back in time. I left with a flat full of herbs and my soul reminiscing of simpler times.

The herbs thrived well at the children's garden, and before long, we had an abundance of produce that we donated to the local food pantry. At the end of the season, we had a harvest supper in the basement of the church. I helped the children make a large pot of vegetable soup, carrot muffins, and zucchini bread. We invited the neighbors, who were mostly older women. They all complimented the children on the fantastic job they did with the garden and even confessed to taking a few green peppers from the garden.

One woman in the neighborhood who took notice of the garden was Pat Martin. When she found out about the project, she asked if I would help her plant an herb garden at her house just a few blocks away. Pat had just recovered from cancer and told me that when she was undergoing treatment, the one thing that kept her going was the thought of starting an herb garden. I helped her design one and shared some of the perennial herbs from the community garden with her. Pat invited me to her house for tea. While we were visiting, she mentioned reading *A Wheel of Life* by Elisabeth Kubler Ross. I borrowed the book from her and read it cover to cover. I started to see patterns in my life coming full circle and knew on a deep level that somehow everything in my life was going to turn out for the best.

The garden project connected me with the community and gave me a purpose in life other than preaching to people that the world was coming to an end. I began to believe that there was hope for the future. I realized how important it is to nurture seedlings, not only of plants but the tender souls of the children. I also learned to be cautious about what I asked for in life. At the end of fall, when the stately maples trees in the community dropped their colorful leaves, I contacted the borough to ask for leaves to cover the garden plot for winter. I didn't expect to get a dump truck load of them deposited in one big pile. Unfortunately, some neighborhood teenagers lit the leaves on fire. The neighbors called the fire department and put the fire out. The ash proved to be a good mulch for the gardens. I was beginning to experience how negative experiences in life could be used to fuel growth for the future.

Count Your Blessings

Each month I drove the winding roads from Emporium to State College, via Wykoff Run, and through the Quehanna Wild Area for monthly staff meetings at the Penn State Campus. On the way home from one of the trips, during the spring, when the coltsfoot was first in bloom, I was driving slowly admiring the waterfalls along Wykoff Run. A camp for sale sign caught my eye.

Gary and I had recently gone to a counseling session with Dr. William Fernan, a psychologist who had an office in St. Marys. Penn State's Employee Assistance Program covered three visits to a psychologist in their plan. I was unhappy in our marriage and thought that if I could get Gary to see a counselor with me, our marriage might work out.

During our visits with the counselor, he asked Gary and me to think of what the two of us liked to do together. We both remembered that we liked to go camping but didn't do it anymore because it was just too much work with four children. Dr. Fernan suggested going on picnics and taking walks in the woods. When I noticed the camp for sale, I thought perhaps this would be the solution to our marital woes. I pulled the car off the side of the road and jotted down the phone number on a piece of paper. As I crossed the Wykoff Run Road Bridge and turned left onto Route 120 I felt excited about telling Gary that I found a camp for sale. I tried to remain calm, telling myself that it was probably out of our price range.

When I returned to the house, Gary was working the second shift, so I called him at work to tell him about the camp. He agreed that I should call to find out the price. When I called the long-distance phone number to ask the price, the woman didn't give me a direct answer. Instead, she asked questions. "Why did I want the camp? What did we intend to use it for? What did we do for a living?"

I told her that my husband and I were looking for something to do together as a family and we enjoyed being out in the woods. In regards to our employment, Gary was a die setter and I worked as a nutritionist for Penn State. Justin had recently moved out of the house leaving only Caleb and Cherey living at home. We thought they would also enjoy time out in the woods.

The woman and her husband lived out of state but said they would be at the camp in a couple of weeks. When we met the elderly couple at Wykoff Run, they invited us into the camp which reeked of mothballs. The small trailer was well cared for and included a vintage General Electric refrigerator and stove. The couple told us how the camp had been in their family for generations, but they were the last of the living family and were too old to keep up with the maintenance. They didn't want the camp to go to people who were going to use it as a party place; they wanted a family to care for their cherished getaway.

When we asked for the price, it was exactly how much money we had in a retirement plan. Still believing that the world would come to an end before we retired, I didn't hesitate to cash in the plan. Although it didn't include a lot of property, the land behind the camp was vacant. There was a path along Wykoff Run that went back to a swimming hole where the kids could swim.

We spent the summer airing out the place and spending weekends at Wykoff Run. The kids enjoyed the creek and spending weekends outdoors.

Brandi brought our grandson William down to spend the night. In the fall, Gary took Caleb hunting at Wykoff Run. During the winter, Gary had different ideas about how to spend time at the camp and started going down by himself on weekends, distancing himself from the family. We started to argue about the time he was spending there and continued to argue about money.

When Justin and Brandi were in their teen years, Gary became more their friend than a parent, leaving all the discipline to me. I was growing frustrated with how things were at home but didn't know how to change them. On more than one occasion, Dr. Francis suggested a separation, but I told him that it was against my religion. The scripture about loving your neighbor as yourself took on new meaning. If God could love me unconditionally, I now had the task of loving myself before I could love anyone else. This insight couldn't have come at a better time, as my older children had left home and my relationship with Gary wasn't good. If I didn't take care of me, no one else was going to.

As I was developing a stronger sense of self-respect, I had a reduced tolerance for lies and deception. Reimbursement checks for doctor appointments wouldn't come in the mail, and I would later find the empty envelopes in the trunk of the car. I started listening to Tracy Chapman's music on a cassette player. Lyrics to the song, *Give Me One Reason* resonated within me. I discovered an inner strength rising in me as I listened to the heavy beat of the rhythmic music. At first, I hummed along to the song and before long I found myself belting out the words when I was alone. "Give me one reason to stay here, and I'll turn right back around. Give me one reason to stay here, And I'll turn right back around." The more I sang the song, the fewer reasons I had for staying with Gary.

When spring rolled around, we decided to sell the camp. A landowner who owned a nearby property offered us three times the amount we paid for it. After we sold the camp, I realized there wasn't any hope for our relationship. Gary had a hard time finishing projects around the house and I found myself saying, "In my next life, I'm going to marry someone who knows how to repair and build things!" After a significant argument, including a fight about a broken window that he wouldn't repair, I had finally had enough. The broken window was symbolic of our broken relationship.

During the fight, Gary asked me if I wanted him to leave. Since Jehovah's Witnesses didn't allow a spouse to separate unless there were grounds of adultery or abuse, it had to be him who made the decision. I told him if that's what he wanted, to go ahead.

He asked, "How much money will you give me?"

"How much do you want?" I asked.

He wanted what we made from the camp. I wrote him a check and he left. He agreed to find a place of his own and to continue making payments on the house, so the kids and I had a place to live. Although it wasn't easy for either of us financially, we were both happy to be out of an unhappy relationship.

Still hanging on to the Jehovah's Witness religion, I had made plans at the beginning of the year to attend one of their three-day conventions, being held in Cleveland, Ohio. The trip corresponded with Gary leaving. He said he would be gone by the time we returned. Cherey was sixteen and Caleb was thirteen at the time. On the way out to the convention, I explained to the two of them that their dad and I were separating. I thought maybe they would be sad but both of them thought it was a good idea since Gary and I didn't get along. I tried to sit through the convention, but the boredom was more than I could stand. The indoctrinating talks consisted of the same information I heard each year for the past twenty-five years. I surprised Cherey and Caleb by leaving the convention early and taking them to the Rock and Roll Hall of Fame.

They both wondered what happened to their old mom who was a strict Jehovah's Witness. The smiles on their faces and the excitement they exuded while at the museum made me feel like I did the right thing for all of us. When we got to the top floor of the museum, where the group Pink Floyd was featured, and I started humming the melody to *Money*, both Cherey and Caleb wondered how I knew the tune. Their jaws dropped when I told them about attending the 1975 Pink Floyd concert at Three Rivers Stadium in Pittsburgh

When we returned home, Gary had moved out with all of his belongings. He rented a furnished mobile home, so there weren't any arguments about appliances or furniture. We both agreed that we didn't want to spend our money on a lawyer, so we agreed to go through Keystone Mediation located in St. Marys to legalize the divorce. A lawyer drew up the divorce papers and the day we signed them I went out in the car and cried. It was sad to end a twenty-five-year relationship and I felt like I had just received an F on my marriage report card. Dr. Francis helped me to see the situation differently. He compassionately reminded me how young I was when I married and rather than a failure, the marriage was a mistake from day one.

At the time, I felt so alone. I didn't know anyone else who was divorced. To help me navigate my way as a single woman, I found the book, *Flying Solo-Single Woman in Midlife* at the library. I started to feel my wings spread when I read words of wisdom by Helen Keller: "One can never consent to creep when one feels an impulse to soar." After finishing the book, rather than feeling alone, I felt empowered. I could feel my wings begin to spread and when I started to fly, I knew not to look down or back.

After the divorce, I wondered if I would ever remarry but discounted the idea. I hadn't met a man I deemed worth marrying and set my standards high, in case one existed. I had three qualifications. The deal breakers were he couldn't smoke, abuse alcohol, or lie. A handyman would be the icing on the cake.

Because Gary and I separated for other reasons than adultery or physical abuse I was 'marked' by the people at the Kingdom Hall. Marked was a term used to punish someone who didn't fall into line. There was a list of other reasons a person could be marked. If someone married an unbeliever or pursued worldly activities that did not fall under the rules, the person would be disfellowshipped. There would be a talk at the Kingdom Hall on the person's misbehavior, and others would know not to associate with that person. To avoid the pain of being shunned, I began attending Sunday meetings at other congregations in the area. I found out that I was marked in the whole area. Instead of love bombing, I received cold shoulders at the meetings.

In the first few months of being single, I felt lonely and lost. I started taking antidepressants to help stave off the low feelings. While working, I had some free time after everything was set up for an after-school cooking class for kids in the basement of the First Evangelical Lutheran Church in Ridgway. Pastor Duffield, the pastor of the church unlocked the door for me and made sure I had everything I needed for the class. Again, I was touched by his thoughtfulness and willingness to help. Pastor Duffield's and his wife, Jeannie had recently moved to Ridgway. Jeannie worked at the Extension office and we had gotten to know each other quite well. They lived their faith in a very practical manner by caring for and adopting children. I found their approach to Christianity more useful than spending countless hours knocking on doors that the majority of people didn't answer.

After making sure I was set for the cooking class, Pastor Duffield left the building, leaving me alone for about fifteen minutes before the children arrived. While waiting, I wandered into a meeting room next to the kitchen where there was a piano. I randomly picked up a songbook and started reading the words to the song. The songbook was opened to the song *Count Your Blessings*. I read the words one by one:

> "When upon life's billows you are tempest-tossed, When you are discouraged, thinking all is lost, Count your many blessings, name them one by one, And it will surprise you what the Lord has done.

Count your blessings, name them one by one, Count your blessings, see what God has done! Count your blessings, name them one by one, Are you ever burdened with a load of care?

Does the cross seem heavy you are called to bear? Count your many blessings, every doubt will fly, And you will keep singing as the days go by."

I returned the book to the piano and put the verses into practice. I started counting my blessings one by one: Pastor Duffield, who was kind and helpful, the church for providing the space for the cooking class, the kids who were coming to the cooking class, my four children who were healthy, the house I lived in and my job. Just like a cloud lifting on a cloudy day, my dark outlook on life felt lighter and brighter. I thanked God when I could actually feel the sun shining through the stained-glass windows of the church. This was a major turning point in my life. I no longer needed antidepressants.

Stephanie invited Dr. Vickie Zeigler, the director of the Center for Medieval Studies at Penn State and me, to do a lecture at the annual Sweet Posie Herb Festival in Johnsonburg. The festival was set up in Stephanie's back yard located on the side street of Church and Mill Street, where artisans displayed their paintings and other artwork. I met Stephanie's daughters Larissa, who was about twelve and Thea, who was about seven years old. Larissa wove sachets using ribbon and lavender stems, and Thea offered guests samples of mint and other edibles from the garden.

Stephanie and members of the Seven Sister's Herb Guild made light bag lunches for the public. Some of the delicacies offered to the public were Tabbouleh salad made with bulgur and fresh mint, and chicken salad sandwiches flavored fresh lovage and water infused with lemon and lavender. I had never tasted so many delicious blends of flavors made from simple herbs grown in a backyard garden. The recipes were compiled and put into cookbooks, which were sold at the festival.

Dr. Ziegler lectured on Herb Gardens in the Medieval Era. I did my homework and learned what herbs to use in cooking and gave a presentation on Culinary Uses of Herbs.

After I finished with my talk, a man sitting on a wood bench, underneath an apple tree carving spoons from wood caught my eye. He was wearing blue jeans, a forest green Carhart T-shirt and a brown suede hat with a broad brim to keep his eyes shaded from the sun. I walked over to where he was carving and watched a log turn into a beautifully carved spoon using hand tools that I had never seen before.

While he was finishing off a spoon, I asked, "Can I buy one of your spoons?"

He handed me a smoothed and oiled spoon.

I asked, "How much do I owe you?"

"Nothing."

At the same time, Stephanie came over and introduced me to her dad and said he was going to be on the Elk County Cooperative Extension Board. When I told her he didn't charge me for the spoon, she relayed that her dad was grateful for what I did to help her with the festival and wanted me to have the spoon. I shook her dad's hand and thanked him for the gift. Inside, I was touched by their father-daughter relationship.

At the November extension board meeting, I met Stephanie's dad again and learned his name was Cliff. After the meeting, while we were socializing over some bran muffins made by Barb Miller, a few of the members, including Cliff, were talking about places they went cross-country skiing. I mentioned I always wanted to cross country ski, and if they were in Cameron County, I would love to learn how to ski. I was familiar with trails at Sizerville State Park, not knowing the trails were for hiking instead of cross-country skiing. After the meeting, Stephanie told me how impressed her dad was with all the programs I was doing to teach children how to garden and cook. He felt they were lost skills and was glad to know someone was teaching the next generation how to be self-sufficient.

On a snowy evening in January, I received a phone call, which I answered from a phone in my upstairs bedroom at my house in Emporium. It was Cliff inviting me to go cross country skiing with him on the weekend. I couldn't believe my ears! I told him I didn't have any skis, but maybe I could borrow a pair from Corinne. He asked what size shoe I wore.

When I told him a size ten, he offered to bring a set of skis with him. We agreed to meet at the Cabin Kitchen for breakfast.

That night I got dressed and scuttled down to the library to check out a book on how to cross-country ski. Instead of a book, I found videos to watch on the VCR. I watched them them from beginning to end, so I at least had an idea of what I was doing.

On Saturday morning, I bundled up in some warm clothes and headed down to the Cabin Kitchen to meet Cliff for breakfast. He was sitting in the backroom in a booth, sipping a cup of hot coffee. I ordered a big breakfast of pancakes and eggs, thinking I had to fill up on carbs for energy. Cliff admired my big appetite. He ordered eggs over corned beef hash, home fries, and sausage. Over breakfast, I told him I had four children and was recently separated. He told me he had two adult children, Stephanie and Stephan, two granddaughters and had been single for twenty-seven years after going through a divorce.

After breakfast, I put on the pair of ski boots he brought along and climbed into his teal green F150 pick-up truck. I started to get nervous as we headed out of town towards Sizerville. It was a Saturday morning, and I knew most of Jehovah's Witnesses were out in service. I was afraid they would see me in a vehicle with a worldly man. I relaxed once we got to the State Park. Cliff parked the truck in the parking lot across from the swimming pool.

When I got out of the vehicle, he showed me how to attach the skis to my boots and how to hold my poles. I told him where the trailhead was and followed him into the woods, patterning my glide after his. We climbed over fallen logs, and I tried to keep my balance on slopes and sidehills, which weren't meant for skiing. I must have fallen in the white, fluffy snow at least a dozen times but I was having fun. I felt the same joy I did as a child when I played in the snow. By the time we made our way down to the campground and turned around, we were on flat ground. I mastered the rhythm of the glide and could now talk and ski at the same time.

I told Cliff, "When my children were small, and we lived in the trailer park a few miles up the road, and we didn't have much money, I dreamt this was our private country club where we swam, picnicked, hiked and rode bikes and ice skated. Now I'm here cross-country skiing. It's a dream come true." I then went on to confess, "I'm one of Jehovah's Witnesses, but I'm not a very good one, or I wouldn't be out here with you."

Cliff talked about politics and his frustration with the Clinton administration. I was barely aware of who the Clintons were. He also told me he recently purchased a house on a piece of property outside of Ridgway, which he planned on renovating. When we returned to the truck, we replenished our energy on a jug of grapefruit juice and bananas that I brought along. When he dropped me off at my house, I invited him to supper the following weekend when Caleb and Cherey would be with their dad. He accepted.

The first meal I made for Cliff was lentil shepherd's pie. I was a vegetarian at the time, and it was the closest thing to a hearty meal. He raved about having a home-cooked meal even though it didn't include meat. He then proceeded to tell me how he purchased sides of beef from a local farmer. I thought perhaps being a vegetarian, having two teenagers, and being a Jehovah's Witness would be deal-breakers for him. Still, at the end of the evening, he invited me to a ski party at the North Fork ski lodge on West Creek Road in St. Marys.

My Jehovah's Witness conscience started to kick in, and I began to conjure up all kinds of thoughts about Cliff. He might be abusive, an alcoholic, or trying to get me to sleep with him. I prayed to God to give me a sign to know what kind of person he was.

The snow was melting, making skiing conditions unfavorable, so we started hiking together. Cliff wanted to take me to see some waterfalls in Quehanna, so I invited him to my house for breakfast. Before he arrived, I put some potatoes in a stovetop pressure cooker and went upstairs to shower. After showering, I lay down and fell asleep until I heard a knock at the door. With my head wrapped in a towel and wearing a white terry cloth robe, I ran downstairs to find the potatoes scorched. By the time I answered the door, I was crying. I felt like such a failure and thought perhaps I was sabotaging myself. If Cliff thought I wasn't a good cook, he wouldn't want to see me anymore.

When I told him what happened, he suggested we go out for breakfast instead. I invited him into the house to wait for me while I got dressed. If he was going to rape me, now would be his chance. Instead, he sat on the couch reading a leather-covered Bible he had brought with him. I felt this was my sign from God. Over breakfast, he talked about God's love for us and the importance of believing in the deity of Christ, God, and the Holy Spirit. This belief was in contrast to a primary teaching of Jehovah's Witnesses; they taught the Trinity was a pagan teaching and anyone who believed it would be disfellowshipped. I didn't feel comfortable with the conflict, so I told him I didn't want to discuss the Bible. Inside, I admired that he brought a Bible with him when he came to my house. He was earning my trust.

After breakfast, we drove through Wykoff Run to get to Quehanna. I broke down crying as we passed the camp Gary and I sold. I poured my heart out to Cliff, telling him everything that happened between Gary and me. Up to that point, I never talked to him about what happened and how I felt about it, and he never asked. I expected him to give me advice like the elders at the Kingdom Hall would do, but instead, he just listened and then told me his story. His wife left him when his daughter Stephanie was eight years old, and his son Stephan was three years old. With the help of his parents, he raised the children. He never remarried because he wasn't sure if he was looking for a mother for his kids or a partner for himself.

By the time we arrived at the Quehanna Wild Area, we both felt good about sharing our backstories with each other. The waterfalls which were raging with the runoff from the melted snow and the sound of the water pouring over the rocks cleared our minds. As I was admiring the water, Cliff had climbed to the top of a rock and could see me from above.

I felt something bump into me from the back. Thinking it was a bear, I let out a scream, until I turned around to see a black lab trying to make friends with me. Seeing how alarmed I was, Cliff scrambled down the rock to comfort me. Together we hiked trails, with me letting him hold my hand as I scaled slippery stones.

The next weekend, Cliff invited me to his house in Johnsonburg. I attended a meeting at the Kingdom Hall in Kersey and went to his house after the meeting. I stopped going to the Tuesday and Thursday meetings. I had skipped a few Sunday meetings but felt a huge void and guilt for not going. Even though people at the Kingdom Hall didn't talk to me, I hung on to the religion by a thread. When I went into his house for the first time, I thought perhaps we weren't meant for each other. The two-story, white-sided house was a bachelor's pad with the kitchen table covered with tools and bike parts, dishes in the sink, and laundry piled on the dining room table. He said he had something to show me, so I followed him into the living room, where there was a brand new, candy red Rockhopper Mountain bike with a tag hanging from the handlebar.

Having no idea why he was showing it to me, I said, "Nice bike."

He said, "It's for you."

"What do you want for the bike?"

"Nothing. I enjoyed cross country skiing with you and would like to ride bikes together."

I firmly told him, "Well, if you expect anything else, it's not happening."

He assured me he just wanted to be friends. I accepted the bike. It had been years since I had ridden a bike, so I got a three-speed out of the shed in the back of the house and tried to ride the bike around town. To my dismay, I couldn't even peddle the bike one block. I didn't know how I was going to ride bikes with Cliff. I told him I wouldn't be able to go up and down any hills. He suggested we ride a short distance on the Clarion Rail Trail in Ridgway. We parked at Island Run and planned on riding the bikes a mile or two for my first time.

Cliff showed me how to shift the gears. When I started riding the bike with over twenty speeds, I felt as if I could ride a hundred miles, so we went longer, and I found it took little effort to pedal up a grade. The red Rockhopper was like riding a Cadillac compared to an old clunker.

I fell in love with the scenic trail that ran parallel to the Clarion River. Every few miles, we stopped to admire the wildflowers along the trail. Cliff told me his favorite flowers were yellow and burgundy trillium peeking through the forest floor. I had never met a man that loved flowers and was deeply touched by his love of nature. I felt as if I had just woken up from a nightmare and was in the paradise I had only dreamed about.

The next weekend he suggested we eat breakfast in Marienville and ride the bikes in the woods. As we headed out of Johnsonburg and were driving on Long Level Road, we started talking about what risks we took in life. Cliff told me about a time he was riding his mountain bike and got caught in a severe thunderstorm and didn't think he was going to make it home. Then out of the blue, he said, "I'm going to do something I never did before."

I braced myself by holding onto the door handle of the truck and asked, "What's that?"

"I'm going to stop at Russell City for gas." I breathed a sigh of relief and broke out laughing. Russell City is so small that if you blink your eyes you would miss it while driving through the Allegheny Forest. The gas station consisted of a gas pump in front of a general store. As we turned right onto 948 and headed toward Marienville, he slowed down and pointed to the house he owned and intended to renovate. All I could see was a white house hidden behind two rows of pine trees with a barn that looked like a windstorm blew it down. I didn't give the place a second thought as we continued to drive, stopping at Russell City to fill up the gas tank and then to the Bucktail Restaurant in Marienville for a hearty breakfast.

My most significant risk was telling Cliff about my childhood and family. I didn't want to tell him about Mooseheart because I didn't want him to feel sorry for me. I hadn't been in contact with any of my siblings for a while and wasn't sure Cliff would understand. I also wasn't sure he would understand I was seeing a psychologist. I was afraid if I told him, he would think I was crazy, and it would be the end of our relationship. In that case, I needed to tell him now before we got any closer. In the back of my mind, perhaps I was afraid of intimacy and thought it would end our relationship.

On the way home from Marienville, I mustered up the courage to tell Cliff that I had six siblings, one sister, and five brothers. With excitement in his voice, he responded "I was an only child and always wanted a brother. Where do they live?"

"Only four of them are living, and the only one I have contact with is my brother Jack, who is in the Army. I'm not in contact with my other three brothers because I've been seeing a psychologist for depression, and he advised me not to see them." There were no words to tell Cliff what my brothers were like and why I had contact with one, but not the others. I made it seem like it was my problem. I was too sensitive to their teasing and brash behavior. I continued to tell him my other three brothers lived in the area. Bill lived in Emporium, Bob was living in Warren, Pa. and Warren was living in St. Marys. I told him a little about each brother and that Warren was severely burned while working at the ink plant in Ridgway a few years ago. All Cliff heard was I had brothers. He didn't pay attention to what I said about not having contact with them as he thought we didn't talk much. He was clueless about Post Traumatic Stress, and I didn't have the words to tell him.

Asperger's Syndrome and Autism were unheard of when I was a child, not that they didn't exist. I first heard of the diagnosis' when a woman started attending the meetings at the Kingdom Hall with her three-year-old son, who was autistic.

When I researched the term, I started learning about Asperger's and self-diagnosed my brothers as having the disorder as it explained their 'abnormal' behavior. The sad part was when we were children, there wasn't anyone to teach them social skills. They teased me to no end. Without an adult around to tell them their behavior was inappropriate I was at their mercy. Learning about Asperger's lessened the shame and embarrassment I felt about my family.

Warren was the one brother of which I thought I might be able to have a relationship. Bob was a Jehovah's Witness and was living in Warren, Pennsylvania. Bill and I didn't have anything in common and he had picked on me the most when I was younger. Warren was two years older than me, and we had spent the most time together when we were younger. I was feeling guilty about not being there for him when he had his accident. I also admired him for taking care of my mother when she was dying. I thought I could manage a relationship with Cliff's support.

When I told Cliff that Warren lived near Taft Road, he suggested we go for a bike ride on the Shawmut railroad grade and visit Warren. The next weekend, after riding about ten miles on the Shawmut grade, we drove the truck up to Warren's house so Cliff could meet him. Warren was home and seemed happy to see me. He told us that he was hosting exchange students. I was pleased that he found something in life to make him happy. I apologized to him for not being there when he had his accident. He graciously told me he understood that I was going through my own stuff. I was happy that we connected. I eventually introduced Cliff to Bill and Bob. It didn't take him long to figure out where a lot of my insecurities came from as they irritated him as much as they did me.

Born Free

While sitting home crocheting an afghan on an autumn evening, I heard a knock at the front door of my house. When I opened the door, two men from the Kingdom Hall, dressed in suits and ties, were at my door. One of them was a brother who had been studying the Bible with Caleb. My intuition told me to tell them this wasn't a good time, but instead, I invited them into the house. Within five minutes of their visit, I wished I would have listened to myself.

The black brother started, "Can we open this discussion with a prayer."

I nodded my head, yes, but all I heard from them was, "Blah, Blah, Blah."

After the prayer, the conversation continued. "It has been reported that you were holding hands with a worldly man in downtown Ridgway?"

Whenever I was doing programs in Elk County with the Extension office, I met Cliff for supper in Ridgway after we were both done working. While walking down the main Street of Ridgway, he put his hand in mine to cross the street. We didn't let go of each other's hands until we reached

Susan's Restaurant, located across from the Rite Aid pharmacy on Main Street. It didn't surprise me that the news got back to the elders.

I asked, "And the problem with that is what?"

They continued to question me. "Do you have intentions of marrying this man.

I felt my face getting red with anger. "No, we are just friends."

"If you don't intend to marry this man, then you shouldn't be holding hands with him. The only reason you should be dating someone is with the intent to get married. You are only permitted to marry one of Jehovah's Witnesses.

I challenged them by asking, "Where is that in the scriptures?"

They asked me to get the Bible and read 1 Corinthians 7:39 that reads, "to marry only in the Lord."

I read the scripture aloud and then proceeded to tell them, "The Bible doesn't say I can't date or marry someone who isn't a Jehovah's Witness; it says to marry only in the Lord. For your information, Cliff is more a man of God than anyone at the Kingdom Hall. He reads the Bible, is honest, treats me with respect, and unlike some elders, isn't an alcoholic."

The brother who was studying with Caleb, quickly changed the subject to Caleb. "I've noticed that Caleb has been disrespectful during our Bible Studies. He doesn't give the correct answers and seems defiant when there are topics he doesn't agree with."

I got up from where I was sitting, walked to the front door, opened it, and said, "This is enough. You can leave my house and do not return. If you try to call me or disfellowship me, you will be hearing from my attorney." I never heard from them again. I read that the elders could be sued for libel by disfellowshipping people. It felt good not to be going by their rules anymore.

After they left, I called Dr. Francis and told him what had transpired. He said, "I was surprised when you got enough courage to separate from

Gary, but you leaving the Witnesses is even more surprising. That took a lot of courage. Let's make an appointment to talk more."

One of the pitfalls of dissociation is that decisions were sometimes made without checking in with everyone on the team. When I visited Dr. Francis, he wanted to make sure leaving Jehovah's Witnesses was a unanimous decision. Dr. Francis taught me to take a consensus with various parts of myself. The one personality who was most conflicted was a little girl named Anna, who felt she needed a religion. At Mooseheart, she was shamed for not being Catholic and feared going to hell. She liked the Jehovah's Witnesses because they didn't believe in hellfire. She asked Dr. Francis what religion she should join. I thought he might suggest his faith, Catholicism, but instead, he said to be a good person. Dr. Francis also wanted to make sure I could handle the shunning that I would experience when I left the religion. He wasn't aware that the shunning had already happened.

When I informed Caleb he wouldn't be continuing the Bible study with the brother; he smiled ear to ear. The next morning when I woke up, I felt free as a bird. I went out and sat on the steps of the front porch, wondering what I would do with my life now that I was free. Sunbeams were shining through the clouds that were breaking up from a rainstorm. I looked over towards the Baptist Church that was catty-corner from where I was sitting and saw a brilliant double rainbow. I knew then that I was going to be OK. I made a promise to myself that I would never put God in a box again, even though I didn't know who or what God was.

For the next month, I sang the song *Born Free* from morning to dusk. I was now free to follow my heart. I missed some of the people during the first few months, but the feeling of freedom outweighed any satisfaction I derived from so-called friends. A couple of women, whom I used to call sisters, wrote me long letters. I didn't read them as I figured they were going to try to convince me to return to Jehovah. My biggest dilemma was to figure out who God was. Dr. Francis taught me to go inside when I had questions. I found myself talking more often to my inner selves than praying to God, who I pictured as a man with a long white beard expecting to punish me for breaking his commandments. I was glad to be free of this image of God. Rather than trying to figure out who God was, I focused on the human form of Jesus and attached Corinne's image of grace to him.

I didn't announce my leaving Jehovah's Witnesses publicly as I wasn't ready to admit to the world I made a colossal mistake joining the religion. I came across a quotation from 1921 by Maurice Arthur that helped me feel better about the mistake I had made. He said, "In reality, those who repudiate a theory that they had once proposed, or a theory that they accepted enthusiastically and with which they had identified themselves, are very rare. The great majority of them shut their ears so as not to hear crying facts, and shut their eyes so as not to see the glaring facts, in order to remain faithful to their theories in spite of all and everything."

I did email my brother Jack and let him know I was no longer a Jehovah's Witness. He was kind and told me he never quit praying for me. He informed me that he would be going overseas to Germany, where he would be stationed for a few years. I asked if he and Connie minded if Caleb, Cherey, and I drove down to Fayetteville, North Carolina, to see him before he left. I had never driven that far on my own and was quite nervous about the long trip. Cherey had just gotten her driver's permit and drove some of the way down and back in a Bravada Gary and I bought before we separated.

It was exciting to see the Atlantic Ocean at the Outer Banks for the first time. Caleb was sick the day we went to the ocean, but Cherey was like a mermaid in the water. Before we parted, Jack gave me the book *The Grace Awakening* by Charles Swindoll. When I returned home, I read the book and it affirmed God's love for me even though I wasn't a Jehovah's Witness

Caleb made friends with some kids who were into the punk music scene and started going to local concerts. He also met Dave and Mary Ann, a couple who had moved to Emporium to start a new church at the old

Fourth Street School. Dave had a brother who was a Jehovah's Witness and befriended Caleb. Caleb hung out with Dave and his wife and attended a few of the church services. Cherey had a friend from school who was Catholic and invited her to attend services at St. Mark's Church. Participating in religious services other than those held at the Kingdom Hall was a big step for them, as Jehovah's Witnesses taught that all other religions were demonic and dissenters were going to experience God's wrath at Armageddon. The Witnesses frowned on attending weddings and funerals of relatives held in churches. Going to a bar and drinking was tolerated more than worshipping in a different church.

As for myself, I wasn't able to attend a church service. It would take me a little longer to deprogram from twenty-five years of brainwashing. When I told Cliff, I decided not to be a Jehovah's Witness anymore, he tried to talk to me about the Bible, but each time he would read scripture, I was reminded of Jehovah's Witnesses' teachings and felt guilty. I did my best to explain to Cliff how they twisted the Bible's teachings, and until I could get them out of my head, I didn't want to read anything from the Bible.

While shopping with Cliff in DuBois, I found a copy of *A Course In Miracles* at the bookstore in the mall. I knew about the book from reading *A Gift to Myself* by Dr. Whitfield, who made quite a few references to the spiritual writings.

When I saw the price was $60.00, I returned it to the shelf as I was living on a tight budget. Cliff took the book back off the shelf and bought it for me. I was so grateful. When I got home, I started reading the text which resonated with my soul. I started reading the daily meditations and began to feel lighter. The book helped me to see a different view of God and aided me to stop judging everything, including myself. For the next few months, the only scripture I focused on was, "Stop judging, and you will not be judged. Stop reviling, and you will not be reviled."

I found walking helpful when I needed to clear my head. Loretta, who I met from the probation office while establishing the children's garden, and I started walking around town together. Loretta was a good listener and had overcome a lot of obstacles in life. While being a single mom, she went back to school and got a business degree. I admired her courage and resiliency. On weekends, we took long walks to the end of Plank Road Hollow and up to the Salt Run Reservoir. When I told her I was dating Cliff, she didn't judge me. When I told her he was fourteen years older than me, she didn't judge me. When I told her my biggest concern was the chance of him dying and me being alone, she asked, "Isn't it better to love and lose than to never love at all?" It was good to have a friend who listened and didn't give advice. I was also relieved not to have to worry about being seen with her and getting reproved by the elders at the Kingdom Hall.

Cliff and I spent the summer riding the bikes on other rail trails and backroads in the Allegheny National Forest with friends of his that also rode bikes. I met Annette Slater, Blaine Stauffer, and Kim Granche. I met Kim through the La Leche League many years earlier, and her husband, Bill, had been my high school English teacher. I enjoyed the camaraderie of people who didn't have any agenda for liking me. Each of them told me Cliff was a great guy. If I had any doubts about Cliff's character, they disappeared.

After Cliff took me to his favorite places in the woods, I invited him to see some places I enjoyed. On a Sunday afternoon, we left the bikes at home and took a ride up to the Chautauqua Institute to hear the Army/Navy Band play at the amphitheater. Listening to a military band wasn't in my comfort zone because of how Jehovah's Witnesses felt about patriotism. Cliff served four years in the Navy, so I thought it was something he would appreciate. While we sat on wood benches and enjoyed the summer breeze, I found myself tapping my foot and clapping my hands to the music. When the band played the Star-Spangled Banner, I sang the words to the melody, which were deeply embedded in my mind from when I was a child. After the concert, we took a walk down to the lake and then ate supper at Webb's Restaurant, where we had our first taste of goat cheese on a spinach salad.

On the way home, we stopped at a used bookstore we had spotted on our drive up to Chautauqua. Cliff loved reading history and was always searching for books by his favorite author, Eric Sloane. He already had an extensive collection of books about Early Americana and woodworking. One book he didn't have was *Ages of Barns* and he was determined to find it. I enjoyed reading non-fiction and cookbooks. While at the bookstore, he found a couple of books to add to his Eric Sloane collection, and I found a book titled *Coming Through the Swamp-The Nature Writings* of Gene Stratton Porter.

Ironically, the book title caught my eye because it described what it was like getting out of Jehovah's Witnesses.

When I showed Cliff the book, his eyes got watery and told me his mother loved Gene Stratton Porter's books with her favorites being *A Girl of the Limberlost* and *Freckles*. He then asked, "Can I buy it for you?"

Already feeling indebted to him for buying me the new bike, I said, "No, I have enough money to pay for it."

"Can't I pay for anything, except for our meals?" When we got to the check-out counter, he insisted on paying for the book. Experiences like this verified to both of us that our relationship was meant to be.

In late summer, we drove to Bedford to meet a cousin, Jan Bassette who Cliff had met at a family reunion before we met. Jan's grandfather, Walter Stump, and Cliff's great grandfather were cousins. Walter Stump was a farmer who lived to be over one-hundred years old. When Cliff learned that he had farming in his bloodline, he felt all was well with the world. Cliff was excited for me to meet his extended family.

When we arrived and Jan's farmhouse in Mann's Choice, she was welcoming and introduced us to her husband, Jeff, and their seven children. While we were in the area, we visited Bedford Village, a retro pioneer village. Volunteers dressed in period clothing demonstrated how to make candles, weave, and make barrels from wood. Music played and German food and beer were served for an Octoberfest.

Although Cliff didn't drink, I talked him into sharing a bottle of the dark German beer with me. I was convinced he would enjoy the taste, which he did to a fault. I didn't realize that Cliff was a recovering alcoholic, nor did I realize how much of a problem one drink could be for an alcoholic. Cliff had told me jokes about his drinking. His friends teased that when he saw the sign "Drink Canada Dry" on the concrete building next to Wilhelm Pontiac Garage in Johnsonburg, he had gone to Canada to see if it could be done. Cliff also told me that after he quit drinking, his dad and grandfather quit. His dad even joked about the drinking. He once said, "Cliff, the only difference between alcoholics and us is that we don't have to go to the meetings." The three of them quit drinking, cold turkey, without ever going to an AA meeting.

In the evening, we attended the play, *Fiddler on the Roof*, which was Cliff's first live theater event. Afterward, we went to Jan and Jeff's farmhouse and had a delicious homemade supper with their seven children.

After visiting Bedford Village, Cliff talked about carving spoons at an Autumn festival at Sizerville State Park. I told him that I had been making hard tack candy at the same festival for a couple of years. We were at opposite ends of the park. I was at the nature center where children were making corn husk dolls, painting pumpkins, dipping candles, and making leaf prints. He was at the far end of the park closer to the campground. We reminisced about the potluck dinner after the festivals and came to the conclusion that we must have met there, and that's why we felt so familiar with each other. Within a few months, it seemed as if we'd known each other for a lifetime. We both agreed it wasn't much fun setting up at the Autumn festival alone and thought it would be a great idea to do it together. For the past twenty years, Cliff had been hoping for a creative, industrious woman who wanted to work alongside him. Since I was a child living in the orphanage, I found it too painful to wish for something I didn't have; therefore, I hadn't thought of having someone to share interests with. I began to dream about the two of us having a life together.

When the annual postcard reminder for the Sizerville Autumn Festival arrived in the mail, I called the park office to make my reservation and put in a request that Cliff and I set up together. I didn't expect that the idea would be met with resistance. My longtime friend, Lisa, had since moved on to another state park. Instead of hearing Lisa's kind voice, in a stern voice, the park manager barked, "You will have to stay in the area where you are, and Cliff has to stay in his area. He is doing a demonstration, and you are doing an activity with children." Her demeanor was as irritating as poison ivy that made my skin itch.

I hung up the phone and after fuming for a few minutes, called the park office back to inform them that I wouldn't be making the candy any longer. It was an abundant year for apples, so Cliff and I came up with the idea to make some apple butter in a cast-iron kettle like Cliff had read about in his Foxfire books. While looking for a recipe, I learned that in pioneer days, every family had a custom recipe. I came up with our own recipe using brown sugar, cider, cinnamon, nutmeg, cloves, and my secret ingredient and favorite spice, cardamom. Cliff crafted a small apple butter paddle to stir the mixture. To demonstrate how pioneers cooked without electricity, I used a whole grain master mix recipe to make biscuits in Cliff's Griswold cast iron Dutch oven, over hot coals.

On the day of the festival, Cliff brought enough dry firewood to build a fire. I hadn't thought of asking for permission to build a fire from the park manager since fire pits were available at each picnic area. In previous years, vendors had fires to stay warm on the chilly Autumn days and the smell of burning wood added ambiance to the event. After having breakfast at The Cabin Kitchen, we arrived at the park around 9:00 A.M. to start the fire early enough to have hot coals to bake some biscuits and have the apple butter made before guests began strolling through the park.

The day before, I had mixed up a large batch of the master mix, using twenty pounds of flour, non-fat dry milk, a pound of lard, baking soda, and salt the night before. I mixed up small batches by adding water to some of the dry mixture and then rolled out the pliable dough on a wood cutting board. My grandson William, who was just tall enough to reach the picnic table, cut out circles using an antique biscuit cutter. The first few batches of biscuits burned as the fire was too hot, but as the wood turned to hot coals, the biscuits came out golden brown.

All was well as people began stopping by to taste samples of the warm biscuits with apple butter until the park manager, who told me we weren't allowed to set up together, confronted us. She was dressed in her park uniform and had fiery red, shoulder-length hair. I recognized her voice from the phone call we had a month earlier. "You didn't get permission to do an activity in this part of the park."

"I'm not doing an activity. I'm doing a demonstration on how to make apple butter and biscuits over a wood fire."

"You are not allowed to do this here."

"I'm sorry, but there isn't much I can do about it now."

She sharply turned and walked away in frustration. The day continued with people stopping by to watch Cliff carve spoons on his Schnitzelbank (German for a carving bench) and to taste the apple butter and biscuits, which we now had to cut in quarters to accommodate the large crowd which had swelled to over a thousand people. It was fun seeing little boys and older men alike stand for hours and watch Cliff carve spoons with his hand tools. A five-year-old boy with red hair who was wearing a checkered flannel shirt stopped to watch Cliff smooth out a spoon with a spokeshave.

"What are you making?" he asked, inquisitively.

"A spoon made of wood," Cliff replied.

The boy thoughtfully said, "Maybe you should make a wooden bowl for your wife's biscuits."

Not knowing how to reply to the lad. Cliff said, "I used to have red hair when I was a little boy."

Seeing Cliff's grey hair under the brown leather brimmed hat which shaded his eyes, the boy said, "Wow, that must have been a long time ago."

As the crowd dwindled and the apple butter and biscuits ran out, the drill sergeant returned, walking slowly towards Cliff and me. She no longer seemed as angry.

"Are there any biscuits and apple butter left? Everyone is telling me how good they taste. People love the smell of the apple butter wafting through the park and are telling me what a great idea it was to have someone making apple butter and biscuits."

I scraped the last of the apple butter from the cast-iron kettle and spread it on a piece of biscuit. I handed it to her and said, "This is all that's left."

She thanked us for volunteering and reminded us next year to get permission first.

I almost told her my favorite motto in life is 'It's easier to ask for forgiveness than it is to get permission' but thought I should probably keep it under my hat. Little did I know I would need her forgiveness again at next year's Autumn Festival.

Recipe for Biscuit Mix:

4 ½ cups unbleached flour 4 ½ cups whole wheat flour
1/3 cup aluminum-free baking powder 1 cup non-fat dry milk
4 teaspoons salt
1 pound lard.

Sift all dry ingredients. Cut shortening into flour until the mixture resembles coarse cornmeal. Store well covered in a crock, dry place.

Biscuits:
2-3 cups biscuit mix

Stir in enough water to make a pliable dough. Knead a few times lightly. Pat into a large circle that is ¼ inch thick.

Cut into rounds with a biscuit cutter. Put rounds on an ungreased baking sheet. Bake in preheated 425degree oven until lightly browned; about 10-12 minutes.

When the snow began to fly, and it was time to cross-country ski again, Cliff and I went to Love's Canoe in Ridgway to buy a brand-new pair of skis. His friend, Dave Love, who owned the outfitter store, made sure the skis were the right fit and length. They were much more comfortable than the borrowed pair I had used the year before. The skis had a smooth glide and didn't flop around. We went to the Laurel Mill Ski trail in Ridgway. The trail was groomed with a machine that made double tracks in the snow. Skiing was a breeze, and I only fell half a dozen times.

As we spent more time together, we realized we wanted to spend our lives together, so we began making plans for where we would live. Cliff offered to move to Emporium, so Caleb and Cherey didn't have to move, but it would be a long drive back and forth to work for him. I was also ready to leave Emporium. Neither of us cared to live in the house he inherited from his parents.

On a warm spring day, we drove out to Montmorenci to see the property Cliff intended to renovate. He purchased the property in 1998 with some of his retirement money because he expected the market to crash in Y2K, a moniker for the year 2000. People were predicting that there would be a glitch in all the computer systems causing a worldwide disaster. Cliff prepared to live off the grid with a coal stove, bags of rice, a wheat grinder, and a fifty-pound bag of wheat he stockpiled in case the predicted disaster brought down the electric grid system. Even though I hadn't prepared for it, I was concerned because Penn State held meetings to inform people how to prepare for the event. Fortunately, nothing happened when the calendar turned from 1999 to 2000.

The house was a fixer upper as it was vacant for a few years. The roof was leaking, and the frozen pipes burst, causing water damage to the drywall. What I liked most was the location. The house sat back from the main road, surrounded by pine trees and a little creek that flowed behind the property. With no neighbors in sight, it was peaceful and quiet, except for an occasional tractor-trailer barreling down the road. When Cliff asked if I would like to live in the house, I was a little apprehensive. What if he was like Gary and didn't finish projects he started?

At forty-five years old, I had enough energy to start a new life and took a chance Cliff would fix up the house with my help. We began to spend the weekends cleaning up remnants of carpet, rotted wood, and other debris that the previous owner had strewn around the four acres of land, located six miles north of Ridgway. We built a fire outside and cooked our meals over the coals. The insurance company required that the old barn be torn down, so that was one of our first projects. The plumbing in the house wasn't working so Cliff built an outhouse from reclaimed wood.

Occasionally we hopped in the truck to go to antique stores and the flea market in Leeper, Pennsylvania to forage for items we might need for our homestead. At the White Swan antique shop near Corry, Pa. we found a hundred-year-old green, porcelain, wood-cook stove for our kitchen with a price tag of six hundred dollars. I told Cliff the stove would make an excellent engagement gift. A diamond ring didn't appeal to me, as I never wanted to feel a man owned me because of a ring on my finger. Without hesitating, Cliff put a down payment on the stove.

At a flea market, we found a wood crate to contain our someday chickens, a hand-operated bread machine, and a kraut cutter in need of repair. As we were carrying our finds to the truck, a fifteen-gallon, copper apple butter kettle caught Cliff's eye. He said, "This is what we need to make apple butter at Sizerville this year." I looked at the price tag of three hundred dollars and went into sticker shock. I recently paid one hundred dollars for a good used electric stove at my house in Emporium and couldn't fathom spending that much money for an apple butter kettle we would use only once a year. Cliff assured me that buying it would be an investment.

After I agreed to the purchase, Cliff walked over to the large man named Bill, sitting behind a glass counter displaying knives, old watches, and other artifacts. Nonchalantly, Cliff greeted Bill and asked, "What's the least you can take for that apple butter kettle?"

"The kettle is dove-tailed, and it's a pretty good one. What's the price on it?"

"Three hundred."

"I'll take the two-fifty."

Cliff reached in his back pocket and pulled out his black and white leather wallet made of cowhide and handed him the needed bills. I tucked the bread machine under my right arm as Cliff gave me the chicken crate he was carrying. He set the kraut cutter in the kettle and lifted it off the ground to take to the truck. On the ride home, Cliff talked about building a tripod using a one-inch black iron pipe that he could get from St. Marys Steel Supply. "It won't fit in my truck, so I'll have to lay it across the back bumper and cut it in three seven-foot pieces with my hacksaw to get it home." I liked the way he planned and thought things out. It told me a lot about his character.

Also, thinking ahead, I said, "We will need a lot more apples than we had last year to fill the huge kettle."

"And we'll also need some fifty-cent pieces to keep the apple butter from sticking to the bottom," Cliff added.

I figured if Cliff knew about apple butter paddles and apple butter kettles, he must know about the fifty-cent pieces. Sensing my skepticism, when we returned to the house in Johnsonburg, Cliff showed me his Eric Sloane book, which illustrated in detail how to make apple butter using the coins.

Summer came and went with us hauling out the musty, dank wall-board, wet from broken water pipes, tearing out kitchen cupboards lined with gold and forest green wallpaper from the 1970s and removing old carpet, which covered a pine floor in the kitchen. Cliff repaired the plumbing and had the house rewired. He set up his table saw in the large room that would be the kitchen and started making paneling and kitchen cupboards out of a thousand board feet of pine he purchased.

In late August, Cliff's daughter, Stephanie, gave birth to her third daughter, Tameryn Estelle. I was also expecting another grandchild; my daughter Brandi was expecting a baby due in March of the next year. As our family was growing, Cliff and I talked about what we would do if something happened and we had to raise a grandchild. Both of us were done parenting but agreed we would support each other if we ever had to help out raising a grandchild or grandchildren.

When apples began to fall from the old apple tree in the back of the house, I was reminded to call the Sizerville State Park Office for permission to make apple butter and biscuits at the upcoming Autumn Festival. When I called, the secretary at the park office was excited to tell me that they had a site set aside a pavilion with, running water, and a little stone fireplace for us. I thought we were set for a great year.

Eric Sloan wrote in his book, *Seasons of America's Past,* that bruised apples are more flavorful for apple butter. Knowing we would need more apples than the tree produced, Cliff contacted his friend, who had an orchard. He gave us six, five-gallon buckets of drop apples. The day before the festival, we cooked down the apples in a large kettle over a wood fire in the backyard. After they were soft and mush, we processed the hot cooked apples through a Victoria strainer attached to a picnic table. Afterward, we had ten gallons of applesauce that would half fill the copper apple butter kettle we bought at the flea market.

Early the next morning, when the rising sun was turning the frost to dew we loaded the apple butter kettle, applesauce, a picnic basket full of spices, ten pounds of biscuit mix in a pottery crock, Cliff's shaving horse, his carving tools, and some chunks of green applewood for carving spoons into the back of the pick-up truck. We stopped at the Cabin Kitchen Restaurant in Emporium for a breakfast of sausage, biscuits, and gravy. Before heading out to the Sizerville we stopped at Olivett's Market for a couple of gallons of fresh apple cider to add to the applesauce. When we drove up to the park office and informed the parking attendants who we were, they recognized both Cliff and me. We were directed to a site past a small creek that ran through the center of the park.

As we pulled into the parking space, I told Cliff, "We'll have to get a fire started right away to have enough hot coals to cook down the applesauce into apple butter." Before we unloaded the truck, he started chopping kindling with his wood ax. I gathered dead tree branches and pinecones to fuel the tender flames in the stone fireplace. It wasn't long before we had a nice fire going. Cliff set up the tripod and built a fire where the apple butter kettle would stand. When both fires were burning well, we began unloading the truck. Out of the corner of my eye, I noticed the drill sergeant walking toward us with a sense of urgency. Knowing trouble when I see it, I wondered what we did wrong. I was soon to find out.

"What are you doing starting a fire in an uncontained area? That's illegal to do in a state park," she scolded.

I pulled out my forgiveness card and apologized. Not being one to apologize, Cliff informed her, "We needed to get the fire started to have enough coals to cook down the apple butter that you thought was a great idea. It isn't our fault that you didn't have a fire ring here for us.

She argued we were supposed to cook the apple butter and biscuits in the little stone fireplace made for grilling hamburgers or hot dogs. We agreed that we failed to communicate that we were going to make apple butter in a huge apple butter kettle rather than a little cast-iron pot.

She responded by pulling her hand radio off of her belt and directed her employees, "Get a fire ring to site number twenty-one as soon as possible. There's an uncontained fire burning in the park."

While we were waiting for the fire ring to arrive, a park employee came with a power blower and began blowing leaves away from the site. The ambiance of the day with people walking through rustling fall leaves was nearly in ruin. Within a few minutes, some friendly park employees pulled up in a white government truck with a cast iron black fire ring and some nice dry firewood. After the fire was contained, I again apologized and asked her to stop the employee from blowing the leaves away from our site. After all, this was a fall festival. By then, the fire was burning nicely as was the park ranger's ire at us. She reluctantly directed the employee to another task.

As the fog lifted and the sun began to shine through the partly cloudy sky, Cliff filled a six-quart white enamel coffee pot with spring water, a cupful of Eight O' Clock and threw in a couple of eggshells that he saved from breakfast. The eggshells kept the coffee grounds down to the bottom of the pot. He balanced the pot on a grate over the hot burning coals. The aroma of percolating coffee attracted other vendors and staff employees to our site for a morning cup of camp coffee.

By noontime, we were on schedule, serving samples of nicely browned biscuits and a taste of apple butter. Cliff carved out five spoons that sold and received orders for three more.

People started asking if we had apple butter for sale. I hadn't thought of selling it but filled some canning jars and sold it for $3.00 a pint until it was sold out. After the festival, we joined the other vendors and park staff at the nature center for the potluck meal. The drill sergeant was there and seemed to have calmed down a bit. She was smiling and commending everyone for all their efforts in making the autumn festival a success.

The autumn festival became an annual event that we enjoyed for over twenty years. As more grandchildren came along, they joined us by selling hot dogs roasted over the fire, apple cider, cookies, hot pepper mustard, and jellies. It was fun seeing old friends from Emporium and meeting new people year after year.

Along with an abundant crop of apples, it was also a good year for sweet corn. Cliff said he would like to dry corn for Thanksgiving. He had two large, flat steamers that we filled with water. After blanching the corn, and cutting it off the husks, we cooked it on top of the steamers until it dried. While processing the corn, Cliff told me he never dreamed he would meet someone who enjoyed canning and homesteading as much as I did. His mother, Agnes Stump, had passed away a year before we met. A few months before she passed away, he helped her to can bread and butter pickles. After she was gone, he wasn't sure he wanted to continue canning food but was happy to be in the kitchen again. After the corn was dried, we stored it in muslin bags his mother had sewn from old flour sacks and saved it for our first Thanksgiving meal together.

For our first Thanksgiving together, we invited Stephanie and her family and his cousin Jan and her family to the house on Clarion Road. I helped Cliff clean off the dining room table and found his mom's terry cloth autumn colored tablecloths and candles in the buffet. Stephanie brought coleslaw, and along with the turkey and all the trimmings, we cooked the dried corn. Both Cliff and I had much to be grateful for as we enjoyed our first Thanksgiving.

When Christmas came, I didn't jump into celebrating. I still felt there was a lot of materialism connected to the holiday. Cliff agreed and said Christmas wasn't important to him either. He was glad to hear I wasn't into decorating as he wouldn't be expected to hang Christmas lights. At my house in Emporium, I decorated a large jade plant with clear lights and hung some blue and white ornaments, made in Holland, that I bought at the Christmas Store in Smethport. We both enjoyed Christmas music that we listened to at his house while playing board games in his kitchen. After supper, as we slow danced to *Walking in a Winter Wonderland* sung by Bing Cosby, Cliff broke into song, singing:

'*Later on, we'll conspire, as we dream by the fire, to face unafraid the plans that we've made, walking in a winter wonderland.*'

After the song ended, we set a date to be married on June 23rd of 2001. On Christmas Eve, we had a meal of lasagna and seafood at Stephanie's. Cliff's son Stephen Hoyt, who was named after Cliff's dad, had recently moved back to the area from the Poconos and was starting up a restaurant in Reynoldsville. He too joined the family for the holiday.

Stephen had a great sense of humor and his presence lit up a room, where he became the center of attention. We announced to the family our plans to marry. When he saw his dad open a can of beer, he got quiet for a minute. Stephen had never seen his dad drink. Before long, the two of them were downing one beer after the other, enjoying each other's company. I was concerned about how much alcohol they were drinking but didn't say anything. Cliff's ex-wife also came for the evening and I admired how respectful Cliff treated her despite their differences. I thought if Cliff could be in his ex-wife's presence without animosity or hate, perhaps I could do the same with Gary.

After our engagement, I told Greg Burns, who was the Extension Agent for Cameron and Elk Counties, that Cliff and I were planning on getting married and moving to Ridgway. I asked if I could relocate my work to Ridgway since there was an empty office in the Extension Office, located in the basement of the courthouse. Greg obtained permission from the commissioners and from his superiors at Penn State, who all approved. Greg and Barb Miller, the family living agent, weren't only happy to have me working out of Elk County, they were both glad to hear I was no longer a Jehovah's Witness. Both of them were Christians and said they had been praying for me.

While working at the Extension office in Elk County, one of the pastors from a local church stopped in for some information on gardening.

The secretary had stepped out of the office, so I introduced myself, and he did likewise.

I asked, "What church are you from?"

"I'm a pastor at the Lutheran Church in town."

Not knowing much about the church, I asked, "What is the difference between your church and the Catholic religion?"

"We are fundamentalists?"

"What's a fundamentalist?"

"The best way I can explain it is when it comes to dogma, some religions are gray, and some are black and white.

I wondered aloud, "Is there a religion with color? The question remained in my psyche as I searched for God.

Cliff and I wanted to learn more about basic gardening and signed up for a Master Gardening class. John and Lois Shoemaker and Emily and Tom Landis, who we knew from the Executive Board meetings, also attended the course. Both of the couples had recently retired and were looking for new interests. Lois and John invited Cliff and me to the Faircroft Bed and Breakfast for breakfast and a breadmaking session. Lois was a retired home economics teacher and made Swedish Rye Bread. Cliff had tried making the bread a few times but couldn't get it to rise. I knew how to make bread but had never heard of Swedish Rye Bread. After a delicious breakfast, we put on our aprons and went to work, to bake bread together.

As we were making plans for the wedding, Lois and John offered to host the wedding at their Bed and Breakfast. To make plans for the occasion, they again invited us back for a beautiful supper served on elegant china. After we finished eating, they gave us a tour of their home. While showing us the bedrooms, Lois mentioned there was a special gift for us in one of the rooms. When she got to the second room, I noticed a smile on her face as she opened the door. The first thing that caught my eye was a quilt designed with earthen colors of burgundy, forest green, tan, bordered in a crème white. When I commented on how beautiful the quilt was, she turned a corner of the blanket down and showed me the tiny stitches that were almost invisible and told me that it was handmade by a Mennonite woman. When I asked if this was our special gift, with John smiling ear to ear in the background, she said it was. My heart was touched by their thoughtfulness and kindness.

While making wedding plans, we had the task of cleaning out two houses and renovating our new home on Montmorenci Road. So I didn't feel overwhelmed, I focused on packing up one box at a time. From my house, there were possessions I wanted to bring with me, and there were items I wanted to let go of, including forty bound volumes of *Watchtower* and *Awake* magazines that I had collected over the past twenty-five years. Each year we were expected to purchase the encyclopedia size books to use when we had questions or needed to do a reference for talks at the Kingdom Hall. When it came time to pack them up, I didn't know what to do with them, so I asked Cliff to burn them for me. He loaded them in his truck and hauled the books out to Montmorenci and made a bonfire with them. It was a good way for me to purge myself of the Watchtower propaganda.

The large, two-story house Cliff lived in on Clarion Road belonged to his parents and his Aunt Wilda. Cliff was born in 1942 when his parents lived on Elk Avenue in Rolfe, a little settlement outside of Johnsonburg. After Aunt Wilda's husband passed away, Cliff and his family moved in with her when he was a teenager. Both Cliff's mom, and aunt, liked to hang on to memorabilia from the past, so all their possessions were still in the house. While sorting, I came across a box of black and white photographs. Cliff was an only child, so there were plenty of pictures of his childhood days from the time he was in a bouncy chair to the day he went into the Navy. Going through the pictures helped me get to know what Cliff's life was like as a child. While sorting through photographs, I recognized a black and white glossy snapshot of two women holding little children at Mooseheart taken in 1959 at Baby Village. I was so curious about the picture that I called Cliff to tell him about the picture. When he got home from work that evening, he recognized the two ladies as his great aunts, Ruth and Wilda.

I told him, "If the picture was taken two years later, they could have been holding me."

Cliff wasn't sure why his aunts were at Mooseheart. We thought the puzzle was solved when we found letters sent back and forth between his Aunt Wilda and Aunt Ruth from Johnsonburg, Pennsylvania, to Aurora, Illinois. I thought when Aunt Ruth lived in Aurora, perhaps Aunt Wilda visited her, and they took a trip to see the orphans at Mooseheart, much like people go to visit the zoo.

After working at the house during the day, we walked around the neighborhood where Cliff grew up. He showed me where the two-story wood frame, Rolfe schoolhouse he attended, was located. He walked home for lunch, but the school wasn't his favorite place to be, so he stopped to play on the way back, causing him to be late. In the morning, when his mom's alarm went off, he snuck over to her room and pushed in the stem of the wind-up clock to turn it off. When he walked in tardy, the teacher played a rhyme on the piano to embarrass him. She sang "A diller, a dollar, A ten o'clock scholar, What makes you come so soon? You used to come at ten o'clock, and now you come at noon."

He showed me where he played Cowboys and Indians in the tall pine trees and pointed out Lefty and Raymond Laughner's basement, where he spent hours playing while his dad helped them build the homes. He walked me by the house on Elk Avenue, where his mom and dad rented their first apartment when he was born. At first, I liked hearing his childhood memories but soon found myself feeling irritable and growled, "I'm tired of hearing all your happy childhood memories. Can't we talk about something else?" I couldn't imagine what it was like to live in the same town for sixty years, and he had no idea what it was like for me to live in an orphanage.

While cleaning out his mom's house, I found handwritten report cards, which described Cliff perfectly. He had all A's in history but didn't do so well in other subjects. Cliff was an only child and was happy to have kids to play with at school instead of studying. He had to repeat the third grade because the doctor had accidentally reversed the lens in his glasses, which he wore from the time he was a tot. He said he didn't get behind; the other students got ahead of him. I liked his positive outlook.

We managed to get the house cleaned out and moved everything we wanted to the house in Montmorenci. We gave the rest of the belongings to Cliff's children, Stephanie and Stephen. Cliff and I offered the house to Brandi and her growing family. After she gave birth to a little boy named Jeremy Matthew Peluso, they moved into the house on Clarion Road where Cliff had lived.

Jeremy was born a few weeks premature. His lungs weren't fully developed so he had to spend a few weeks in the NICU unit in DuBois. When Brandi couldn't be with him, I drove to the hospital to see him. To my dismay, I learned grandparents couldn't hold the babies. The nurse explained that some parents don't want grandparents or relatives holding their babies. I was appalled. The baby needed to be held and cuddled, not only by nurses but by someone who loved him.

The day I went to visit, Jeremy's skin was ashen gray, and I wondered if he would live. Since I couldn't hold him, with heart monitors beeping and the nursery lights dimmed, I put my hands over him and prayed for his life. He had an infection from an IV, which wasn't put in properly and was now on antibiotics. When I suggested giving him acidophilus, the nurse scolded me, saying acidophilus for infants wasn't research-based.

At the same time, I noted a box of rice cereal with bananas that they were using to tube feed him. When I asked her what research was done on giving infants bananas, she rudely told me not to think of giving him bananas because there wasn't any research on that. I then asked why the hospital was giving him bananas and pointed to the box next to his incubator. She gasped and said that was an error from the dietary department.

The next day, Dr. Siars, the head doctor of the NICU, who was nearing retirement, came in to examine Jeremy, who's cheeks were now turning rosy. After examining the baby, the doctor turned to me, and asked, "What do you know about probiotics?"

"I've never heard of the word. Why?'

"A nurse told me that you wanted to give your grandson acidophilus."

I related, "When my oldest son had thrush, I learned it was a yeast infection from me taking antibiotics while I was pregnant and know that acidophilus counteracts the effects of antibiotics."

He raised his eyebrows. "I'm scheduled to attend a conference on administering probiotics (the new name for acidophilus cultures) to infants. It seems you are a few years ahead of the medical profession." Now, nearly twenty years later, they make infant formula supplemented with probiotics.

After Jeremy came home and thrived, I wrote a letter to Dr. Siars and the NICU suggesting if parents didn't want grandparents holding their infant, they should make that the exception, not the rule. I received a nice thank you note and was told the rule was now changed. Grandparents and relatives were more than welcome to cuddle the preemie. When Jeremy was two months old, I learned my daughter Cherey, was expecting a baby in January.

Vows

•————————————————•

While planning the wedding, I found a cross-stitch wedding pattern with the scripture from Solomon 6:3, *I am my beloved, and my beloved is mine*. At the same time, I found a set of rings with the same inscription in Hebrew letters and knew that this would be the theme of our wedding. I spent evenings completing the sampler, and after it was finished, I framed it in a white and gold frame I found at a yard sale.

John and Lois helped plan the wedding and didn't miss a stitch when it came to minute details. Lois was an experienced planner, and we were appreciative of her suggestions. Since neither Cliff nor I attended a church, Tony King, the local magistrate, officiated at the wedding. Although he usually performed marriages in his office, since he knew Cliff, he agreed to participate in the wedding.

For the big day, I wore a floor-length sage green dress, and Cliff wore a pair of tan casual slacks, a cream-colored dress shirt, and a floral tie. Lois and John stood for us, Greg Burns, my supervisor from the Extension office, opened the ceremony with a prayer, my friend, Corinne read from *A Course In Miracles*, Cliff's cousin, Jeff Bassett read from the scriptures. Dr. Francis blessed our rings and said the concluding prayer Our vows came from a beautiful book on second marriages. When we read them aloud to each other, tears were streaming down our cheeks. It seemed as if they were penned just for us.

My love,
I waited so long for you
That I had begun to believe
There was no such thing as true love,
That my life would be lived out
Alone, that nothing precious
Would come in the form
Of someone to love.

Finally, after so many sorrows,
Missteps and losses,
After I had given up all hope,
You were given to me like a miracle,
Like a single elegant star in the darkest
Of night. Now I feel joy
Now I feel whole
Now I feel anything is possible.

Thank you for coming into my life;
Thank you for loving me well.
I have waited so long for my heart
To be glad, for my soul to be full

I, Clifford Allan, take you, Jeanette Elizabeth
To be my beloved husband and friend,
To give you, from this day forward,
 The gift of my tender love.
To honor you with my body,
To fill up the wounds
In your heart;
To sleep in your bed and stand at your side

In good times and bad.

I choose now to take this journey with you
Wherever it leads
Whatever the outcome
No matter what may befall us
As God is my witness
Through all the days
Of our lives.

Startled awake
At this late and unexpectedly beautiful
Hour, long after sorrow, long after love,
Long after hope,
I receive you into the breath
Of my soul
To make my light with you,
To fill with joy my glad heart,
And to love you far more and dearly
Than ever before in all our
Imaginings you could have imagined.

With the sight of my eyes,
With the wings of my heart,
With the milk of my soul.
I have come to you with the plain grace
Of a small bird to love you
And I will love you:

I, Jeanette Elizabeth, take you, Clifford Allan
To be my beloved husband and friend,
To give you, from this day forward,
The gift of my tender love.
To honor you with my body,

To fill up the wounds
In your heart;
To sleep in your bed and stand at your side
In good times and bad.

I choose now to take this journey with you
Wherever it leads
Whatever the outcome
No matter what may befall us
As God is my witness
Through all the days Of our lives.

Barb Miller, Lois, and Jeannie Allenbaugh prepared a delicious buffet of food, and Rebekah Burns made a beautiful strawberry cheesecake. Although it rained the day of the wedding, we enjoyed celebrating under the white event tent. Cliff kept thanking me for how simple I kept the wedding.

More than one person told us the rain meant our marriage would be showered with many blessings, which proved to be true. Afterward, we opened gifts that included a beautiful wood clock from my brother Warren.

For our honeymoon, we drove to Cook's Forest and stayed overnight at the Gateway Lodge and then traveled to Harper's Ferry. Cliff had been to Harper's Ferry and wanted to show me the many shops and places. I preferred to explore places on my own and wasn't used to someone wanting to be with me wherever I went. I felt as if I needed some space, so I suggested we go our own way for a little while and meet back at a central location. Cliff was deeply disappointed we weren't going to be together all the time. We called a truce and decided to have lunch at a restaurant that overlooked the conflux where the Shenandoah and Potomac Rivers met.

While eating, I told Cliff when two mighty rivers converge, the water is turbulent and not to forget the Shenandoah is still part of the Potomac. I was having a hard time giving up my newly formed identity after getting divorced from Gary and didn't ever want to lose myself in a man again. I held onto the framed quotation by Kahlil Gibran: "And stand together yet not too near together, for the pillars of the temple stand apart," which I hung in our new home.

From then on, our trip was much more enjoyable. We hiked a small leg of the Appalachian trail and stood on a rock where Thomas Jefferson once stood. On the way home, we stopped at the Jean Bonnet Tavern in Bedford, Pennsylvania, just north of the Mason Dixon Line and stayed overnight in a bedroom with a four-poster bed decorated with lace and a handmade quilt. The tavern is a 1760 historic landmark where soldiers stayed to quell the Whiskey Rebellion. While we were eating in the stone-walled dining room with a large fireplace, we fell in love with the hardwood chairs made of hickory. We both thought they would look beautiful in the kitchen Cliff was renovating. We looked on the bottom of the chairs to see where they were made and jotted down the phone number on a napkin. When we returned home, we called the phone number and found the chairs were handcrafted by two older men who were brothers. Their shop was located in Mann's Choice. We ordered six chairs that would be ready for pick up in two months, just about the time we expected the kitchen to be finished.

Cliff worked tirelessly, building cabinets that I painted with confederate blue stain. We found wallpaper with blackberry brambles that matched the green porcelain cookstove and the stained cabinets. His final touch was a nine-foot kitchen table he built from Louisiana Yellow Pine, two and a half inches thick that he salvaged from a building the paper mill had razed in 1983. The table was so big that he and Mike Shrefler had to bring it in pieces. The two of them bolted it together and Cliff stained and varnished the table that seats up to twelve people. We've had many family gatherings and guests from all over the world join us at the table. It's become the centerpiece of our kitchen.

As we were working in the kitchen, a robin that was building a nest on the windowsill in the soon to be kitchen caught my eye. I marveled as she instinctively wove twigs and branches into a round nest. I wondered why she chose the open windowsill when she could have picked a place in the safe confines of the tree branches. I wondered if this was just for me to see? My question brought to mind the scripture verse: "Even the sparrow finds a home and the swallow a nest for herself, where she may lay her young, at your altars, Lord of hosts." Psalm 84:3.

In the back of mind, I was concerned about my seventeen- year old daughter, Cherey, who was expecting a baby in January. Even though Cliff and I invited her to come live with us, she chose to stay in Emporium to finish up her senior year of high school and to be near her boyfriend and classmates. When building nests, eagles are known for weaving in a few thorns, so the baby birds will be sure to leave the nest when they are older. I worried there were too many thorns in my nest. Maybe the divorce was too much for her.

I was also concerned because she didn't seem to have a maternal bone in her body. As a little girl, she didn't take an interest in baby dolls and never cared to babysit younger children. She was sassy, independent, and taking risks with her life. And just like any other teenager, her main concerns were friends, shopping for name brand clothes, and having her make-up applied perfectly. The black eyeliner she wore shadowed the deep sadness in her brown eyes.

As Cliff and I continued to work on the house, I noticed blue eggs in the nest. It wasn't long until there were four beaks wide open waiting for food. The mother diligently delivered the hungry peeps fresh earthworms she pulled from the soil every day. Shortly after that, they outgrew the nest and left one by one.

It was then I quit fretting about my grandchild's life. If a bird knew by instinct how to care for her young, then I had faith my daughter would be able to care for her baby. After Cliff and I married, her dad moved back into the house on Fifth Street, so she had a place to live. To my delight, Cherey began gathering infant clothes. In her home economics class at school, she made a patchwork, pastel quilt for the baby and set up an oak spindle crib I found at a yard sale in the corner of her bedroom. Once a month, I traveled to Emporium, to take Cherey to her monthly prenatal appointments in Coudersport. The first time I saw the flutter of the baby's heartbeat on the ultrasound I wondered about her future. I prayed that God would watch over and protect her.

My concern for her and the future of all my grandchildren's futures was heightened on September 11, 2001, when I was working in the Extension office located in the basement of the Elk County Courthouse. We received an alert that a plane in Somerset County, located two hours south of Ridgway had been bombed. My co-workers and I rushed up the steps to see what had happened. I think we all expected the sky to be bomb-ridden but instead saw a beautiful blue sky with white clouds. The air was still and somber. There weren't any birds chirping or squirrels chattering.

When we returned to our office, the scene on the television was completely opposite. My heart grieved for the people scattering from the Twin Towers, billowing with smoke and debris in New York City. My heart grieved more for the people trapped inside of the buildings. It was a sad day, reminiscent of the day I watched John F. Kennedy's funeral on television when I was in kindergarten. It was a day I knew I would never forget. It was a day when I, and many others no longer felt safe in the world.

After leaving Jehovah's Witnesses, I didn't know the difference between a Republican or a Democrat. After 9/11, I found myself caught up in patriotism and found myself leaning toward conservative values. Cliff believed strongly in the Constitution and felt that the Republican Party supported his values. Because of not being exposed to politics, I was influenced by his views and registered to vote as a Republican.

After the attack, President George Bush declared war on terrorism. My brother Jack was still in the service at the time and received orders to go to Iraq. I feared for him, and all the soldiers, protecting our country from another fateful attack. Cliff had a penchant toward conspiracy theories and felt strongly that our government may have orchestrated this tragic event. He read extensively about the JFK assassination and other ploys by our government to cover up the truth behind atrocities. I was confused and didn't know what to think. I had just left a religion who taught the world was going to come to an end any day and didn't want to live in fear any longer. I chose to see the good in people and the world.

When my brother Jack received orders to go to Iraq, my heart was heavy with concern for his safety. While working at the courthouse, I started running during my hour lunch break and prayed for Jack's safety while running up the hill to Portland Mills and back through the rail trail. When it came time for the annual triathlon in Ridgway, I felt as though I was in good physical shape and asked Cliff if he would like to do the event together. He talked about how much he enjoyed doing the triathlon in his younger years and was excited to have a partner. He biked, I ran, and together we canoed. While running, I lagged behind the last runner but reminded myself I was ahead of all the people sitting home on their couch. We aced the canoeing and placed in the upper half of all the contestants.

Thankfully, Jack returned home safely from Iraq. Cliff and I visited with him and his wife Connie in Williamsburg, Virginia a few months later. While having supper together at a restaurant, he showed us stacks of pictures of the arid desert landscape in Iraq. To us, the pictures all looked the same. He didn't share much about his experience in the war. All he said was, "Things are not what they seem."

Sugar and Spice

On a cold, wintery day on January 11, 2002, Paige Elizabeth was born at the Coudersport Hospital. Cliff and I were present to welcome her into the world. Cherey graduated from high school in June and moved into an apartment in Emporium with her boyfriend. I made trips to Emporium to help Cherey out as much as I could. When she needed a break from parenting an infant, Paige stayed overnight at my house.

For Paige's first birthday, we had a party at Memorial Hall with balloons, cake, and lots of gifts. I regretted not having birthday parties for Cherey and supported her in making Paige's first birthday fun. I spent the next few years of my life, painfully realizing what I had deprived my children of by raising them as Jehovah's Witnesses. Both Brandi and Cherey jumped into celebrating Christmas and birthdays with their children to make up for what they hadn't had. I apologized to all my children, more than once, for all the mistakes I made. The greatest gift they gave me was their understanding and forgiveness. Rather than blame me, they held the religion responsible for misleading innocent people. I had a lot to learn from them.

When Paige was two years old, she developed a severe diaper rash that wouldn't clear up. Cherey had taken her to the family doctor and was told that it was a urinary tract infection and was prescribed antibiotics. When the rash didn't clear up, I became concerned. She was extremely thirsty and would gobble down a whole bag of cookies. I urged Cherey to make another appointment with the doctor and told her I would go with her to find out what was wrong. I left work early and drove to Emporium in time for her appointment at the Cameron County Health Center. The physician's assistant who examined Paige said that maybe she still had a UTI and that he would do another urinalysis. I wondered if the rash were a yeast infection.

As we were leaving the office, Dr. Freeman, who was my family doctor when I lived in Emporium, spotted me and said hello. I was holding Paige while Cherey set up a follow-up appointment. Dr. Freeman, smiled and asked, "Is this your little one?"

"No, it's my granddaughter. Cherey is her mom."

He remembered Cherey from when she was little and asked, "What brings you here?"

"The baby has a severe diaper rash that won't clear up."

His smile turned to a frown, and he asked, "Did they order a finger prick for her?"

"No, why?' His face turned beet red. He turned to the nurse and said, "Get a glucose reading from Paige, ASAP."

We went back to the lab while the nurse pricked her finger and did a urinalysis. Within minutes, Dr. Freeman came in and broke the news to us. Paige's blood sugar was over 800, and her urine was high in ketones. I had no idea what any of it meant. Dr. Freeman explained she had juvenile diabetes and would need to be life-flighted to a larger medical facility. He gave us a choice between the Children's Hospital in Pittsburgh or Geisinger Medical Center in Danville. We chose Geisinger because it was closer to Emporium. Dr. Freeman spent over an hour with me explaining juvenile diabetes. He practiced at a camp for children with type 1 diabetes and knew about the disease first- hand. My biggest concern was how Cherey was going to take care of her.

In a state of shock and disbelief, we drove to the Coudersport Hospital, where she was life-flighted to Geisinger Medical Center. I asked to fly with her but wasn't allowed.

Cherey and I wrapped her up in her favorite blue and white checkered baby blanket with bunnies that she called her 'bunny foo-foo' blanket and kissed her goodbye. She was so frightened, and tears were streaming down her cheeks. Cherey and Paige's dad drove down to Geisinger and arrived around midnight. How they found their way, I'll never know. I drove back to Ridgway, praying the whole time that God would comfort Paige and keep her safe.

Cherey and Paige's dad had to stay at the hospital with Paige until they learned how to check her blood sugar levels and give her injections of insulin. Cherey just about fainted at the sight of a needle but eventually learned how to give Paige the needed injections. Cliff and I drove down to learn all we could to help care for Paige. At first, it was devastating to know that she would be dependent on insulin injections for the rest of her life. I didn't know anyone personally that had diabetes, but Cliff knew a few people and was more familiar with the disease than I was. When we arrived at the pediatric floor and saw children who had cancer and children in vegetative states, it didn't take us long to quit feeling sorry for her or ourselves. It felt as if she were the healthy one, walking around and talking to everyone she met.

Within a month, we knew how to prick Paige's finger to check her blood sugar, how to count carbohydrates, how to measure insulin, and give injections. The whole process was overwhelming. At a health fair in St. Marys, there was a table with resources from JDRF-Juvenile Diabetes Research Foundation. As I picked up a few of the handouts, I told the woman representing the foundation, about Paige being diagnosed with diabetes. She introduced herself as Tracy and told me about her five-year-old son, who had juvenile diabetes. After talking to Tracy, I no longer felt alone and knew that this was manageable. She gifted us with a teddy bear and books explaining the disease. Tracy invited us to the JDRF walk that was held annually in Johnsonburg.

I designed t-shirts for our first walk and named our team Paige's Path. Although we didn't raise a lot of money, we benefited from the camaraderie of other children and families living with diabetes. We faithfully attended the walk for five years at the Johnsonburg Fire Hall, where Elk County was recognized for raising the most money in the region.

On one walk, Paige was looking for a cure alongside Silver Creek Road and asked, "Gramma, did we find a cure yet?" It saddened me that she didn't understand what a cure was, and I felt like the walks were promoting false hope, especially after reading the book *Cheating Destiny* by James Hirsch. While the author was writing the book and doing research at the Joslin Research Center, his son was diagnosed with type 1 diabetes. Hirsch wrote about promising research that wasn't being funded. If a cure were found, insulin pump companies and pharmaceutical companies would go out of business. I spoke about this at one of the diabetes walks and then lost interest in JDRF.

Having a toddler with diabetes took a toll on Paige's mom, who felt overwhelmed and unable to care for her twenty-four hours a day. Blood sugars needed to be checked in the middle of the night, and every bite of food she ate needed to be measured. Insulin needed to be measured according to her blood sugar levels and what she ate. When Paige turned three years old, I resigned from my job at Penn State to care for her full time in our home. The only room available was a storage room upstairs, so we cleared it out and painted the room lavender and set up a toddler bed. Every night I read her stories and taught her the alphabet using cut out letters from sandpaper and tracing them with her fingers.

The experience of caring for a child with diabetes was like riding a roller coaster. There were days when Paige's blood sugar levels were high, and she needed extra doses of insulin, and then there were days when her blood sugars dropped so low, I had to give her glucose injections. And she handled it like a champ. I wiped away a lot of tears.

Diabetes didn't affect her vocabulary or brain function. We realized early on that Paige was highly intelligent and articulate. When her glucose level dropped to 15 (normal blood sugar levels are between 90-110) she had to be rushed by ambulance to the emergency room. After being doused with pancake syrup and glucose injections, the nurse informed the doctor that she was 80. Paige sat up in the bed and said, "I'm not eighty; I'm only three years old."

At one of her well-child check-ups, Dr. Siars, the pediatrician, was evaluating her development. He pointed to paper with pictures of zoo animals and asked her what the name of an animal was. She replied, "A giraffe."

He pointed to an elephant and asked her the same question. She asked him, "What's the matter? Did you forget?"

He chuckled, closed her chart, and said, "You have a bright little girl on your hands."

In between the twenty-four-hour care Paige required, we had fun reading children's books, singing songs, dancing, and doing crafts. Paige was by Cliff's side, helping him hold a tape measure or pound nails into boards. While working at Head Start, I read extensively about the Montessori method to child-rearing and education and wished I knew about it when my children were young. I wished I had had all the experience, wisdom, and support when my children were young. The aphorism, 'Experience is the comb life gives you after you have lost all your hair' rang true for me. I wanted to be the supportive mother and grandmother that my children and I never had.

I realized Paige needed social experiences but didn't feel comfortable enrolling her in a day-care because of her medical condition, so I started attending the Trinity Methodist Church in Ridgway so she could attend Sunday School. The people at the church were welcoming and kind. I met a woman named Liz, who was also insulin dependent. When Liz learned that Paige had juvenile diabetes, she invited us to her house and gave Paige a three-story dollhouse that belonged to her daughter Alison. When I attended church services, I couldn't get Jehovah's Witnesses' interpretation of the scriptures out of my head. Teachings about the trinity, communion, and the cross flooded my psyche, not letting me enjoy the services.

Deep down, I felt as if I were doing something inherently wrong.

I also signed Paige up for the Parents as Teachers program. Each week, an early childhood educator visited her at our house and did activities with her. When the program learned she had juvenile diabetes, they assigned Nancy Osgood to be her teacher. Nancy's son had type 1 diabetes. It was helpful to talk to someone who knew what it was like to care for a child with diabetes. Paige and I both looked forward to Nancy's visits.

I stayed abreast of diabetes treatment and learned about the insulin pump. At an appointment at Geisinger, I inquired about the availability of it for Paige, but they told me she was too young. After doing more research, I learned that younger patients do well on the insulin pump and pushed for her to get one. My persistence paid off, and when she was a little over three years old, she was sporting a bubble gum pink insulin pump. Although managing the carbs was easier, inserting the cannula into her little leg was heart-wrenching. The needle was much larger than the insulin needle and was much more painful for both of us. Injecting the needle into her leg was one of the hardest things I ever had to do. After inflicting pain on her, I would go to bed, bury my head in my pillow and cry myself to sleep. In the morning, the sun would rise, and she would come running into my room and crawl into bed with me and wait for the rooster to crow. Then she would tell me, "Gramma, tell the rooster that we are already awake."

Even with the insulin pump, managing diabetes was a challenge. Low blood sugars caused Paige to hallucinate and see what she described as spiders and bugs. In the middle of the night, Cliff drove us to the Geisinger emergency room, where she was admitted for a few days over the Easter holiday. While there, Paige's outgoing nature brought joy to many of the patients, including a little girl with a malignant tumor on her arm. She enjoyed visits from the therapeutic dog and art activities provided by the hospital staff. In between tests to rule out other reasons for the hallucinations, Paige's stay at the hospital, for her, was like a vacation, but for me, it was like being in prison. The courtyard was fenced in, and we weren't allowed off the grounds. It brought back memories of being confined to the hospital at Mooseheart. The medical staff wasn't compassionate when it came to diabetes education. It felt as if they were shaming me for not providing her with adequate care.

When I was at wits' end and after all of Paige's test results came back negative, Cliff and I took her off-grounds, pulling her in a red wagon. We hopped in Cliff's truck and went to Wendy's for lunch. When we returned, the staff treated us like criminals by telling us we would be turned in to the authorities for removing Paige from hospital grounds. I called Dr. Francis for advice, and he told me to discharge her and find better medical care where we were treated with dignity and respect. I took his advice and switched her care to the Pittsburgh Children's Hospital, where we were referred to a top endocrinologist. The diabetes education was much better, and we were much happier.

We were given a lot of books that explained juvenile diabetes, but none a toddler could understand, so I started writing our own story in a pamphlet form I titled *Sugar and Spice*. I had two hundred and fifty of the books printed at a local printing business and distributed them to children who were diagnosed with Juvenile Diabetes. When Paige went to Head Start, I gave copies to each child in her class so they would understand her condition. The teachers invited me to read the book to the class.

Cherey visited Paige on weekends and became more confident and involved in managing her diabetes. When life stabilized for everyone, Paige went back to live with her mom in Emporium. Although I was sad to see her go, I knew it was best for everyone. I felt raising children helped me grow as a person, and I didn't want to deny my daughter the opportunity. I also didn't want Paige to someday resent me for keeping her away from her mom.

Not long after Paige was gone, Cliff retired from the paper mill where he worked for thirty-three years as a pipefitter. We now had time to spend with each other, riding bikes, cross-country skiing, and traveling.

Vietnam

———•—————————————•———

When Cliff and I had married, Caleb moved to Ridgway to live with us and enrolled in Elk County Catholic High School. He adapted well to the new school and enrolled in a Theology class. One day he brought home a book about Buddhism. Thinking Buddha was a false god; I reacted by telling him that Jesus is our savior. I now wish I would have taken the time to read the book rather than react. The teachings of Buddha fit Caleb's easy-going nature and despite my ignorance, he adopted some of the beliefs.

At school, he met a classmate whose mom knew my brother Warren. After Warren recovered from the burn accident, he started hosting exchange students who attended ECCHS. Caleb connected with his uncle and the exchange students. Warren invited Caleb to go to Thailand with him the next summer. I was a little apprehensive after the 9/11 tragedy but told myself that I wasn't going to live in fear. Warren convinced us to host an exchange student. We agreed, believing that learning about people from other cultures would be an excellent way to contribute to world peace.

Our first exchange student was a girl from Thailand, named Earn, who hardly spoke a word of English. Because of her poor English skills, she didn't qualify to come to America through the exchange student program but was able to get here because her parents paid an independent party that knew Warren. Earn was a pleasant, talented girl who played the piano and kept her room neat as a pin, but it was tough to communicate with her. Warren hosted two boys, a Thai boy named Tul and a Vietnamese boy named Tien.

While the kids were here, I learned quickly that they didn't care for American food. On Thanksgiving, I was excited to serve them a traditional turkey dinner, but when I put the mashed potatoes and gravy on the table, they moaned, "That looks like school food." They picked at the turkey but didn't touch the mashed potatoes or stuffing. I asked them what they liked to eat besides rice, but they had no words to describe their food. Warren knew a Vietnamese family who lived in Clarion. They invited us to their apartment for Vietnamese Beef Noodle Soup called pho. The soup was delicious, so I asked for the recipe. They told me it took at least twenty-four hours to simmer the broth and required ingredients that I didn't have in my kitchen.

Warren and I took a trip to an Asian Market in Pittsburgh, where exchange students stocked up on Asian Ramen Noodles. I picked up a Vietnamese cookbook, pho noodles, fresh ginger, Thai basil, cilantro, mung bean sprouts, limes, daikon radish, Hoisin sauce, Sriracha sauce, fish sauce, and pho seasoning packets. We had beef bones in the freezer, so thawed them out and filled a large kettle with water and added celery, onion, ginger, daikon radish, and seasoning packet. Our kitchen was swirling with the aroma of anise, black cardamom, cinnamon sticks, and beef. The students were so happy and said our house smelled like home.

When Tien and Tul returned the next year, we had a cookout to welcome them back and invited friends and family who knew them from last year. My friend, Kathleen Lawrie, brought a Japanese friend named Yuriko and her seven-year-old son, Akila. Kathleen was friends with Kim Granche, who told Kathleen that I lived a natural lifestyle and knew about eating healthy. Akila, whose nickname was Piyo, had just been diagnosed with leukemia. Yuriko had read about the importance of strengthening the immune system to beat cancer and wanted to start eating healthy. Yuriko had a peaceful presence. While we were talking, she told me about a book she was reading called *The Power of Now* by Eckhart Tolle. Not long after that, another friend was reading *The New Earth-Awakening to your Life's Purpose* by the same author.

When something knocks on my door twice, I pay attention. After reading both books, my life was transformed from worrying and fretting, to a life of peace and living in the present moment. I realized how much time I wasted thinking I should be doing something else other than what I was doing. If I was washing the dishes, I thought I should be working out in the garden. If I was working in the garden, I thought I should be inside doing dishes. If I was at the beach, I thought I should be out in the woods hiking. When I was out in the woods hiking, I thought I should be at the beach. My thought processes were maddening. Once I learned to keep them in the present moment, I felt a deep peace, and stillness like being deep in the ocean, far beneath the waves and turbulence of the sea.

When Yuriko met Cliff, she had a sense that her husband, Mike and my husband would get along. We invited them over for gatherings. I did as much as I could to teach Yuriko about preparing healthy foods, and she taught me how to make sushi rolls, California style, without fish. Cliff and Mike connected and arranged to do some contracting work together.

Along with undergoing chemotherapy, Yuriko put Piyo on a strict diet of no sugar or meat, lots of vegetables, and gave him Noni juice and other elixirs. Cleaning was an art form for Yuriko, and she fastidiously made sure no germs reached her beloved son during the treatments that weakened his immune system. The cancer went into remission, and Piyo grew into a handsome young man who graduated from high school and joined the U.S. Air Force.

Unfortunately, Yuriko was diagnosed with lung cancer shortly after Piyo was cured. She had left Japan when she was a teenager after marrying an American soldier from Ridgway, who was stationed in Japan. Her mother wasn't happy with her decision, and the two of them didn't talk for many years. When Piyo acquired cancer, Make-a-Wish sponsored a family trip to Japan. Yuriko was able to reconcile with her mother. She never told her mom that she had cancer but talked her into coming to the States to visit. As sick as Yuriko was, she planned on taking her mother and brother to see Niagara Falls. Mrs. Matsuda arrived in the states and was able to see Yuriko one day before she passed away at the young age of forty-seven.

A couple of days after Yuriko's death, I spent the day with Mrs. Matsuda. Although we couldn't communicate verbally, I sat and looked at family photos as she grieved the loss of her daughter. She talked to me in Japanese and I listened not only to her foreign words but to the universal language of facial expressions and body language. Through Mike, I told her what a good friend Yuriko was. I invited Mrs. Matsuda over to my house for supper. I had all the ingredients ready for us to make sushi together. When I showed her what Yuriko taught me, she beamed with pride. Mrs. Matsudo gave me extra tips on making sushi. I think of the two of them whenever I eat sushi.

In 2004, Tien's parents gifted us with a trip to Vietnam for taking care of their son while he was our exchange student. At first, Cliff and I were hesitant to travel to an underprivileged country but we couldn't pass up the offer. Cliff and I both read extensively about the Vietnam war. Cliff served in the Navy on the USS O'Brien from 1961-1965 in Long Beach California as a third-class boatswain's mate. When his four years were coming to a close, he was asked to ship over to Vietnam. He heard President Johnson proclaim the North Vietnamese had two hundred torpedos in Tonkin Bay, located on the coast of North Vietnam. Cliff thought it was a false flag and didn't want any part of it. Also, he hadn't had any leave for over two years. Four years away from his hometown of Johnsonburg and family was enough for him. He declined the offer to reenlist.

I still remembered the Vietnam war from when my brother Jack enlisted, in lieu of being drafted, in the early seventies and served in Vietnam. The resistance to the war was still fresh in my mind, with the chant, 'Hell No, We Won't Go' from the anti-war protesters ringing through my head as if it were yesterday. I still felt the grief of my friend Ruby Gilson at Mooseheart, when her brother Tim, was killed in the war.

Although it happened thirty years earlier, I still recalled attending the ceremony at the auditorium where his mother was awarded her son's purple heart medal.

To Tien, the war was just a small part of history, which he learned from Vietnamese history books, that took place when his parents were ten years old. We called it the Vietnam War. Tien knew it as the American War. Cliff and I were curious to learn more about the conflict.

Our flight from Pittsburgh to Vietnam was over twenty-four hours long with a layover in Japan and overnight stay in Singapore. Orchids and gardens made the airport feel like paradise. People in the food courts wore masks and gloves. During our layover, we took a bus tour of the Singapore coast with white sand and palm trees. The city was sparkling clean. The fine for littering in the country was death. I felt excited about spending two weeks in a tropical area.

The descent into Vietnam was another story. My heart dropped as the plane descended over tattered rooftops of buildings in the war-torn country. The airport was manned by men in uniform who ordered us from one place to another as we processed into the country. I didn't know what to expect next and wondered what we got ourselves into by coming to Vietnam.

Tien's parents, Mai and Huy, (pronounced My and Wee) greeted us with warm smiles. The couple didn't speak English, so Tien translated for us. Both Mai and Huy were originally from North Vietnam and relocated to Ho Chi Minh City-formerly Saigon-after the war. Tien's father spoke five different languages and was now learning English. We all piled into a Mercedes van they rented to transport us to the hotel where we would be staying.

I was relieved to know we wouldn't be sleeping on dirt floors. The hotel had marble floors and walls that didn't show a speck of dust. When we checked in, the staff asked that we relinquish our passports, which made me extremely nervous.

What if there was a coup during our stay and we couldn't leave the country? I felt trapped, but Tien's parents convinced us everything was alright.

For supper, they took us to our first Vietnamese restaurant located on the third floor of a building. While we were walking up the steps, Cliff noticed smoke pouring out of the building and thought it was on fire. Tien explained that the steam was from the humidity in the air colliding with a fan.

When Tien's parents told the owners we were American guests, they rolled out the red carpet for us, especially Cliff. They were partial to men, especially American men. The South Vietnamese were grateful for the help they received while trying to free themselves from the communist rule of North Vietnam. The waitresses brought Cliff large servings of food and kept him supplied with cold cans of Tiger beer.

Before we left for Vietnam, I tried to prepare myself for the heat by not using air conditioning in the car while I was driving during the summer. Nothing could have prepared me for the noise and smells of Ho Chi Minh city, populated by over six million people. Motorbikes crowded the streets that reeked of urine and fish sauce. Horns on the vehicles beeped incessantly. Trying to cross a road was like crossing a raging river. We stepped into the traffic and walked gingerly as the moving bikes made their way around us.

Tien's parents were fantastic hosts and took us to see many sites in Vietnam, including a boat ride on the Mekong Delta, where people were bathing and washing their clothes in the muddy water. We also went to remote islands and to Nha Trang Beach along the China Sea, where we spent two days aboard a bright blue painted boat with wood benches for seats. After the Americans pulled out of the war in the mid-1970s, refugees used the boats to flee the impending punishment of the North Vietnamese. It was hard for us to envision the vessel crowded with South Vietnamese refugees crossing the Atlantic Ocean to America. We snorkeled and saw beautiful corals and fish in the clear water while birds flew in and out of mountainous caves. Tien explained the birds were called swiftlets and they made nests from salvia, which the Vietnamese harvested to make Bird's Nest Drink and other delicacies that they believed were aphrodisiacs.

The second day on the boat, I became seasick and began thinking of American food to stave off nausea. I had visions of spaghetti, turkey and stuffing, ham and mashed potatoes, and juicy hamburgers cooked on the grill. When we got off the boat, I was famished. We found a seaside restaurant that served square burgers served on a white piece of bread. Catsup wasn't available in Vietnam. As I was gobbling down the burger, a large rat, the size of a housecat, ran in front of our table. I couldn't finish my meal.

The majority of the restaurants were open-air. Before each meal, we were presented with a clean white washcloth to wash our hands before we ate. After we finished eating, little children would sneak up and steal the leftover food. For a big treat, Tien's parents took us to a restaurant that served crocodile. It tasted like fatty pork. At some of the restaurants, we grilled meat that was brought to the table raw, on a Hibachi burning with fiery red coals. The only food I wasn't able to eat was goat brains.

Before going to Vietnam, I told Tien I would like to learn how to cook Vietnamese food while visiting his country. I wanted his mom to know that we didn't expect to eat out and that I was willing to help out in the kitchen.

Tien's house had a little stove and refrigerator, which they used to store food. They didn't cook as it was easier to buy food from street vendors. Every morning we had a bowl of pho at an outdoor restaurant and then went swimming in the public pool.

Mai honored my request and arranged for me to attend a cooking class. Cliff, Mai, and I traveled to the course together. After the class, Mai commented on how good Cliff was to me. Translated through Tien, she said, "American men are so nice. It's uncommon for Vietnamese men to help with domestic chores. Wives are treated like hired help."

I communicated back, "Not every American man is as kind as Cliff."

One evening, Mai and Huy prepared an out of season Tet New Year dinner for us in their home. It was like having Christmas in July. When we went to their house the table was decorated with beautiful dishes and food. Mai had a big smile on her face and couldn't wait to tell us that Huy helped her prepare the meal, just like Cliff helps me. Huy was smiling and said how happy he was helping Mai. We loved the dragon fruit, freshly squeezed orange juice, Banh Chung, Vietnamese rolls, and other delicacies, but more than that, we felt good about helping Mai and Huy improve their relationship.

Tien's parents took us to the Cu Chi tunnels that the Vietnamese used in the French war. The Vietnamese dug down three stories through ground that was hard as cement, to make underground kitchens, school rooms, sewing rooms, and rooms to make primitive traps for the enemy. Cliff and I squeezed into one of the tunnels where there were large underground rooms. An escape tunnel led to the Saigon River, where they could swim to freedom if the tunnels were discovered. During the Vietnamese/American conflict, our soldiers unknowingly set up a military base above the site that the Vietnamese built during the French war, losing numerous soldiers until they found the tunnels. They then doused the tunnels with napalm to kill the Vietnamese.

We also visited a Vietnamese museum where deformed babies were preserved in formaldehyde filled jars. The Vietnamese claimed that Agent Orange, a defoliant chemical used by the Americans caused birth defects.

Medals and letters of regret from American soldiers were displayed in glass cases. Out of their regret for having devastated their beautiful homeland, some American soldiers relinquished their battle medals to the kind people of Vietnam. It was a sobering experience for Cliff and me; neither one of us had heard the other side of the war. We bought a little paperback book titled *The Sorrow of War* by Bao Ninh. When we returned to our hotel room, I read the book cover to cover in one night. The novel helped me see the similarities between American soldiers and Vietnamese soldiers. No one won the war.

While traveling through the Vietnamese countryside, we stopped at a house where a young boy, wearing tattered blue jeans and no shirt, was sitting on a marble floor carving images of Jesus and the Blessed Mother for the Catholic Churches. Ten percent of the country is Catholic; the majority of people practice Buddhism mixed with Confucianism and Taoism. Tien's parents had a shrine to Than Thai, the God of wealth in their home. Each day they placed fruit and flowers around a locked safe where they kept their money. Tien's parents strongly believed in luck, and eight was a lucky number. When one of the eight fish in their fish tank died, they had to immediately replace it with another fish. Also, they told us that the Mekong Delta has eight rivers when it actually has nine.

Their beliefs sounded hokey to us until we bought a statue of the crucifix. When they asked us who the man on the cross was, we tried to explain Christianity to them. I tried to explain that there's a Being in the sky who loves us and to whom we pray. Jesus was a man who came to earth from heaven to forgive us of our sins. While trying to explain God and Jesus so they could understand, it felt as if I was talking about Santa Claus. Our belief in God sounded as irrational to them as their belief in luck did to us.

After spending two weeks in Vietnam, both Cliff and I couldn't wait to eat American food. On our return home, when we stopped in Singapore, we ran to a McDonald's restaurant and devoured quarter-pound hamburgers and French fries. This was the first time that Cliff and I ate fast food since we met.

When the plane was landing in Buffalo, I couldn't quit singing the song, *God Bless America*. I felt grateful to live in a free country with modern conveniences. The next week, when I went to the YMCA to swim, people were complaining because the water was a little cloudy. I thought if they went to Vietnam and swam in the Mekong Delta, they would be grateful for the lovely pool at the YMCA. I dove into the water and swam laps with the words of *God Bless America* going through my head.

Visiting a third world country changed my perspective on life. Although Cliff and I aren't wealthy, we have more than many people throughout the world. There's not one day I take what we have for granted. Over the years, I've mastered making pho, and each time I taste the soup, I thank my brother Warren for making the introduction which led to our deep exposure to the Vietnamese culture.

When Tien returned to America for his senior year of high school, we learned that Tien's parents expected us to help Tien through college. From their point of view, we were rich, but by American standards, we were lower middle class. At the time, it was all we could do to take care of our own family.

Caleb was ready to graduate from high school, and I was caring for a grandchild with a life-threatening illness. Tien went back to live with my brother Warren who helped him further his education.

Marcellus Shale

C liff and I attended a political event in 2004 where Pennsylvania Representative, Dan Surra, spoke about the Marcellus Shale and the economic boom it was going to bring to Elk County. When we returned home that same evening, we looked up Marcellus Shale online. According to the State Impact website, Pennsylvania Marcellus Shale is a sedimentary rock buried thousands of feet beneath the earth's surface. It stretches from upstate New York, south through Pennsylvania, into West Virginia and western parts of Ohio. Named after a town in upstate New York, the rock itself is millions of years old, formed from mud and organic material.

The natural gas created as a by-product over millions of years of decomposition is trapped in tiny spaces and fissures within the rock. The Marcellus Shale is just one of many shale formations across the world. A technique called hydraulic fracturing (a.k.a. fracking) that involved injecting water, sand, and chemicals at high pressures into the shale to release the fuel trapped inside, used to allow huge amounts of unrecoverable natural gas to be accessed.

Not long after we heard Dan Surra speak, there was a talk from our neighbors about the money they could make from leasing their gas and mineral rights to gas companies. It sounded like we were back in the times of the gold rush.

Because Cliff had read about the dangers of fracking, in Wyoming, Colorado, Texas, and Oklahoma, he became alarmed when it began hitting close to home. He was aware that the procedure compromised the land and water. Growing up hiking, biking, skiing and walking the woodlands in Elk County, he now felt as if his sacred land was being invaded. Like Paul Revere, Cliff set out to warn our neighbors and friends about the dire consequences of the drilling.

Farmers and were selling the mineral rights to their properties without being aware of the environmental dangers of fracking. And some were being taken advantage of financially. One of our neighbors attended a meeting sponsored by Penn State and signed a five-year lease for $350 an acre of his farmland. Not long after that, other farmers were being offered up to $2500 an acre. Our neighbor felt cheated.

Before long, wires with electrical currents were installed along roadways to determine the depth of the Marcellus Shale. Next, trucks laden with sand and concrete flooded the Pennsylvania roads. Cliff got wind of a drilling pad being built close to the headwaters of the Clarion River.

Fracking had the potential to contaminate water, making it unsafe to drink. Noise pollution from trucks and escaping fumes were also concerns. And then there was a flow back fluid called brine that needed to be disposed of. The brine was a by-product that contained radioactive waste and other chemicals. Trucks marked 'residual waste' started dumping the waste into the Clarion River that flowed downstream to people's drinking water in Pittsburgh and other communities. In protest, we wrote letters to the editor, attended local meetings to voice our concerns, and contacted the media.

Cliff read about a group that was meeting in DuBois to address the environmental concerns of the Marcellus Shale drilling. When he attended the meeting, he met a woman named Jenny Lisak from Falls Creek, who owned an organic farm and was concerned about the drilling in her backyard. Jenny invited a group called the Community Environmental Legal Defense (CELDF) that was helping people to protect the land. Cliff was dismayed to find out the corporations had more rights than the people. At the meeting, he picked up a No Fracking sign and hung it on the side of the barn facing the road. We wanted people to know where we stood on the issue.

We met some like-minded people who were concerned about the environment and organized a local group called CARES (Citizens Advocating for Responsible Environmental Stewardship) in Elk County. Kim Forsythe had a degree in environmental science and had recently moved to Ridgway with her husband Tom, who was the superintendent of the Ridgway School District. The couple's uncle had six hundred acres of farmland in Tioga county that he had leased to the oil and gas companies. He gave Tom and Kim thirteen acres of land, but they didn't want to build on it because the water was polluted from fracking. Kim had done extensive research on the chemicals used in fracking. Mike Kamandulis, taught Earth science in Johnsonburg and presented well-researched information to the community. Bill and Kim Granche, who were both educators, tirelessly wrote letters to the editor voicing their environmental concerns.

When we learned another Marcellus Shale Well pad was scheduled to be built close to the Ridgway Reservoir, we became alarmed and attended township meetings to raise our concerns. I made a sign that read 'We Can't Drink Money' and invited the local news channel to the meeting. Cliff learned that local rules could be changed by having a shift in the township's way of governing to Home Rule. He decided to run for township supervisor. Rick Glover, who was a township supervisor at the time, pitched in and led a letter-writing campaign to educate people living in the township. I did my best to promote his effort by making up business cards and campaigning, but we lost the election by a narrow margin.

A Marcellus Shale well was installed not far from our house, and at night we could see an eternal flame of gas being burnt off. Cliff was on the phone with people day and night trying to convince them to join us in the fight to stop the drilling. He succeeded in getting more people involved with CARES but not enough to stop the drilling.

The situation started to divide the community. A county commissioner, elected to represent all the people, wrote a Letter to the Editor published in the Ridgway Record where she likened us to anarchists. It was hurtful to read this from someone who previously called us friends. It seemed community interest went from procuring local foods and eating healthy to getting money from the Marcellus Shale.

The situation felt hopeless. I became weary of hearing Cliff complaining and warning people about the violation of our constitutional rights and the possible danger to the environment. Every day it felt like a raincloud was hovering over us. During this time, Cliff's son Steve passed away at the age of forty-two. Due to all this stress, Cliff's immune system was compromised and resulted in a severe case of shingles that endangered his eyes. I believed the stress of trying to stop the fracking was taking a toll on him and our relationship.

I found myself wanting to dissociate from everything. I didn't want to talk to Dr. Francis because he had recently lost his wife and was having health problems. I came across the book *Coping with Trauma-Related Dissociation* by Dutch authors, Suzette Boon, Kathy Steele and Onno Van Der Hart. The book helped me to stay in the present moment by taking the time to be aware of three things: what I could hear, what I could see and what I could taste. The book was full of other tips to help me get through stressful times.

I finally told Cliff, "I can't live like this anymore. I know firsthand what it feels like for someone to come in and take over my property. It happened to my father's farm when I was a child. For twenty-five years, when I was a Jehovah's Witness, I believed the world was coming to an end every single day. I had no hope for the future. I don't want to live in fear one day longer." Although it wasn't easy for Cliff to give up something he believed in passionately, he toned down his rhetoric, and the stress eased up.

I learned from the Marcellus Shale experience that Republicans not only have conservative values, but they promote capitalism. I also believed in capitalism, but not in putting money ahead of human well-being and environmental safety--what I call capitalism run amok. On the other hand, I didn't believe in giving handouts to people who are capable of doing work or community service in return for their benefits. I had worked with children whose parents and grandparents were generationally dependent on public assistance. I switched my party affiliation to Independent.

One day while Cliff was working in the barn, Dunk, a guy he knew from Johnsonburg stopped by to tell Cliff that one of his childhood friends, Dennis Glover, nicknamed Nip, had moved back to Johnsonburg and recently lost his son in the Iraq War. Cliff didn't hesitate to find out where Nip was living in Johnsonburg and stopped by to pay his respects. The two friends parted ways when they entered the Navy but even after forty years, they picked up where they had left off. They reminisced about playing tag, kick the can, and even getting in trouble for stealing beer when they were teenagers. The two of them had been made to go down to the police station and make amends.

Nip was in a state of deep grief after losing his son Michael who had enlisted in the Marine National Guard after the 9/11 attack. While in Iraq, he was shot down by a sniper. Cliff invited Nip out to the house to meet me. Nip was smitten by the goats and enjoyed spending time in the barn, helping Cliff with barn chores. He told us he was dating his high school sweetheart, Barb Ross. The two of them soon married and lived in Pittsburgh.

As a diversion from his grief, Nip started writing and decided to write an entertaining children's book about our goats creating anarchy in the barn. He hired an artist from Pittsburgh to illustrate the book and included my two granddaughters, Ariana and Paige, in the story. I later read the book to elementary school children. It was an especially big hit when I read it to my granddaughter's classes as a guest reader. Their classmates wanted to know how they got to be characters in a book.

Life After Fifty

I n 2007, I turned fifty years old and decided to have a birthday party for myself at the end of August. It was my first real birthday party and I wanted it to be something memorable, so we had a pig and goat roast. Cliff and my son Justin stayed up all night cooking the meat so that it was well done on the day of the event. Friends and family, including my children's friends from the years of growing up as Jehovah's Witnesses, joined us for the celebration.

Chelsey, who was living in upstate New York, had recently left Jehovah's Witnesses. She was struggling with family members who would no longer talk to her. Before my birthday, her younger brother Nathan had stopped by to say hello while passing by our house. I wasn't home at the time, but Nathan told Cliff I was like his second mother when he was growing up. Although being raised a Jehovah's Witness, he never followed his sister's footsteps of being baptized in the faith. Even though he wasn't following the religion, he didn't have the same struggle with his family not talking to him that his sister did. Chelsey was suffering the consequences of a decision she made to be baptized when she was an impressionable young teenager and wanted to fit in with other Witnesses her age.

Justin's best friend John and his partner Stacy, who were both raised in the religion, also joined us for my birthday celebration. Since I had left the faith, John's mom, Sharon Scarpelli, had committed suicide while she was a Jehovah's Witness. The pain of not being able to talk to her disfellowshipped children was too great, so one night, she took a pistol, drove to a hotel, and shot herself. John's brother Dan had since died of an overdose of grain alcohol.

After spending a few years in prison, John was in an immense amount of psychological pain and extremely angry at his parents for raising him as Jehovah's Witness. He and Stacy had two children, and they were doing their best to be a family, but the hurt and pain overcame John. On a rainy night, he didn't come home. When Stacy went looking for him, she found him in the truck with his wrists slit.

Numerous studies regarding Jehovah's Witnesses verify that mental illness is higher within that demographic than that found in virtually every other American religion. According to Jerry Bergman, Ph.D., "Jehovah's Witnesses have carefully cultivated a public image of a God-fearing devoted people, determined to ferret out God's truth from the scriptures and live their lives fully accordingly. Behind this façade, lies a nightmare which results in a rash of mental illness and social problems." Not only do Jehovah's Witnesses have a high rate of mental illness, but they are also discouraged from receiving professional help for psychological problems. The Scarpelli family is a case in point.

I was able to stay in contact with other kids who were Jehovah's Witnesses on social media. Ami, the young girl who was sent away by her mom for wanting to have a boyfriend when she was a teenager, was a few years older than my children. After leaving the religion, she attended college, married her teenage sweetheart and was working at Cornell University. The two of us met at Watkins Glen. I met her little girl Lena, who her own mother hadn't yet met. Her mother had told her sister that she went to a convention and was instructed not to talk to grandchildren because baby snakes grow up to be big snakes.

While hiking the gorge, Ami told me how much I meant to her while she was growing up, and that she often wished I could have been her mother. At times I had survivor's guilt that I was able to get out of the religion, but their parents had not.

One of my greatest joys was hearing from Beth Bracken, who was now living in Nebraska. She had recently left Jehovah's Witnesses and was going through a custody battle for her teenage daughter. I flew out to Nebraska to testify about Beth's good character. When Beth picked me up from the airport, she had just purchased a beautiful turquoise prom dress for her stepdaughter, Paige. The sequins in the dress matched the sparkle in Beth's eyes that came from giving a teenage girl something she lacked in her, and now, her daughter's life. Beth's daughter was being instructed not to talk to her mother. Beth was also struggling with the emotional trauma of being shunned by her oldest son, mom, and siblings who were Jehovah's Witnesses. It was painful to see first-hand how damaging the religion is to families. I was able to help Beth by giving her books that I had read, by Bonnie Zieman, who wrote about her experience leaving Jehovah's Witnesses. I was honored to learn I had become known as the 'Mother Hen' for the adult children who left the religion.

After turning fifty, as I reflected on my life, I felt grateful for everything I had; all of my dreams had come true. I was free and living on a beautiful piece of property, growing my food, and raising animals. I was back at where I started in life before my father died. Living off the land was deeply embedded in my soul during the first three years of my life.

This time my life had a different ending. I had a partner who loved and supported me. Instead of asking God for anything more, I looked up at the blue, cloudless sky and asked, "God, what can I do for you?" I began to wonder just who God was. This question took me on a spiritual journey that I never imagined.

On a Sunday before Easter, on my way to the Methodist church, I drove by the Grace Episcopal Church and at the last minute, decided to check out their services. The attendance was sparse, so I tried to sit discreetly in one of the back pews but was noticed by a woman who made sure I had the program, songbook, and Book of Common Prayer before the services began. I felt overwhelmed by all the literature so placed it on the pew. The Episcopal Church was unlike any protestant service I had attended. A woman priest dressed in a white robe gave an eloquent sermon. The music was a little dreary, and I couldn't keep up with all the prayers and answers to prayers, so I decided not to participate but to observe.

After the service, everyone was invited to have coffee in the social room. Before I could sneak out the back door, the priest came over and introduced herself as Mary and thanked me for visiting. I was drawn to Mary's humbleness and sincere warmth. She invited me to have coffee, but I told her that Cliff and I had a bike ride planned for the afternoon. I felt like I might have found a church home. In the back of my mind, I heard a voice reminding me never to put God in a box again.

I pondered on who or what God was and found I no longer viewed God as an authoritative male figure. Instead, I sensed God to be a loving presence tinged with a bit of mystery. Reverend Mary invited me to read the Bible with her and to discuss what we read each week. Initially, I was concerned about Jehovah's Witness teachings coming back into my head. Reverend Mary suggested not to read the scriptures literally but to look for allegories in the Bible. I found reading the Bible much more comfortable as I wasn't trying to make sense out of all the events and verses. Together we read the book of Daniel and Ruth. I enjoyed spending time with Reverend Mary and having spiritual discussions with another person.

Everyone at the church was kind and welcoming.

Ironically, Brandi's first-grade teacher, Mrs. Masson, who lived in St. Marys, was a devout Episcopalian. When I told her she had taught my daughter, who was now in her thirties, she welcomed me with a warm hug.

I continued to attend the Sunday services and volunteered to teach the children Sunday school, which was only one or two children. When my grandchildren visited on the weekends, I took them along, and we planned activities in the social hall. The children performed a Christmas play. On Easter, Paige and Ariana were baptized by Reverend Mary.

On Wednesday mornings, I attended the healing mass. Reverend Mary's words were always wise, kind, and soothing. At one of the masses, I had a vision of a beautiful rainbow shining through the stained-glass windows. The vivid colors that made one rainbow, depicted all the separate parts of myself that blended into oneself. For the first time in my life, I felt whole.

Reverend Mary invited me to be received in the church. I wasn't quite sure what was required and told her that I would do it, with the understanding that I was only traveling through and wouldn't be staying. I came across Margaret Guenther's spiritual writings and read all her books cover to cover. I learned that the Episcopal Church originated when King Henry VIII split from the Roman Catholic Church in 1534 when the pope refused to grant the king an annulment. I was on a mission to find out where religion originated.

At about the same time, Reverend Mary was being transferred to a different parish, Cliff and I stopped at a yard sale near Marienville. An older man, who was recently widowed, was selling all of his wife's belongings. While rummaging through her journals, I came across three missals about St. Francis and purchased them for a few cents. When I returned home, I read the journals cover to cover and felt that following the life of St. Francis was my path. His experience of simplicity and his fondness for animals resonated with me. I felt a calling to follow the path of St. Francis. I searched online for a community of Franciscans and found one in upstate New York. The only problem was that it required that I belong to the Catholic Church. I began attending mass at St. Leo's Church, which had recently been remodeled. I enjoyed the beauty and light of the church, compared to the dark ceiling of the Episcopal Church. I also liked the fact the masses were well attended so I could remain anonymous.

As I was reading the Sunday announcements in the weekly bulletin, a retreat at the Bethany Retreat Center in Frenchville, Pennsylvania, caught my attention. While working for Penn State, I attended programs at the Retreat Center, located in a picturesque setting with a beautiful chapel. The grounds were well kept with a boxwood shrub bordered labyrinth. I was familiar with labyrinths from my friend Pat Martin who designed one for the hospice Serenity Garden in St. Marys. Labyrinths have long been used as meditation and prayer tools. They are patterned walkways that represent a journey to our center and back again out into the world.

The retreat I attended was on finding purpose in the second half of life. The instructor was a former Dominican nun. We did a variety of activities, including making a mandala from pictures we cut out of magazines. My mandala included a little girl writing, who I thought represented my ten-year-old granddaughter, who enjoyed writing. After meditating on the mandala, it dawned on me that there was a little girl inside of me that needed to write. I listened to that voice and started to attend classes and workshops on writing to inspire me. I always thought of writing a book about the years I spent at Mooseheart but couldn't get past the first chapter, which I rewrote over a dozen times. It felt as if I were spinning my wheels in a foot of mud.

While foraging around in a second-hand store, I discovered a book titled *Blackbird--A Childhood Lost and Found* by Jennifer Lauck, for fifty cents. When I returned home, I read the book cover to cover and was in awe of how Jennifer was able to write about her painful childhood that was similar to mine. I wondered how she managed the emotion that I knew went hand in hand with writing her story. I did an internet search on the book and came across her writing website that had free podcasts. I watched a few of them and then signed up for her online mailing list.

In February of the next year, when I was experiencing cabin fever, I received an email from Jennifer inviting people on her mailing list to a writer's retreat in Manzanita Beach, Oregon. I was sitting at my writing desk, and Cliff was in the kitchen preparing our usual breakfast of fried eggs, bacon, and toast.

"Hey Cliff, what would you think of me going to Oregon for a writing retreat?"

"How much does it cost?"

When I told him the price, he said, "I think you should go." I never expected him to take the idea seriously.

"We don't have enough money in our bank account right now. Maybe next year."

"When is it?"

"August."

"I have a road bike I've been thinking of selling that will help pay for the trip." I couldn't believe my ears. One minute I was only dreaming and the next minute, my dreams were coming true right before my eyes.

Within a month, Cliff sold the road bike to a young man. When he came out to the house to pick up the bike, he asked why Cliff was selling it. Cliff told him about the writing retreat. The young man handed me an extra one hundred dollars. Never in my life had I felt the wind beneath my wings as I did in that minute. I hadn't prayed for this to happen; it just did. I booked a flight to Portland, Oregon, and made arrangements to stay at a rental with three other women who were writing their memoirs.

From the minute I got off the plane in Oregon, I felt at home in the airport lined with stores selling clothing in earth tone colors made from natural fibers. Remarkably, the airport bathrooms had composting toilets. I connected with Chloe, who flew in from the southwest. She was writing about her childhood years being raised in the wilderness. We hopped in a rental car and drove from Portland to Manzanita Beach together. I fell in love with the rugged west coastline. When I set my eyes on the Pacific Ocean, I thought back to the time that Dr. Francis had told me my mother was as far away as Oregon. The nurturing, gentle sound of the waves soothed my soul. I felt surrounded by pure love. My heart was filled with gratitude to Cliff and the universe for helping me arrive.

My three roommates arrived the next day. Angela was writing about losing her father to gun violence, Sherry was writing about her experience of being coerced by a Muslim man to have an abortion, Beth from Philadelphia, (we were the only two from the East coast) was writing about an abusive childhood, and I was writing about the ten years I spent in an orphanage.

Along with twenty other participants, over five days, I learned the craft of writing memoir from Jennifer. In the evening, we sat around a fire and listened to each other's writings. I was surprised when people took an interest in my story and felt as if I had something worthwhile to write about. We also had time to enjoy Manzanita Beach, which my roommate, Angela, described as 'granola town' with hippies, health food stores, and massage spas.

When I returned home, I began in earnest to write my memoir and set an intention to have it published by the time I was sixty years old. I read multiple books on writing and attended creative writing classes at Pitt Bradford and the Chautauqua Institute in New York state. The writing tip that helped me the most was what I gleaned from a book written by Ann Lamont. Her suggestion was to quiet the inner critic. The writing process began to flow, and I was well on my way to finally writing my memoir.

Coldwater

———•———————————————————•———

Cliff's granddaughter, Larissa had moved to Galena, Illinois after graduating from Full Sails Film school. She and her partner Matt, now had two daughters, making us great grandparents. Larissa and Matt invited us to their house for Easter. I told Cliff that I would like to visit my sister-in-law, Dottie, in Michigan on our way out. It had been twenty-five years since my brother, Paul, had passed away. I hadn't been to Michigan since his funeral. Before we left for the trip, I checked out three audiobooks from the Ridgway Public Library. We listened to the two shorter ones on our drive out. I saved the longest audiobook, *The First Phone Call from Heaven* by Mitch Albom, for the long trek home.

While visiting Dottie, I felt Paul's presence in the house the minute I walked in. When I couldn't find a light switch in the upstairs bathroom, I asked Paul where it was at and immediately located it. While checking out Dottie's book collection, the book *The Light Beyond* by Raymond A. Moody, Jr., M.D., about near-death experiences caught my attention.

When Dottie noticed my interest in the book, she told me reading it helped her immensely after Paul had passed away. She let me borrow the book to read and I promised I would return it to her. As we were driving from Michigan to Illinois, I thought of Paul when we passed road signs to the Sand Dunes on Lake Michigan. Paul had enjoyed camping there with his family.

After a two-day visit with our granddaughters in Illinois, we headed back east. We decided to drive through Chicago on a Sunday night to miss the traffic and stay overnight in Indiana. Cliff drove as we left Galena. I popped in the first CD of the set and we began listening to the book. It wasn't long before I decided I didn't want to finish listening to the book about five people who lost their loved ones.

After ejecting the CD I said to Cliff, "This story feels depressing. I'm enjoying my time off from working with the elderly and hospice volunteer work." I was in my third year of providing respite for caregivers whose loved ones were dying. As fulfilling as the work was, caring for people who were in their final days was draining and often sad.

I put the CD back in the case and turned on the radio.

We stayed overnight at a hotel on the Illinois-Indiana state border. In the morning, while we were having breakfast at Bob Evans, as Cliff was sipping on a cup of hot black coffee and I was eating a veggie omelet, he said, "I was enjoying the book we were listening to yesterday. I often wonder what I would say to Stephen if I had one more phone call with him."

The morning sun was beginning to rise when we got in the car to head home. I told Cliff, "You can put the maps away because I know the way home like the back of my hand." I thought the drive from Illinois to Pennsylvania was indelibly etched in my mind. I would never forget the long journey on Interstate 80 when I finally got out of Mooseheart in 1971. It was my first ride to freedom. After entering the four-lane highway, I put in the first CD and started listening to the story from the beginning. I decided not to judge the story but to listen to the plot and character development. It didn't take long to get enthralled with the characters and storyline. The setting of the book was in Coldwater, Michigan, which I assumed was a fictitious location.

As we were driving for a few hours, I noticed a sign to Battlefield, Michigan. I ejected the CD and told Cliff we must have gotten off a wrong exit while listening to the book. I started beating myself up for adding extra hours to an already long trip. I pulled the car over and took the map out of the glove compartment. When I got oriented, I noticed we were only forty miles off course. A southern route from Battlecreek to Interstate 80 would get us back on track quickly.

As we resumed listening to the book, I began to wonder what it would be like to have one last conversation with Paul. I thought about how I felt his presence while visiting Dottie. My mind was jolted from daydreaming, when I caught a glimpse of a green sign with white letters that read COLDWATER.

I said to Cliff, "Did you just see that sign?"

"What? Are we on the wrong road again?"

"No, the sign said Coldwater. That's the name of the setting of the book we are listening to."

He replied, "Don't tell me this is another one of your miracles."

"It is!"

As clear as day, I heard Paul chiding me for taking a wrong turn. Teasing was his nature.

Then he said, "Thanks for keeping in touch with Dottie, Coleen, and Jim."

I silently told my brother how much everyone missed him and thanked him for getting me out of Mooseheart. It was comforting to feel his presence the rest of the way home through the long state of Ohio and into Pennsylvania.

After returning home, I read *The Light Beyond* in one day and ordered more books by the same author. Moody's testimonials and thorough research about life after death convinced me that our loved ones do not suffer after death, and neither should we. After hearing from my Uncle

Henry years earlier, and now from my brother Paul, I don't doubt the presence of loved ones in our lives, when we choose to think about them and engage in conversation with them. They are only one breath away. I feel the presence of my ancestors when I'm working in the garden and enjoying walks in the woods, just as they did. I hear my parents apologizing for what happened in my childhood. These experiences bring me an immeasurable amount of comfort and peace.

Autobiography of a Yogi

O ur cottage industry at Little Mill Creek continued to grow, and we began selling goat milk soap, baked goods, apple butter, hot pepper jelly, and spicy mustard at festivals. One year we set up at the Ridgway Rendezvous, an international chainsaw carving held in Ridgway each year. When we heard that Liz and Rick Boni were looking for people to host carvers from different countries, we offered our home but didn't want to host anyone who smoked or who needed driven back and forth to town. That eliminated the majority of carvers that required accommodations. In early January, I received a phone call from Liz asking if I would be interested in hosting a woman from Israel who didn't smoke and leased her car.

Maly was in her mid-forties and had visited Ridgway with her husband, who was writing a botanical book about plants in America. While in America, they wanted to see the elk in Benezette and on their way, they drove through Ridgway. The carvings in front of the Appalachian Arts building on top of Boot Jack caught Maly's eye. She told her husband to stop because she wanted to learn how to carve wood. Her profession in Israel was a stone carver. They stayed at the Royal Motel for a week while she learned the basics of wood carving from Rick Boni. She returned to the States for the Rendezvous and needed a place to stay.

Cliff and I enjoyed learning about different cultures and were excited to learn more about Israel. Maly was Jewish and taught us about the Jewish faith, in addition to teaching me how to make eggplant with tahini sauce, falafel, and pita bread with Zaatar, a seasoning she brought from Israel. Cliff helped her get her saw running and pulled her out of the snow when she was stuck in our driveway. She had never driven in snow before.

On a cold day in January, Liz called to tell me that a journalist from the *Pennsylvania Pursuits* travel magazine was on the way to our house to interview us. Cliff and I weren't prepared for guests but invited the young woman and her fiancé, who was traveling with her into our home. The young woman from the Philadelphia area told us that Liz spoke highly of us and thought our business would be an excellent addition to the article she was writing about Elk County.

Cliff and I were sitting down for lunch and served the sojourners a bowl of black bean soup that had been simmering on the stove. As they were finishing up the soup, the fiancé, who was studying for his bar exam, asked, "Can I look in your refrigerator?"

The journalist's face blushed, "Why would you ask them that?"

"I'm curious what's in their fridge since they don't eat any processed foods."

I told the couple that they were more than welcome to peek in our fridge. When I opened the door, the gentleman was surprised to see half-gallon glass canning jars of goat milk, fresh vegetables, cheese, and plastic containers with leftovers.

After visiting, they thanked us for our hospitality. The journalist told us she would send us a copy of the magazine when it was published. To our surprise, when the magazine arrived in the mail, we were the main feature of the piece about Elk County.

Within a month, we received a phone call from a woman named Diane. When I answered the phone, it was as if I were talking to a long-lost friend.

"Hey Jeanette, we want to visit your goat farm. My husband, Howard, told me that I could do anything I wanted for my birthday. I told him I wanted to visit you and Cliff."

In a guarded voice, I asked, "Do I know you?"

"No, my name is Diane, and I read about you and Cliff in a travel journal, and after reading the article, I knew I wanted to meet you. We have two home-schooled teenage daughters, and they would love to visit your goat farm. We also want to see the elk featured in the journal."

I told Diane when we would be home, and we coordinated our schedules for a visit. She and her family drove from Kent Island, Maryland, and arrived at our place just as we were eating supper. We invited the four of them, all dressed in tie-dyed t-shirts, to join us for supper. Diane had packed food and brought lentil pate and other local foods that matched our healthy cuisine from her car. Paige, who was visiting me for the weekend, got along well with Liza and Emma. Howard and Cliff got along well, and within an hour, we felt as if we had known the family forever.

As it was getting dark, they asked where the closest hotel was. We told them that it might be difficult getting a room so late and invited them to camp out in our living room. In the morning, while enjoying breakfast together, I suggested that perhaps we could visit them as Paige wanted to see the ocean. They told us they had a beach house rented at the Outer Banks at the end of August and invited us to stay with them for a week. Paige, her mom, and her boyfriend, Lee, and I took them up on their offer and had a fantastic vacation together, enjoying the beauty of the Atlantic Ocean.

The next spring Cliff and I drove the grandkids out to Howard and Diane's house in Kent Island. While visiting, I was perusing their book collection for something interesting to read. Howard handed me a paperback copy of *Autobiography of a Yogi* and said, "I think you will like this book."

He was right! The spiritual book resonated with me. I liked how it didn't bash other religions but explained what the Hindi religion taught. It made sense that there would be prophets, other than Jesus, whom God sent to the earth to reach people spiritually. I often wondered how the millions of people in Africa, India, and other third world countries would receive salvation if they hadn't heard of Jesus. The practical suggestions for practicing meditation and quieting the mind to connect with God were helpful. Finding this book was like finding a map to the spiritual path I was navigating.

I started searching for more information on the Hindi religion and met a young man from Ridgway who had moved from Los Angeles, California. Fritz had spent time at an Ashram and was familiar with the spiritual practice of meditation. He introduced me to *The Gospel of Sri Ramakrishna*. After reading the book, I felt I got more out of it in one reading than I did reading the Bible a dozen times.

Although Ramakrishna was a Hindi, he traveled the world to experience different religions. He concluded that there is good in every religion. He recommended being like a bee that extracts nectar from all the beautiful flowers; take all the good out of each religion, but don't ever let one of them tie a noose around your neck. I was impressed that the book didn't criticize other religions as Christianity sometimes does.

Fritz invited me to meet a Swami who was visiting him from California. I gathered up some friends who I thought might be interested and attended an event that included a meal afterward. The peace that the orange-robed Swami exuded was calmer than any other religious leader I had met. The Swami instructed us on how to conquer the mind by using illustrations such as keeping the flame of a candle still. He also likened the mind to a monkey that likes to run all over the place, but we needed to gently bring the mind back to our center. While having a lunch of Indian dishes prepared by Fritz and his wife, Abbi, I sat next to the swami. After we finished eating, he put his fork down and said to me, "Whatever you are doing, do it for God. If you are cleaning the floor, do it for God. If you are cleaning the toilet, do it for God, and know that God is doing everything."

Not long after reading the two books on Eastern religion and meeting the swami, I discovered the Peaceful Valley Ashram in Sligo, Pennsylvania. I invited my friend Marylisa who enjoys travel and is open to different belief systems to join me. Marylisa and I met through Cliff's granddaughter, Larissa, who was in high school. Marylisa taught French and sponsored an exchange student program.

When Marylisa's sister, Kathy, had Stage 4 lung and brain cancer Marylisa asked if I could give some nutrition lessons to Kathy in hopes of curing the cancer. Kathy and I became quick friends after I noticed a copy of *A Course in Miracles* on her bookshelf.

I visited Kathy once a week and soon learned that her condition was terminal. I found myself feeling comfortable listening to Kathy talk about death and what she wanted her funeral to be like--including violin music. Her only problem was that she didn't know how to talk to her sister, who was hanging on to hope, about dying. I became a mediator. When Kathy passed away, Marylisa honored her sister with the perfect funeral that included a violinist.

After sharing this experience, Marylisa and I became close friends. When the two of us arrived at the Ashram located in a retired elderly facility, we felt as if we landed in India. We were welcomed by a young woman with long brown hair, parted in the middle. Darshanie, who was a spiritual intuitive, was barefoot and wearing a turquoise blue silk sari that complimented her dark skin. Before entering the building that was painted bright colors and smelled of sandalwood, we instinctively removed our shoes, knowing we were in a sacred space. Darshanie spent time with us talking about what led us to the Ashram and answering our questions.

I wanted to know the difference between Buddhism and Hinduism. Darshanie explained that Buddhism was a split from the dogmatic Hinduism, much like the protestant religion was a split from the authoritarian Catholic Church. She told me about the *Bhagavad Gita and* suggested I study the text, which I have since done.

The Gita is called the spiritual gem of India and is a story about a man named Arjuna who needs to stand up and conquer family members. He prays to Krishna, and in turn, Krishna helps him find the courage to find the inner strength he needs to accomplish the task. The Gita is full of metaphors that resonated with my soul.

Through studying Eastern Religion, I learned that the rosary beads Catholics use originated from mala beads that were used by Buddhist monks to meditate. Also, Centering Prayer originated in Tibet. Three Trappist Monks, Fathers Thomas Keating, Basil Pennington, and William Meninger traveled to Asia to study the practice and incorporated it into Catholicism. I was fascinated to discover the origins of religious practices.

Darshanie introduced us to her mom, Leela Mata, who welcomed us with a beautiful smile and warm hug. Mary Lisa and I spent the night at the Ashram soaking up the calming atmosphere. In the evening, we joined in on a meditation and evening service. Afterward, both Mary Lisa and I felt as if we experienced a higher level of consciousness that was unlike any spiritual experience at churches we had attended. Leela Mata ended the meditation with the St. Francis prayer, which left me pondering on the words:

> Lord, make me an instrument of your peace,
> Where there is hatred, let me sow love;
> Where there is injury, pardon;
> Where there is doubt, faith;
> Where there is despair, hope;
> Where there is darkness, light;
> Where there is sadness, joy;
> O Divine Master,
> Grant that I may not so much seek
> To be consoled as to console;
> To be understood as to understand;
> To be loved as to love.

For it is in giving that we receive;

It is in pardoning that we are pardoned;

And it is in dying that we are born to eternal life.

Hearing the poem reminded me of my resolve to follow the life of St. Francis. I visited the Ashram a few more times and learned that yoga is a deep spiritual practice, unlike the physical fitness programs that western people use for. Neither Darshanie nor Leela Mata tried to convert me to Hinduism. They both spoke highly of the Christian religion and encouraged me to follow and respect whatever path I was on, although I wasn't exactly sure what that was at the time.

After the visit to the Ashram, in the spring of the year, before the mass at the Catholic Church began, I was sitting outside the church on a cement bench surrounded by flowers and watched the bees extracting pollen. I thought of what I read in *The Gospel of Ramakrishna* about not letting anyone tie a noose around my neck. I found some of the rules of the Franciscan order and Catholic church rigid, so I decided to follow the life of St. Francis on my own.

I decided that serving people at the basic level of humanity would be a good place to start. I came across an advertisement in the *Ridgway Record* requesting people to care for the elderly at Ridgmont, an assisted living facility in Ridgway. I always regretted that I wasn't able to care for my mother. I had worked briefly with the elderly at the Adult Day Center in St. Marys but found myself worrying about who would take care of me if I ended up with dementia. At the time, I was practicing the act of living in the present moment, so I resigned from the job.

I applied for the job at Ridgmont and was delighted to be called for an interview within a week of submitting my resume. I was hired immediately to help shower residents. What I didn't know was that the employee turnover rate was over ninety percent. My biggest fear was how I was going to handle cleaning bowel movements. My friend, Sandy, who is a nurse, told me to have a small bottle of Vicks in my pocket and to focus on helping the person maintain their dignity.

I went to the Goodwill store in St. Marys and picked up a few sets of scrubs and ordered a pair of nursing shoes. When I walked into Ridgmont on my first morning, the large, white water tower reminded me of Mooseheart. Besides showering the residents, I was expected to check blood sugar levels, transfer an amputee patient, and change an ostomy pouch.

Because I wasn't trained to do the tasks, I politely declined and focused on washing the residents, thinking that each of them was Christ. In turn, the majority of residents expressed gratitude for what I did for them. I was surprised when they told me repeatedly how kind I was. It didn't take me long to figure out why when I witnessed other employees yelling at the residents as if they were naughty little children. I would later learn that what they were experiencing had a name: compassion fatigue.

An opening came available on the second shift, and I applied for the position, thinking that I could help the elderly even more, and I would also have health insurance. I was now required to administer medical treatments and dispense prescription medications without adequate training. I tried to remain optimistic around the residents but found myself exhausted and at times, becoming unkind to residents who rang their call bells frequently. I found it challenging to be caring for a resident while thinking of the twenty other residents who needed care at the same time. I tried to take my concerns to management but didn't feel heard.

While I was working at Ridgmont, I received a call from my Mooseheart friend Valerie, whom I wrote about in *The Red Caboose-An Orphan's Journey*. It was at this time that I had a flashback when asked to use the rotary phone to call for assistance when needed. The institutional setting of Ridgmont that reminded me of Mooseheart and poor management of the facility was more than I could handle, so I resigned after six months.

Caring for the elderly relieved some of the guilt that I had for not caring for my mother. I viewed the work as a self-imposed penance. One of the tasks I enjoyed the most was filling resident's water cups each morning as it gave me time to visit. They always thanked me for listening to them. It was like having grandparents that I never had. One of the last patients was Helen Hughes, who was a friend of Cliff's. Helen was a historian and explorer. As I was showering her, she asked me if I believed in heaven. I told her all I knew was that my life on earth has only gotten better, and I believe when we leave this earth, that pattern will continue.

While working at the assisted living facility, I found myself comfortable with people who were on hospice and thought I would like to be a hospice volunteer. Also, many of the residents just wanted to go home. I decided I would be better suited to meet the needs of people in their own homes, caring for them one on one. After leaving Ridgmont, I applied to be a hospice volunteer and sent in a resume for a job with Community Nurses as a personal care aide. I was hired for both positions.

To prepare myself to work with hospice patients, I took an online course and started reading books about grief, death, and dying. The Eastern philosophy of dying, which I read about in *The Tibetan Book of Living and Dying*, resonated with me more than the teachings of Western religious philosophies of heaven and hell. I observed that people who were dying and believed in a reward or punishment afterlife, often didn't feel good enough to get into heaven. One elderly Catholic woman who I thought was pure, sincere, and honest and said the rosary religiously, asked me if I thought she was going to heaven. I told her, "You have done so much good in the community. If you don't get into heaven, no one will."

Working with hospice helped me confront my anxiety about death. I've come to believe that death is a transition from one experience to a different experience, although I'm not sure what that is for every person. The majority of people who had Near-Death Experiences all report that they felt pure love, majesty, and indescribable beauty while they were clinically dead. It didn't matter if they were Catholic, Protestant, Buddhist, or agnostic.

While I was learning about the afterlife, I came into contact with a young man named Chip. We had met his brother Sean who moved to Ridgway from New York with his partner Stephanie and their little girl, Luna. Chip was living in Iceland, studying nomadic folklore to further his degree in library science. For a few years, we had Chip and his family over for the holidays when they all gathered in Ridgway. After eating a delectable meal of roast lamb with rosemary roasted potatoes and other side dishes, Chip asked if I read any of Florence Scovel Shinn's work. I hadn't. Chip strongly suggested I read her work, which I did. Her collection of books changed my whole outlook on life and led me to Ernest Holme's book *The Science of the Mind*. I thought back to when Dr. Francis told me that the one thing no one could take from me was my mind. What he didn't teach me directly was the power of *my* mind. I felt as if I were beginning to tame the eye of a hurricane.

A patient's wife I was caring for in St. Marys was from Norway. I was drawn to her accent and kind manner. I told her my father immigrated to America from Holland. On one of my visits, she gave me a Euro coin and told me I could spend it in Holland someday. At first, I thought that would be impossible, and then I remembered Ernest Holme's writings. Not long after she gave me the coin, I came across a paperback on Holland. I kept the Euro in my wallet as a good luck charm, believing someday, I would get to visit Holland. Within a year, Cliff and I had enough money in the bank to pay for a trip overseas. My brother, Jack, and his wife Connie were stationed in Germany. Jack had told me about the beautiful Keukenhof Gardens, where tulips were in full bloom in the spring. I planned a trip by booking our flight, a five-day stay at a Bed and Breakfast in De Zilk, Holland, and paid for tickets to the Keukenhof.

When we arrived in Holland, I felt as if I were home. The fragrance of hyacinths filled the air, and the fields of colorful flowers made the country look like a calico quilt. We rented a car that was a standard. I hadn't driven a stick shift in over twenty years, but just like riding a bike, it all came back to me. I felt a calling to go to the North Sea, and after checking into our room, we took a drive to the sea. Cliff asked how I knew where I was going, and all I could say was that I had a knowing.

The Keukenhof Gardens were stunning with people from all over the world taking pictures and strolling through the gardens. Jack joined us for two days and was our guide. We visited a cheese and wooden shoe business and went to the town of Alblasserdam, where our father lived before coming to America. We stopped at Kinderdijk to see the stately windmills that kept the country above sea level. Before leaving Holland, we spent a night in Amsterdam, where we toured the Anne Frank House and Rembrandt's home. It was a trip of a lifetime. I never spent the euro that my patient's wife gave me, but instead kept it as a reminder that dreams do come true.

On November 29th of 2014, just one day after Thanksgiving, I was blessed with my sixth grandchild, Camdyn Lee. After caring for people who were dying, I appreciated the miracle of birth with new eyes. I began seeing similarities between the two experiences. Both the newborn and the dying are entering a new life. I felt honored to provide comfort to the latter as they passed on to their new life. I try to convey to patients who are near death, that they are loved, that they are safe, and that it is okay to let go. I heard a well-renowned spiritual teacher say that being with people while they were dying was the highest calling in life. I admired the hospice nurses and family members, who were doing so much more than I was, to comfort and care for people at such a fragile time in life.

Although I conquered my fear of death, I hadn't conquered one of my greatest fears, that of losing my mind to dementia. I was about to learn. The agency I was working for trained personal care aides in basic care and what rules to follow for safety and government regulation, but they did not prepare employees to care for people suffering from dementia and Alzheimer's. One of my first experiences was caring for an older woman who didn't want me in her home. She went after me with a fly swatter when I wouldn't leave. Seeing the fly swatter come near me, reminded me of the times matrons at Mooseheart hit me with a fly swatter when I didn't follow orders. I wasn't about to let this woman boss me around, whether she was in her right mind or not. I stood up to her and asked her if this is how her religion taught her to behave. It felt good at the time, but I left the house in tears, feeling defeated.

Not long after, I was assigned to another woman diagnosed with Alzheimer's. This time I was warned that the patient had pulled people's hair and had an aggressive nature. I said I would give it a try. When I arrived at the well-decorated home on Dewey Circle in Ridgway, I met a woman named Shirley. As I looked around the house, I noted books on nursing. When I asked her daughter, Paula, about the books, she told me that her mom was a psychiatric nurse for thirty years at the Ridgway Hospital. I wondered if she cared for my mom when she was a patient on the fourth floor.

Shirley seemed sweet and kind until I tried to get her to the bathroom. When I finally got her to sit on the toilet seat, she started hitting me and pulling my hair. Neighbors began to notice my car in Shirley's driveway. They thanked me for taking care of her and told me what a kind and patient nurse Shirley was. I heard this again and again throughout the community. I was determined to find a way to give the same compassionate care back to Shirley that she had at one time given to her patients.

I started researching Alzheimer's online and came across courses from the Alzheimer's Association. I signed up for a couple of classes and learned the basics of caring for people with dementia. The class was a game-changer. When I visited Shirley, I introduced myself and sat on her bed and talked to her before giving her care. When she went to the bathroom, I guided her by holding her hand. When I bathed her, I started at her feet instead of her face. Shirley's whole demeanor changed.

When I met her daughter Paula, I asked where she found support in caring for her mother. She said online and at work; the only support group was thirty miles away in Emporium, Pennsylvania. I decided to begin an Alzheimer's Support Group in Elk County at the Fox Township Senior Center. Leanne, who was a nurse at Camp Flutterbye, volunteered to help facilitate the meetings.

Another woman, Phyllis, who had recently moved to Ridgway from New Jersey, also volunteered to help with the meetings. Cliff and his partner Craig helped renovate a house on East Ave that Phyllis and her husband, Dwight transformed into a Bed and Breakfast. When Phyllis heard about the Alzheimer's Support Group, she wanted to share what she had learned caring for her and Dwight's elderly parents who had dementia. Phyllis was compassionate and listened intently before she offered words of wisdom to people who attended the group and were grappling with how to care for their loved ones.

Phyllis and I traveled together to conferences sponsored by the Alzheimer's Association in Erie together. I was happy to have her support and friendship. A year after she agreed to volunteer, she was diagnosed with an aggressive form of cancer and passed away within a month after the diagnosis. I was devastated and at a loss as to how I would keep the meetings going without her support.

In the meantime, Cliff's Uncle Bobby was diagnosed with dementia. Uncle Bobby was Cliff's dad's youngest brother, who was fifteen years older than Cliff. Cliff and I offered to help the family by cooking meals and eating with him a few times a week. While his uncle still had his long-term memory, the two of them reminisced about hunting and fishing together. As Uncle Bobby started to hallucinate and slip from reality, Cliff felt lost and confused. He began attending the support group with me and benefited from hearing other people's experiences. I was glad to have Cliff's support at the meetings and was able to keep the meetings going with his encouragement and belief that the meetings were truly helping people cope with such a brutal disease.

While caring for Shirley, I received a call from my brother Jack, who was now living in Chester, Virginia. He called to tell me that Mrs. Gulley, one of his house parents at Mooseheart was celebrating her 90th birthday and asked if I would call her. I couldn't believe she remembered me. When I returned home from work that evening, I dialed the number Jack gave me. On the other end was a shaky voice that said hello. After I introduced myself, Mrs. Gully and I proceeded to talk for over an hour, reminiscing about Mooseheart. She remembered more about my childhood than my mother did.

Before she hung up, she asked if I could come out and visit her in Southern, Illinois where she was living with her daughter. I didn't hesitate to book a flight to see the woman who treated me with kindness as a child. For three days, the two of us couldn't get enough of each other. Her husband Charlie had passed away and she remarried when she was in her eighties. I wanted to soak up all the love and attention she gave me as a child. She wanted to soak up all the admiration I had for her.

She was suffering from a bout of pneumonia, so I accompanied her to the doctor. I told her I was writing a book about being at Mooseheart. When I read to her what I had written, tears streamed down her cheeks as she told me that was the nicest thing anyone had ever said about her.

Before I left, she gifted me with a photograph of her and her new husband, Earl, a statue of an angel, and a little bird with fragile wings. Her only request was that I would never forget her. I told her that would be impossible, because her kindness had left an imprint on my heart that could never be erased.

A Lesson in Forgiveness

O ne of my first home visits with Community Nurses was with an older woman living in a little shack out in the country. When I pulled in the driveway, a snarly looking dog was on the front porch barking. I wanted to get in my car and leave but instead asked myself what Mother Theresa would do. I said to myself, "Jeanette, this is your Calcutta."

When I entered the house, the sweetest lady with gray hair and wearing a lavender, cotton dress with knee-high nylon stockings was sitting on a tattered couch singing hymns. She welcomed my company and asked if I would read to her from the Bible. She nodded off as I read Psalm 23 from her King James version. I felt affirmed that this was my path in life. This was verified when I started caring for an older man in Ridgway.

The first time I knocked on Mr. Allegretti's door, questions ran through my mind. What level of care does he need? Was he friendly, or cranky? I knocked loudly on the glass storm door shielding the main entrance that displayed a wreath of spring flowers.

While waiting for someone to answer the door, I silently said part of the St. Francis Prayer "Lord, help me to console rather than be consoled, to understand rather than be understood, to love rather than be loved." After a few minutes, when no one came to the door, I opened the glass storm door and turned the door handle of the main door and let myself into the home.

"Hello," I called, sending out my voice like a scout checking out enemy territory.

"Come on in!" a loud voice bellowed.

As I removed my street shoes and changed into my brown nursing Crocs, I felt at ease, and a little confused to see a variety of shoes including women's dress shoes, little pink flip flops, size ten soccer shoes, and a pair of boy's black Adidas sandals taped together with neon yellow duct tape and a pair of men's size 13 white sneakers with Velcro straps.

"I'm in here," the man's voice called from the living room of an elegantly decorated house with swag lighting, wood floors, and large comfy sofas. A wooden rocking horse with a red cowgirl hat propped on the head of the horse was standing at attention next to a large screen television. Stuffed animals, crayons, and coloring books were piled neatly in the corner. A large burly man, with blue eyes and a bald head wearing forest green plaid pajamas, a navy-blue terry cloth robe and a pair of brown leather sandals was sitting in a recliner in the corner of the room. He reminded me of Daddy Warbucks from the musical Annie. Stationed next to the recliner was a brown oak end table with a telephone, a red, white, and green Italian derby, and two rosaries.

Remembering his name from my task order sheet, I put out my hand to shake his large hand that spoke of hard work. "Hi Ernest, I'm Jeanette."

"Call me, Ernie." He replied.

"I'm familiar with the name Allegretto, but not Allegretti."

"The original name is Allegretti. The damn nuns changed it to Allegretto, but my dad kept the proper spelling of the name." Ernie went on to speak fondly of his son Jimmy who lived in California and proudly of his daughter, Jeanne, her husband JJ, and his four grandchildren. He told me he was a bricklayer before retiring.

After chatting for a few minutes, I asked, "What can I do for you while I'm here?"

"Do you mind refilling my cup of coffee, and then would you help me put these white stockings on?"

I went to the kitchen and poured him a cup of black Folger's coffee in the ceramic mug imprinted with his four smiling grandchildren dressed in tie-dyed t-shirts. I set it on the stone coaster next to the pile of newspapers and Italian cooking magazines stacked on the end table.

As I knelt on one knee to put on the compression stockings, he asked, "Where are you from?"

"My husband and I have a little goat farm in Ridgway," I replied.

"Have you always lived here?" he inquired further.

"No" I answered shortly, attempting to direct attention away from myself.

"Where did you grow up?"

I usually exercise caution before telling someone, especially my patients, I lived in an orphanage. They have enough problems of their own and don't need to be burdened by my misfortune in life. But as I stretched the stockings up to his knees, I blurted out, "I lived in an orphanage as a child." Sometimes when I mention being in an orphanage for ten years, people aren't sure how to respond and change the subject to something else. I was hoping for that response. But in a decibel lower, Ernie inquired, "Where was the orphanage at?"

"Mooseheart, Illinois, fifty miles west of Chicago."

"You were one of the lucky ones." He stated with a firm voice that wasn't going to feel sorry for me.

"Why's that?"

"I did time in St. Joe's," he answered.

I looked up at his blue eyes that were as watery as the ocean as I gently asked, "St. Joseph's Orphanage in Erie?"

"That's the one. My mom died when I was eighteen months old in 1926, and my father had to work, so he put me in the orphanage. It wasn't very nice. Those nuns were meaner than the devil."

I was familiar with St. Joseph's Orphanage. A former co-worker had also grown up there after her mom had passed away. St. Joseph's Orphanage was a five-story structure located on West Sixth Street in Erie, Pennsylvania, that housed between four and five hundred crowded orphans. The boy's dorm, where Ernie lived, was on the fifth floor of the orphanage. The Italian boys were called "dirty old WOPS"(which meant without papers) and the Polish boys "dirty old Pollocks" by the nuns. Ernie didn't fare well. His mother was first-generation Polish, and his father was first-generation Italian.

I tried to console Ernie. "Mooseheart wasn't that great either Ernie. Once I was sent to a dark, dank basement of a hall, with one light bulb hanging over my head, to copy scriptures from the Bible for two hours in a notebook because I wore my street shoes in the house instead of my slippers."

Ernie was surprised Mooseheart wasn't as nice as he had dreamed. With his eyebrows raised, he asked, "Really? We played football against them a couple of times. Everyone at St. Joe's was trying to get to Mooseheart. I couldn't get adopted because my father was living and had to work to send money to the orphanage."

"Kids at Mooseheart couldn't get adopted either Ernie. The majority of us had one parent living, and Mooseheart received all our social security checks." I told him about a little friend I had when I was six-year-old. Mimi had a hole in her heart and had open-heart surgery at Children's Hospital in Chicago. One of the doctors wanted to adopt her but couldn't even though her father was deceased, and her mother was in a mental institution.

In a matter of minutes, Ernie and I instantly had a connection beyond words. We both knew the feelings of abandonment, being treated harshly by matrons, not feeling loved, or worthy of love. We both knew what it felt like to be valued only for our ability to do chores and 'make the floors shine like the top of the Chrysler building.' We both knew what it was like to have mush for breakfast, peanut butter with no jelly sandwiches for lunch, and slop for supper. We both knew what it was like to 'dream about a place far away where clouds would be far behind us and troubles melt like lemon drops.'

I helped him slip into his sandals and secured the Velcro heel straps. As Ernie gave me his hand to help me to my feet, I said, "Ernie, I'm sorry about what happened to you."

"It wasn't your fault."

"I know it wasn't. I had it much better than you did, though. What happened to me at Mooseheart was done in the name of white supremacist men. What happened to you was done in the name of God. That would be hard to reconcile."

Ernie thanked me and said, "You are the first person that I've met that truly understands what it was like to live in an orphanage. Whenever I've tried to tell people how awful the place was, they don't believe me because the nuns ran it. They don't want to think that they could have treated us that bad."

I wanted to ask Ernie a hundred more questions about his childhood, but he needed lunch before my two-hour shift was over. I also needed to use caution in how many stories we shared. I didn't want to trigger Post Traumatic Stress Disorder in him or myself.

My visits to Ernie took place every Monday and Wednesday. Over the next few months, I found myself caring for Ernie as though he were my father. Not only did I miss having a father as a child, but I missed having a father with whom I could help grow old, with grace. Taking care of Ernie filled that void. I brought him homemade bread and homemade chicken noodle soup for his lunches. I helped him shave and walked beside him as he hobbled with his two wood canes from room to room. We did crossword puzzles together. He instructed me in Italian pronunciation. He told me about Burma Shave signs and how to make homemade noodles. He played "You Are My Sunshine" on the harmonica, and together we sang "School Days" and other songs from his era.

He told me about working on his aunt and uncle's farm after they took him out of the orphanage in 1939 when he was in his early teens because he cried and pleaded with them to take him in. I told him about how I got out of Mooseheart in 1971 when I was thirteen years old because I cried and pleaded with my older brother and his wife to take me in. We talked about how some kids made out at the orphanages because they were compliant, but how strong-willed we were and wouldn't take shit from anyone as soon as we were old enough to stand up for ourselves.

Even though I was curious to hear more about Ernie's childhood in the orphanage, I tried to steer away from talking about it, but Ernie wanted to tell his story. When I told him I was writing about my childhood, he told me he wanted me to tell his story. I needed to make sure we had an anchor before we went out any further into the turbulent sea of memories and abuse. I asked how he was able to reconcile his relationship with God after being treated so poorly by the nuns. He told me that he never blamed God for what happened. It was God that got him through the terrible loss of his mother and his wife, who had passed seven years before. He said the rosary multiple times a day for years.

The noon news was on T.V., and a story came on about a teenage boy that had killed someone. Ernie said, "You know when I see experiences like that on television, I can understand how someone could kill another person. If I could have killed one of those nuns and gotten away with it, I would have."

I couldn't fathom what could have happened to make Ernie feel that way, and I wasn't sure I was ready to hear his story. I acknowledged his anger and quickly asked him how the stock market was doing. He unearthed a white folded letter from underneath the stack of newspapers and gave it to me to read. The return address was from the St. Joseph's Orphanage Alumni. I unfolded the top half and the bottom third of the letter to see a black and white picture of about two hundred children dressed in suits, ties, and dresses attending a mass at the St. Joseph church that he attended as a child.

Ernie pointed to the exact pew he sat in and proceeded to tell me what happened to boys who wet the bed. "The nuns would hang the soiled sheet up in the back of the church, and the humiliated boy who wet the bed had to stand beside the sheet as all the children left the church."

In a whisper, he continued, "The nuns would tie the boy's penis with string at night if they wet the bed and would then tell the doctor they were sore because the boys were playing with themselves. When we were showering, the nuns would come in with brooms and swat us like animals. For punishment, we had to get down on our hands and knees, and they would beat us with a wooden ball bat, and it wasn't on our backside where we had a little bit of padding. I've had back pain all of my life."

"Ernie, that is so sad."

He replied, "You don't know how much it means to me that you believe me. When I tried to talk to my wife about how I was treated, she would say, "It couldn't have been that bad, Ernie."

Ernie didn't need to explain how much it meant to have someone believe his stories. I was blessed to find a counselor over twenty years earlier to understand and help process memories from my years at Mooseheart. One of the painful memories of being raped by a dentist while under anesthesia when I was three years old was fresh in my psyche. My phobia of dentists was so intense that I had been to at least ten different dentists in the area but discontinued seeing every one of them. I started traveling three hours out of town to a dentist who specializes in treating dental anxiety. At my last visit, the dentist apologized on behalf of his colleagues for how I was treated. The floodgates of anger, fear, and bitterness and forgiveness were unleashed when I received a simple apology.

Ernie wanted to enlist in the Marines but was rejected because he was flat-footed. In 1943 the Army drafted him, and he fought in World War II. I asked if he hunted. He told me he destroyed all his guns after the war. He confessed how he hated the Japs for how they tortured people. His anger nagged at my heart.

I met his daughter Jeanne for the first time a couple of months after I began taking care of Ernie. I was visiting St. Leo's Catholic Church and was sitting in the back of the church, observing people receiving the Eucharist. I recognized Jeanne, her husband, and four children from family photos.

After the mass, I made my way over to say hello and to introduce myself. Jeanne was as kind and friendly as her dad. She thanked me for caring for him and said she never realized what a godsend it was to have someone help with his care while she worked. As we were talking Father Brian, a priest in his mid-fifties was in the pew next to me speaking with her husband, JJ.

After the two men had ended their conversation, I asked Father Brian if I could talk to him for a few minutes. I explained that I was caring for Ernie, and he had spent time at St. Joseph's Orphanage, and it wasn't a pleasant experience. I asked if it would be possible for someone to apologize to Ernie on behalf of the Catholic Church. Father Brian told me he knew Ernie but wasn't aware he had been in St. Joseph's Orphanage. Without denying, minimizing, or excusing the abuse at the orphanage, he assured me that he would visit Ernie and apologize.

Father Brian was good on his word and visited Ernie to offer an apology for what happened at the orphanage. On my next visit, Ernie told me how much Father Brian's visit meant. We talked about forgiveness and how important it was to let go of the anger and hatred towards those who mistreated us.

Ernie said, "I sit here and wonder why God has kept me alive for over ninety years, and now I know why. It was his plan that we would meet, so I didn't have to take all the pain and anger to the grave with me. You are such a blessing."

I remembered my calling to serve the elderly after studying the life of St. Francis. I said, "Ernie, I began taking care of the elderly in response to a call from St. Francis. God guided me here to care for you and for our lives to come together. Jesus died on the cross with his arms open wide to forgive us and others for whatever sins we have committed. We have to remember the need to forgive those who have trespassed against us." We both agreed that all the glory belongs to our Creator, who loved us from the day we were knit together in our mother's womb. Psalm 139:13

Ernie requested that I write his story to share with others. When I read back what he told me, he asked, "How did you know all of that?" He forgot what he told me. I sent the essay to the Sisters of St. Joseph and received a reply that included an apology. For me, the apology was negated when I read the last paragraph that read, "We are sorry you have carried this pain for so many years. Hopefully, having shared this with us, you will find it unnecessary to send this onward to the Diocese or the Catholic Digest."

After Father Brian apologized to Ernie, he never talked about the orphanage again. I wonder how Ernie would have felt to hear about the sexual abuse scandal in Erie Diocese when it was finally made public, but he passed away at home, peacefully with his family by his side, before the news broke.

Although I was sad when Ernie passed away, I felt honored to have been a part of his life and wrote the following eulogy, which I read at his funeral on April 20, 2015:

Eulogy for Ernie Allegretti

Two years ago, I was called to be a caregiver for Ernie. I knew I was in the presence of greatness from the very beginning.

Ernie was larger than life and taught me quite a bit. He taught me about history, language, and the stock market. He also taught me not to procrastinate.

One day I was refilling his water cup with ice and water. The ice maker on the fridge wasn't working, so I told Ernie. He said, "Give me the damn phone book, so I can call and get it fixed.

I replied, "Ernie don't you want to wait? Maybe a line is frozen and it needs to thaw. J.J. will look at it when he comes home."

"Wait is what broke the wagon. I'm going to call them right now." And he did.

Ernie was the kind of man that didn't wait for anything. He didn't wait to get mad.

He didn't wait to get over being mad

He didn't wait to get over being disappointed by sickness and physical limitations.

He didn't wait to offer everyone he met a beer or a glass of wine.

He didn't wait to tell each nurse or caregiver that they were the best.

He didn't wait to say thank you, even for the smallest act. He didn't wait to tell someone how nice they looked.

He didn't wait to forgive. He didn't wait to apologize.

He didn't wait to say the three most important words to his daughter, Jean, his son-in-law JJ, his son Jimmy, his grandchildren Dominic, Vincent, Anna and Sara, his nephews, his friends, his nurses, nor his caregivers. He didn't wait to say I love you. When he couldn't say the words anymore, he breathed them. Two nights before he passed away, his seven-year-old granddaughter Sara came in to say good night to her Papa. He tried to say "I love you" to her but couldn't get the words out. She said, "That's OK, Papa. Save your breath. I know what you mean."

Just like Sara, we all knew that not only did Ernie say I love you, he meant it. Ernie came into this world alone. But Ernie didn't leave this world alone.

Despite having a meager beginning in life, he made a name for himself in the community and left this world brimming with love for his family and friends who loved him in return.

To quote Victor Hugo, "To Love another is to see the face of God." Thank you, Ernie, for showing us the face of God.

While caring for Ernie, I thought I might like to join the Catholic Church so I could receive the Eucharist. I enjoyed the music and seeing people from the community at church. I had read a book titled *God's Brain* by Lionel Tiger and Michael McGuire. The authors did studies and learned that being with people in a social group can elevate one's capacity of happiness and well-being. For two years, I attended a small Faith Sharing Group held at the Knights of Columbus building on Tuesday evenings. Although the Catholic Church sponsored the class, it was non-denominational. We shared our stories and struggles in life and got to know each other on a deep level. After each lesson, we had an assignment to put into practice what we were learning.

One of the assignments was to do something for the poor in the community. I suggested a soup supper at Dickinson Apartments. Some members of our group weren't familiar with the housing project for people with limited resources. Everyone liked the idea of a soup and sandwich supper on the last Sunday of the month during January, February, and March when many of the residents might be experiencing cabin fever and be low on food at the end of the month. We took turns making large kettles of homemade soups, sandwiches, and desserts. I made homemade rolls. We were delighted to have over thirty people from the apartments join us for a meal and an evening of socializing.

The event was well-received, although the Bible study group did disagree as to whether we should allow the residents to donate money for the meal. The majority voted no. I voted yes as I believed that most people, including myself, want to pay for what they get. At our first meal, the residents started passing around a coffee container to collect donations for the meal and gave us more than enough money to cover the cost of the food. One of the members suggested playing bingo after the meal and giving gifts cards bought with the extra money for prizes.

I tried attending a few of the RCIA (Rite of Initiation Classes of Adults) but dropped out after the first few sessions. The dogma of the church reminded me of Jehovah's Witnesses; I couldn't go along with all of the church teachings. One, in particular, was the view on birth control. After talking to members of the church, they assured me that not everyone who belongs to the Catholic Church believes in all the teachings. I met with Father Brian and told him I would like to join the church.

He asked if either Cliff and I were married before. We both were, but my ex-husband had passed away. Cliff and his ex-wife married at the Holy Rosary Church in Johnsonburg over fifty years ago. She had remarried after their divorce.

Because she was still living and they hadn't gotten an annulment, I wouldn't be able to join the church and receive the Eucharist. When Cliff's ex-wife died or if they got an annulment I would be able to receive the Eucharist. This rule was ludicrous to me.

I talked to Dr. Francis about my dilemma. He set up a meeting with the monsignor of the parish, whom he knew personally. At the meeting, the monsignor told me the same thing I heard from Father Brian. I asked, "You mean to tell me that if Jesus were here today, and we sat down for a meal, he wouldn't include me because of what my husband had done?" The monsignor had no answer but wouldn't budge.

I attended mass a few more times and received the Eucharist, knowing in my heart, that Jesus would never exclude me from breaking bread with others. Soon afterward, news of the sexual abuse scandal in the Erie diocese was made public. I thought about how Ernie would have felt vindicated. I could no longer attend mass, thinking and wondering about the children that had been abused in the name of God. It was time for me to move on.

I've concluded that organized religion isn't for me. God isn't a figure outside of myself. I understand God to be a divine intelligence within; I'm at my best when I take the time to have conversations with my higher self and see the best in others. I feel as John Muir did when he penned, "I would rather be in the mountains thinking about God, than in church thinking about the mountains."

Camp Flutterbye

Twenty-five years before I started volunteering for Hospice, a close friend had lost her young adult daughter to cancer, leaving behind two preschool aged children. While she was grieving, she said to me, "Losing a child is the hardest death."

I disagreed with her and said, "Losing a parent when you are a child is the hardest thing." In retrospect, I would have been more empathetic with my friend and acknowledged how much she was hurting after losing her daughter. At the time, I was young and insensitive, not knowing what to say to people who were grieving. To teach myself how to be a more compassionate person, in regards to dying, I started reading books about the subject and signed up as a volunteer for Hospice. Presently, I have at least five books about children's grief and twice as many on adult grief on my bookshelf. I've learned that although it wasn't the time and place for me to tell my friend what I believed, I still feel the same. I'm probably biased because of losing my dad when I was three years old, and my mom wasn't able to care for my six siblings and me. When a child loses a parent, their whole support system is pulled out from under them.

In most cases, the child relied on their parent for love and financial support. In my opinion, this is one of the hardest things in the world to experience. When I signed up for hospice I was invited to volunteer for Camp Flutterbye, a two-day grief camp for children held at a lodge called The Pines, which is nestled in a grove of pine trees in St. Marys, Pennsylvania. Because I had never processed the grief of losing my father, the first year I attended the camp, I found myself caught up in the grief and unable to help any of the children. For an introductory activity, Joanne Straub, the Hospice social worker who facilitated the camp, instructed about a dozen children and as many adults to sit in a circle. She held a ball of white yarn in her hands and introduced herself and shared who had died in her family. Holding the end of the yarn, she threw the ball to another person. After catching the ball, they said their name and their loved one's name, who had died. Each time the ball was passed to someone else, the yarn connected everyone. The circle was beginning to look like a massive spider web. When it was my turn to catch the ball of yarn, I felt like a child when I stated, "My name is Jeanette, and my daddy died when I was three years old."

After introductions, Joanne told the group that we were all connected by grief because everyone has lost someone. I was reminded of the story about a woman who lost a child and went to the village guru to ask him to bring back her child. He told her to knock on all the doors in the village, and if she could find someone who hadn't lost anyone to death, he would bring her child back to life. As she went around the village knocking on doors, instead of finding someone that hadn't experienced death, she heard stories about loved ones that had died. She realized she wasn't alone and returned to the guru to tell him she didn't need him to bring back her child.

At Camp Flutterbye, when the children were doing another activity to get in touch with their emotions and feelings about the loss of their loved one, I wondered what it would have been like for my siblings and me if someone cared enough to talk to us about how we felt about losing our daddy and going to an orphanage. I felt anger and jealousy in my gut because I didn't have this opportunity. My eyes welled up with tears, and I felt as if I were going to cry an ocean. I was of no use to the children at the camp, so I went outside to get some air. I didn't return for day two of the camp.

The next year Camp Flutterbye was different. I arrived late—probably a Freudian slip—so I missed the introductions. As I entered the building, Katie, the Hospice volunteer coordinator, welcomed me and gave me a bright yellow T-shirt with butterflies on the front, that all the volunteers were wearing. I wasn't sure where to change my shirt, so another volunteer, Lisa, who I've known for several years, suggested I put the new shirt over the one I was wearing, as she did. When I did, I felt a part of the adult group.

While the children were busy doing an activity, Lisa started telling me about her dad, who I cared for at the Adult Day Center a few years back. He had dementia and she eventually had to place him in a nursing home, which she regretted. We shared similar stories about our childhood and how we felt about our 'awful moms.' Her mom was abusive; my mom was neglectful. Lisa had a master's degree in writing and was my first Creative Writing teacher. Because she was a quiet, introspective person, I was surprised at how much she was sharing with me. I told Lisa about what had happened at last year's Camp Flutterbye, and she immediately picked up on the dissociative experience and said to me that she had been in counseling for the same diagnosis. I felt as if I found a long-lost friend who understood first-hand what I had experienced in life. When there was a lull in our conversation, I glanced over at the group of children seated at the tables and noticed an empty chair at the end of one of the tables. I thought about sitting in the seat but didn't want to leave Lisa hanging, nor did I feel ready to interact with the children.

During lunch, Lisa and I sat at the bar, away from the children. While eating my lunch with Lisa, the empty chair caught my eye. While eating, Lisa shared that she didn't feel comfortable around children and told me about the struggle she had when she gave birth to her first child. After lunch and outdoor play, the children gathered back inside for another activity. The chair at the end of the table was still empty, so I took a seat at the table of six children. After lunch and outdoor play, the children gathered back inside for another activity. The chair at the end of the table was still empty, so I took a seat at the table of six children. Lisa took a seat at the opposite end of the same table. The assigned activity was to write about something good the child remembered about their loved one. Instead of writing, a ten-year-old girl with blonde hair and bright blue eyes, who was sitting to my right, started telling me about how she lost her mom in a car accident when she was in kindergarten. She was in the car with her mom at the time of the accident. Her hair was pulled back in a hairband. She pointed to a scar on her hairline and told me she was scalped when it happened.

A tall twelve-year-old girl, with wavy hair and a beautiful smile, sitting to my left, told me about her mom dying of a heart problem, just over a year ago. The girl couldn't get the picture of finding her mom dead in the living room out of her mind. A few days earlier, she had told her brother that she felt there was something wrong with her mom and pleaded with him to call the ambulance. But he didn't, and now her mom was gone. She was angry at her brother for not calling the ambulance.

I reflectively listened to both the girls and told them how sad it was that they lost their moms. A younger boy joined our conversation and talked about losing his daddy. I then said to the children that I could relate because I lost my daddy when I was three years old. The boy asked, "Who took care of you after your daddy died?"

"I went to an orphanage in the state of Illinois to live."

"What's an orphanage?"

The ten-year-old girl interrupted, "An orphanage is a place where kids go to get adopted."

I added, "Except I never got adopted."

The children knew they had a hearing ear of someone who understood first-hand what they were experiencing and started to share more of what it was like to lose a parent. After our conversation, each of the children were able to write down something they loved about their deceased parent.

When I returned home, I was tired and didn't feel like talking to anyone, including my husband. When the phone rang three different times, I didn't answer it. I took a warm bath and went to bed but couldn't sleep. I started to listen to a voice inside me that didn't want to go back to Camp Flutterbye the next day because it was just too sad. I talked compassionately to the voice and said I was sorry it was such a sad day and that she didn't have to go back tomorrow. I also told the voice how much she helped the children by listening. Not many people understand what it's like to lose a parent as a child, but she did.

When I woke up the next morning, I felt refreshed and thought about wearing the yellow butterfly shirt. I heard a voice telling me *You made a difference to the children. They need to hear it wasn't their fault that their parent had died. They need to know that their mom and dad loved them.* My mood lifted, and I headed off to the second day of Camp Flutterbye.

When I arrived, the children were decorating wood frames with pictures of their loved ones. Again, the seat at the end of the table by the two girls was empty. I didn't hesitate to fill it. The girls smiled at pictures of their mommies as they decorated the frames. The girl to my left told me again about seeing her mom dead on the living room floor and telling her brother to call for help. I told her that it wasn't her fault that her mom died and that her mom loved her. She broke down crying. A little girl sitting next to her put her arm around her for comfort.

The children finished their projects and, by the end of the day, were smiling more than crying. Both of the girls thanked me for being so kind and invited me to be friends with them on Facebook. I had to leave early to pick up my grandson from work, so I missed the parting ceremony in which they received a candle they decorated and released a helium balloon in memory of their loved one. As I drove out of The Pines and onto the main road, I felt as if I had made a difference and thought about the story of the man who was picking up starfish and throwing them back in the ocean.

Someone came along and asked him why it mattered because he couldn't save all the starfish. He replied, "Because it makes a difference to this one."

Broken Wings

●———————————————————●

About five years into my caregiving, just as I was turning sixty, my knees began to ache and was limiting my mobility. I always loved to swim but the pain in my knees was excruciating when I attempted to propel myself forward by kicking my legs. At the time, I could barely walk or climb up and down the pool steps and thought I would never swim again. I thought I would never cross-country ski the Brush Hollow Trail again. I had also given up the idea of ever riding my mountain bike on the Rail Trail. Working in the garden was exhausting. I was feeling depressed and hopeless at the thought of not being in the outdoors enjoying nature, gardening, feeling the sun, wind, rain, and snow on my face and, most of all, breathing in the fresh air. The last time of doing what I loved was piling up.

Three years earlier, I began experiencing severe knee pain after stepping into a deep snowbank to get to my car after visiting a patient. When I fell, I felt my knee twist and afterward could barely walk. I took advantage of the workman's compensation. I made an appointment with a local orthopedic office that referred me to a physician's assistant who ordered x-rays and told me that I had arthritis in my knees and would need an MRI to determine further damage. The MRI revealed that I had a torn meniscus. The surgeon didn't advise surgery; just six weeks off work so

I could avoid steps. When the pain subsided, I attempted cross-country skiing, trying to avoid the hills to prevent falls. At the recommendation of an osteopath, I began taking Osteo Bi-Flex, hoping it would relieve the stiffness in my knees.

The work required to care for the goats became too much for Cliff and me. He could no longer heave dense bales of hay into the loft of the barn, and I could no longer help him stack them. Cleaning out their stalls was becoming a burden. We decided to sell the goats. The same year, our neighbor who supplied us with hay every year didn't have enough fodder for his cows. It was a sad time for both Cliff and me, but we felt grateful that we had a few years in this life to be farmers.

Two years later, after the pain worsened. I could barely hobble up three steps. Working in the garden was nearly impossible. I felt like a bird with broken wings. In desperation, I finally made an appointment with a different orthopedic surgeon. My husband, Cliff, dropped me off at the ground floor of the medical center so that I could walk gingerly to the elevator to the second floor. Stairs were out of the question.

I wasn't fond of the doctor's office from the minute I entered. The white walls, stainless-steel armed chairs, end tables littered with old copies of Better Homes and Garden magazines, and a television blaring in the background felt like negative energy. The receptionist was behind a closed window and didn't seem friendly--she was all business. After an x-ray, I was then led into an examination room, where black and white images of my knees were displayed on a computer screen. I could visibly see the bone on bone. The inflammation from the arthritis was an ominous cloud. Not only were my knees bone on bone, but they were both severely bowed. I felt sick to my stomach. I asked the nurse if my husband could see the x-rays. We both knew it didn't look good.

The surgeon, a man in his fifties, with sandy colored hair, wore plastic black-rimmed glasses. Tattoos on his arms and upper chest were visible underneath the sky-blue scrubs. Matter of factly, as if I were another cog on the wheel, he delivered the diagnosis, Stage 4 arthritis, and a bilateral total knee replacement. He quickly explained the surgical procedure, making it sound like a walk in the park. He added that it would take a year for my brain to get used to my new knees.

I only had one other unpleasant operation when I was six years old and had my tonsils removed. Going under anesthesia scared the daylights out of me. As I was walking out of the doctor's office, tears welled up in my eyes, and I felt like fainting. It was as if I were in a downward spiral that was pulling me further and further into a dark vortex.

Before the insurance company would approve the procedure, I would have to undergo a series of injections that weren't promising and were quite expensive. I opted for Euflexxa, which is purported to lubricate the knee joint. The cost of the injections was $1600.00, which would go toward my $2500.00 deductible. While researching the drugs, I found that the prescription was available through Canada Drugs at half the cost. After some wrangling with the receptionist at the doctor's office, I was able to get the physician's assistant to begrudgingly agree to administer the weekly injections, which they did with extreme caution, fearing they were tainted. I waived them of their responsibility.

At home, I watched videos of the actual surgery on *YouTube*, thinking that might reduce my anxiety, but it only increased. The procedure looked more invasive than the doctor described. Another concern was that if I had both knees done separately, I would be off work for nearly six months. I wasn't sure my employer would carry my insurance to cover both knees. I also learned it would be challenging to find a doctor to replace both knees at the same time. In preparation, I amassed a used stairlift, a walker, and toilet seat riser to get me through the recovery process.

Providentially, at the same time that I was preparing for the surgery, my friend, Kat told me about going to a myofascial release physical thera-pist, named Margo, for plantar fasciitis.

The first time I met Margo was when Kat invited me to a gathering in Ridgway. I felt an instant connection with Margo as we sat around the table and talked about the law of attraction and energy work. Kat's brother brought his guitar, and I danced to folk songs, with Margo in the background eyeing up my weak knees.

Kat believed that she would be able to help me before I went through with the surgery, but I wasn't convinced. Not until she posted a video online of another friend who had a hip replacement. She regained full range of motion after seeing Margo for a few weeks. The higher my anxiety level rose, the more I considered physical therapy. What did I have to lose?

The next week I called for an appointment. When I requested a prescription for physical therapy from the surgeon's office, the Physician's Assistant warned that physical therapy would probably make my knees worse. I was undeterred. I scheduled an appointment with Margo on the same day I had an appointment for the injections. When I entered Margo's office, located on the side of her home, the calming rainstorm blue color of the waiting room, decorated with healing art and a shelf full of books about the body, health, women, and energy, put me at ease.

Instead of being dressed in scrubs, Margo was barefoot and dressed casually in yoga pants. After giving her a brief description of my diagnosis, she described in detail what I was experiencing better than I could myself. She told me what the doctor failed to; the total knee replacement would require cutting into main muscle groups, and that would require weeks of physical therapy.

She ended the conversation by asking, "So what is your goal?"

I answered, "Not to have surgery."

"OK. We'll work on that but no promises. At the very least, if you still need surgery, you will be in optimal shape to get back on your feet as soon as possible."

"Do you need copies of my x-rays?" I asked.

"I can tell what's wrong just by the way you walk." We went through the insurance protocol of ADL's (Activities of Daily Living) that I could no longer do. Walking up and down steps, cooking, baking, carrying laundry to the basement, and groceries in and out of the house were tasks I could barely accomplish. Margo explained that these were more important to the insurance company than the recreational activities that I enjoyed.

Margo led me into a room with bright orange walls that exuded energy. I undressed down to my bra and underwear so that she could evaluate my physical condition. Her diagnosis without seeing x-rays was bowed knees, a frozen right shoulder, sloppy posture, and crooked toes. My reflection in the mirror on the back of the door felt dismal, but I silently told myself I'm not my body. After I got on the table, she shook her head and commented that one leg was an inch shorter than the other, and we had much work to do. She asked if I was in my body. I told her that I had spent my whole life trying to get out of my body. She assured me that would change. After the first session, she showed me some simple poses to do at home.

At the next weekly appointment, Margo explained in detail precisely what fascia is and how it affects the body. Fascia is a thin fibrous connective tissue that covers the outside of the muscles, tendons, and bones; think of the thin membrane that coats the outside of a chicken or meat. When injured or stressed, it hardens, pulling the skeletal structure out of shape, causing pain in other areas of the body. One of the goals of myofascial release is to soften the fascia by doing poses on foam rollers; that I would have to do at home. When a specific part of my body was hurting, Margo educated me by referring to a worn copy of *Grey's Anatomy.* In a second, she could turn to the page she was looking for, and I wondered if she had a photographic memory.

At subsequent visits, Margo showed me pictures of energy in the body and how we are more than skin and bone. Our bodies are fields of energy that can heal and regenerate with the right type of therapy and mindset.

The energy body holds onto ancient wounds-emotional and physical-that block the flow of energy. Energy workers, such as Margo, have the ability to release the blocks allowing energy to flow freely throughout the body. The healing requires the willingness of the person's spirit, which can be hindered through old thought patterns and beliefs. When Margo explained this to me, it was as if she were telling me something that I already knew on a deeper level.

With healing music playing in the background, we worked on releasing energy that was stored in my body from past trauma, such as car accidents, falls, and breaks. The hardest thing I had to learn was to get out of my head and let my body heal. After each visit, I felt my strength being restored and was determined to help the healing along by spending an hour a day on the foam rollers and doing the prescribed poses.

Once the fascia covering my thighs was softened, Margo began straightening my knees. As she gently manipulated the femur bone to line up with the tibia, I could feel my knees popping back into place. When I got off the table, I was awkwardly walking straight. I felt like a newborn goat finding its legs for the first time. The pain in my knees eased as I went up and down steps. Slowly but surely, the knee pain declined, but other parts of my body began to ache. For a few days, I had severe pain in my ankle joint. Margo explained that I was now using joints that weren't utilized before and assured me the pain would dissipate.

Each week she gave me a new set of poses that not only stretched tight muscles and fascia but cleared my mind. When I talked to other people who had been through physical therapy, I learned that Margo's approach is entirely different from traditional physical therapy. She doesn't recommend damaging joints and bones further by doing exercises, running, and biking. What works is to give the muscles, bones, and fascia a restorative rest.

When a debilitating back pain appeared, she asked, "What were you doing when it began?"

"Just sweeping the floor."

"Has anyone ever taught you how to use a broom?"

Using a broom, she demonstrated how to keep it close to my body while I swept. I was shocked that I had been using a broom wrong all my life. It was a wonder my back didn't hurt more. When I started using the technique at home, the back pain subsided. Margo taught me about proprioception-the awareness of my body, in particular, my feet and movement. I became more conscious of how and where I was walking, and in the process, regained balance and mobility. We worked together to heal my beaten-up and neglected body. Margo challenged me to take care of myself rather than sacrificing my needs for other people. Work had defined my worth from the time I labored scrubbing floors on my hands and knees and doing chores at Mooseheart when I was a child. I slowly gave up the idea that I needed to be slaving in the kitchen baking loaves of homemade bread, preparing big meals and canning quarts of food every year.

After six months, I had regained the ability to do ADL's, except now I chose not to be in the kitchen slaving away at the stove any more than necessary. Day by day, I felt my knees getting stronger and stronger. When there was enough snow on the ground, I dusted off the cross-country skis and headed to the trail. I was delighted to find skiing with straight knees was more comfortable than it had ever been before. Thanks to beautiful snowfalls that winter, I skied more that winter than I had in the past five years. When my knees began to ache, I put into practice what Margo taught me.

Rather than pushing myself to the limits, I gave my body rest when it was hurting. When the weather warmed up, I could feel my body getting stronger, not only physically but emotionally and spiritually. I unearthed the mountain bike that I hadn't used for three years and took it for a spin. The only thing sore afterward was my bottom from using the bicycle seat for the first time.

When the weather warmed up enough to take my dogs for walks, I noticed the pain in my knees was minimal. When Margo invited me to kayak with her on the Clarion River at Cook's Forest, I didn't know if I could get in and out of a kayak. She believed I could, and to my surprise, I did! It was pure joy to kayak the river with bald eagles soaring through the mountains.

Shortly after getting back on my feet, I was carrying thirty pounds of extra weight, which was hard on my knees. I read that each pound of weight exerted four pounds of excess pressure on knees. I was convinced I couldn't lose weight because of my metabolism. Through a friend, I came across the book *Bright Line Eating* by Susan Pierce Thompson. After reading the book, I felt confident I could lose weight. All I had to do was follow four bright lines: no flour, no sugar, weigh my food and no eating between meals. I thought I knew a lot about nutrition, but I didn't know that flour and sugar contributed so much to weight gain. I also had never read about the brain connection to eating. I learned that sugar is eight times more addictive than cocaine. I followed the protocol, and within a year, I lost the extra weight. My knees and joints felt even better.

The next year when I slid into the pool and kicked my legs, there wasn't an inkling of pain in my new knees. I swam a few laps relishing the feeling of gliding through a refreshing pool of water. A month later, I took a trip to the Finger Lakes. One of my goals was to hike the gorge at Watkins Glen State Park. That night I had a dream that I hiked the gorge in my bare feet. At the beginning of the canyon, I took off my Merrill sandals and hiked in my bare feet without any pain. The energy surging through my body was intense. I felt energized and healed, but most of all, I felt an immense amount of gratitude to Margo for helping me fix my broken wings. I remembered back to a year ago when my life felt like it was in a downward spiral to today when my life was now spiraling upward.

Eternally Grateful

———•———

I've learned that being grateful is the best antidote to life's woes. Every morning, I have a journal by Susan Ban Breathnach in which I write at least three things I'm grateful for each day and when I go to bed at night, I thank my higher power for all my blessings in life.

Shortly after Ernie had passed away, Cliff and I were having supper at Luigi's with Dr. Francis. While we were eating a meal of pasta, Dr. Francis gently told us that he had recently been to the doctor and found out that he was dying of kidney failure. After he broke the news, I could barely finish my meal. Even though I had outgrown my need for his advice, I took comfort in his presence.

For the past thirty years, since I began counseling with Dr. Francis and adopted him as my father, I dreaded the day he would die. It was one of my greatest fears that stemmed from my father's death when I was three years old. Years earlier, when I shared my fear of his death with him, he didn't try to fix my anxiety. Instead, he jotted down his youngest son, Dan's phone number on a piece of scrap paper, and told me that if anything happened to him, I could call Dan for support. I knew Dan from a few counseling sessions that he sat in on while he was working towards his degree in psychology and felt safe with him. I tucked the slip of paper in my wallet and carried it with me for many years.

Unfortunately, his son had recently been diagnosed with cancer, and his prognosis wasn't good. As I briefly reminisced back to a time when I thought I couldn't survive without Dr. Francis to now when I knew I was going to be okay, and I knew he was, too. My healthy mental state is a testimony to the excellent care I received from Dr. Francis.

I took some deep breaths to regain my composure and asked, "How do you feel about dying?"

He replied, "I'm ready any day." His wife Marge, who he adored, had passed away a few years earlier, and he missed her terribly.

I thought to myself, "If he's ready, then I'll be ready." As much as he would have liked to die quickly, he lingered on for a few more years. He lived on the same street as the physical therapist who I was seeing for my knees. After my appointments and whenever I was in DuBois, I visited him at his home, bringing fresh flowers to brighten his days. As the seasons changed and he became more homebound, he would comment on how beautiful the fall leaves were or point to a bird sitting on a tree branch that he could see from his living room window. He lived long enough for me to publish *The Red Caboose-An Orphan's Journey*, which I dedicated to him.

I worked through my grief by writing a poem. As I read it to him, we laughed and cried together.

Eternally Grateful

When I was drowning in depression and despair
you gave me an anchor of acceptance and kindness
The Ray of light that shone through your eyes
made me feel like I mattered
and belonged to the human race.

When I was overcome with shame and guilt,

you assured me I had done nothing wrong
to carry such a heavy burden in life.
How others treated me wasn't my fault.

When I heard voices in my head,
you explained that I wasn't crazy.
They were unique and creative
survival techniques.
We muddled through memories
that caused me to disassociate.
You held on and didn't let go.

When I hated myself for all of my
wrongs and mistakes,
you taught me to love and forgive
the shadow sides of myself.

When I never felt good enough or
thought I was better than others,
you taught me not to compare myself
with anyone else.

When I was lost and wandering,
you gave me a compass,
always telling me to look within
for answers and direction.

When my son was threatening to commit
an act that would land him in jail
You said to tell him,
"He won't look good in stripes."
Your words worked like a charm.
I felt like I had a father for the very first time.

When I questioned the cult, I was in,

you told me my mind was
the only thing someone couldn't take.
I thought for myself and was free
from judgment and fear.
You taught me the meaning of grace.

When I left a bad marriage,
after twenty-five years of misery,
hanging out on a limb by myself,
you made extra appointments,
stayed late hours to make sure I wasn't alone.
The number 371-0794 was my lifeline,
permanently etched in my mind.

When I didn't have money
to pay for my visits,
you told me just to pass it on
"What's in it for you?" I asked.
You said, "I like to see
people smile."

When I needed a job to pay the bills,
you cheered me on and told me I had talent.
Because I knew no one else,
you gave me a reference
that landed me some pretty good jobs.

When I found love for the very first time,
you attended the wedding and
blessed our rings and union of bliss.
You visited our farm.
We broke bread
and you made friends with Cliff.

When I began to search in earnest for God,
and wondered what path I should trod
You told me to be a good person,
that God loves us all,
and to always forgive.

When you told me
you were going to die
'I stuck out my chin and grinned.'
Knowing you would receive your eternal reward,
together with your bride
in your loving Father's arms.

During our last visit, in a weak voice, Dr. Francis told me to tell Cliff that dying takes a long time. I asked, "Why are you still here?"

Trying to move his elbows ups and down, much like a fledgling bird trying to fly, he gathered his words that were no more audible than a whisper and said, "I can't seem to get my wings."

I replied, "You will when you are ready."

I knew that from all the times I didn't feel like I could fly but did when boughs gave way. I believe that some of us are able to find our wings and rise above the burdens of life while we are here on earth. Others, who are carrying the weight of the world, have to wait until their physical bodies die to be free of the constraints of abuse, rigid institutions, learned helplessness and illness. I'm grateful each day for the opportunity to climb out of the life I was born into and to be flying free.

Afterward

A s of the printing of the book, Jehovah's Witnesses are again vehe-mently preaching that the final part of the end of the system is here. In March of 2020, the Corona/COVID 19 Virus was declared a worldwide pandemic. The virus is a respiratory disease that affects the lungs and has a high contagion and death rate. All schools have been closed and will remain that way for the rest of the school year. That means no prom, senior class trips, or graduations. All non-essential businesses have been closed for over a month; restaurants, going to the beauty shop, getting a massage, or taking the dogs to the vet are all out of the question. Social distancing is a new word that has been added to my vocabulary. People are being instructed to stay six feet away from each other and to stay home except for essential business so as not to spread the virus. Except for losing my home when I was three years old, it's the greatest crisis of my time, yet I'm not fearful of the time of the end or dying. I've lived a good life and am grateful for all I've experienced in this life.

Just as I don't know how my life would have turned out if I hadn't gone to Mooseheart, I don't know how it would have turned out if I hadn't become a Jehovah's Witness. By joining the religion, I was able to quit smoking, quit drinking, develop morals (to a fault) and learned how to speak in public. I learned how to study and read voraciously. I made friends who helped me raise my children. I didn't feel alone in the world. I had a purpose and a group to belong to for a time.

It's been twenty years since I've been free of the mind control of Jehovah's Witnesses. Cliff and I have come to the conclusion that we don't regret anything that we experienced in life, as it's made us into the people we are. Also, if not for our personal traumas, we may have never met. Both of us are thankful for a second chance at love. What I have experienced in the past twenty years has more than made up for the twenty-five I spent in the religion.

As painful as it was for me to see the consequences of my children being raised in a religion that deprived them of birthday celebrations and social experiences, it brings me great joy to see the good people that they've become. My two daughters, Brandi and Cherey have done an amazing job parenting their children, making up for what they didn't have by providing opportunities for them to participate in scouts, dancing, cheerleading, and music. Both Justin and Caleb have a great work ethic and are caring individuals. One of our favorite times is at Christmas, when we get together and exchange gifts with the tree lights twinkling and joy in our hearts.

When I left Jehovah's Witnesses, there weren't many resources to support and help people who were disfellowshipped to move forward in life. Now there are online support groups and books on cults and mind control. There is even a television series on mainstream cults. Recently, *Arts and Entertainment* aired a poignant documentary about Jehovah's Witnesses and the pain the religion has caused people because they wanted to think for themselves. Some of the resources I recommend are *Combatting Mind Control* by Steven Hassan, *Shunned* and other books by Bonnie Zieman and the Empowered Ex-Jehovah's Witnesses Facebook group.

When the topic of Jehovah's Witnesses comes up, people want to know what to say to them when they come knocking on your door. I hope that my story helps people have compassion and to treat them with kindness and to inquire if they know about the concept and beauty of Grace. Maybe, just maybe, that will be the key to open the cage and they too may one day fly free.

Book Club Questions:

1. What did you like best about this book?

2. What did you like least about this book?

3. What feelings did this book evoke for you?

4. If you got the chance to ask the author of this book one question, what would it be?

5. What do you think of the book's title? How does it relate to the book's contents? What other titles might you choose?

6. What do you think of the book's cover? How well does it convey what the book is about?

7. What do you think was the author's purpose in writing this book? What ideas was he or she trying to get across?

8. If you could hear this same story from another person's point of view, who would you choose?

9. What aspects of the author's story could you most relate to?

10. What gaps do you wish the author had filled in? Were there points where you thought he shared too much?

11. Think about the other people in the book besides the author. How would you feel to have been depicted in this way?

12. Why do you think the author chose to tell this story?